The Christian Life

Second Edition

THE CHRISTIAN LIFE, SECOND EDITION

Modified May 2021to correct typos and incorrect answers

For information regarding permissions or special orders, please contact:

BEE World
International Headquarters
990 Pinon Ranch View, Ste. 100
Colorado Springs, CO 80907

ISBN: 978-1-937324-33-9

Second Edition

Printed in the United States of America

1 2 3 4 5 6 7 8 9 10

07082020

Contents

The Christian Life

Course Introduction

Welcome to *The Christian Life* course. When you made the decision to become a Christian by believing in Jesus Christ as your Savior, you began an adventure that will continue for the rest of your life and for all eternity. While there may be no obvious difference in appearance between a Christian and a non-Christian, the life a Christian lives differs from the life of an unbeliever in some significant ways. At the heart of those differences is one's relationship with Jesus Christ. This is central to Christianity.

The Christian life is not complex; in fact, it is really quite simple. It is defined neither by a set of religious disciplines nor by an academic collection of doctrines. The Christian life is a growing relationship with Christ that is lived out day by day. Of course, to say the Christian life is simple does not mean that it is easy; it is not. It may involve both disciplines and doctrines. But what is central is a growing love relationship with the Lord Jesus Christ, a relationship that impacts every aspect of the Christian's life. God's goal for you as a Christian is to deepen that relationship, and this course is designed to help you toward that goal.

Description of the Course

You may find *The Christian Life* course to be a bit different from other courses you have taken in that its goal is not the acquisition of knowledge. The course is intended to help you grow in your relationship to Christ and to equip you to help others grow in that relationship. People will be at different levels of maturity in their relationship with the Lord when they begin this course. Likewise, they will differ from one another in maturity when they finish the course. But no matter where you are in your journey as a Christian, taking this course should help you deepen your relationship with Christ.

In the first unit, you will begin to explore the nature of the Christian life. Unit two will focus on some ways to build a growing intimacy with the Lord. The third unit deals with how your calling as a Christian affects your life and relationships. The last unit examines some of the challenges involved in living life as a Christian.

Course Organization

The twelve lessons in this course are divided into four units of three lessons each. If you are taking the course online, clicking on the "Course Outline" button will display the course outline for you.

Unit 1: Foundations: Discovering God's Plan for the Christian Life

Lesson 1: Discovering God's Plan: Understanding and Pursuing the Goal of the Christian Life

Lesson 2: My Identity in Christ

Lesson 3: The Holy Spirit: How God Lives in Me

Unit 2: Intimacy: A Growing Relationship with God

Lesson 4: Building Intimacy through Worship: Responding to God

Lesson 5: Building Intimacy through the Word: Listening to God

Lesson 6: Building Intimacy through Prayer: Communing with God

Unit 3: God's Family: Finding My Place as a Responsible Christian

Lesson 7: Called to Community and Service: My Relationships with Others and My Role in the Church

Lesson 8: Called to be a Steward: Using Wisely All God Entrusts to Me

Lesson 9: Called to Follow: Making Wise Decisions

Unit 4: Faithfulness: Trusting God in Life's Challenges

Lesson 10: Trusting God when Life Hurts: Making Sense of Suffering

Lesson 11: Trusting God in the Face of Temptation: Living As an Alien

Lesson 12: Trusting God in the Spiritual Battle: Living As a Victor

Using This Course

You can take this course either as an independent study or as a facilitated class, and both of those methods have value. However, taking the course with other students who are being guided by a facilitator will likely increase the benefit you receive from the course. Remember that the goal of the course is to help you grow in your relationship with Christ Proverbs 27:17 says, "As iron sharpens iron, so a person sharpens his friend." That "sharpening" is what you want to see happen in your life as you study this course. You should expect to find the process of interacting with others who are on the same journey to be helpful to you and you helpful to them as each of you grows in your relationship with the Lord.

Patience and pacing will be important for you. Growth takes time, and so it is important that you not rush through these lessons. The readings and assignments in each lesson can usually be completed in about three hours, but you should spread that time out over several days. It is important to give yourself time to think through and respond to the material you are studying. Completing a lesson in about a week or three lessons in about a month is a reasonable pace; if you move more rapidly, you risk losing some of the potential growth.

Remember that you were created to enjoy a relationship with God who loves you. As you work though this course, you will be growing in your understanding and enjoyment of that relationship.

Unit 1: Foundations—Discovering God's Plan for the Christian Life

Unit Introduction

When you became a Christian, you began a dynamic relationship with Jesus Christ with the potential to affect every area of your life. You are probably still discovering all that it means to live life as a Christian. Since that discovery begins with understanding what God intends for your relationship with Him, the first unit in this course focuses on the foundations of God's design and intention for your life as a Christian. Lesson 1 deals with the goal Jesus expressed for His followers, namely, to enjoy a growing relationship with Him. Lesson 2 looks at how our identity is shaped by that relationship. Lesson 3 focuses on the role of the Holy Spirit in developing that healthy relationship with the Lord.

Unit Outline

Lesson 1: Discovering God's Plan—Understanding and Pursuing the Goal of the Christian Life

Lesson 2: My Identity in Christ

Lesson 3: The Holy Spirit—How God Lives in Me

Lesson 1: Discovering God's Plan—Understanding and Pursuing the Goal of the Christian Life

Lesson Introduction

One of the things that sets Christianity apart from the world's religious systems is the reality that Christianity is a relationship rather than a religion. Christ's intention was not to establish a new religious system when He came. His purpose was to enable a restored relationship between God and people, a relationship that had been broken by sin and rebellion. This relational characteristic is crucially important in understanding the nature of the Christian life.

When we become a Christian, our life is suddenly different because we now have a relationship with Jesus Christ. Discovering the ramifications of this new relationship takes time. Our understanding of religion was likely shaped by our previous religious convictions and practices. Perhaps our views had more to do with what a person *did* than what a person *believed*. The idea of a personal relationship with Jesus Christ is central to Christianity and may be a concept that is hard to grasp for new believers. In this Lesson we will explore what Scripture has to say about having relationship with Jesus Christ.

In this lesson we will look at some of the things Jesus said about our relationship to Him and our lives as Christians. In the first topic we will look at how Jesus called His disciples into a relationship. Topic 2 will explore Christ's conversations with two people who were not among the twelve disciples but became His followers. Topic 3 explores three signs of discipleship—things that Jesus said were evidence that someone was one of His disciples. The fourth topic explores one of the metaphors Jesus used to describe the Christian life. In Topic 5 we will see that the relationship is permanent, lasting beyond our life here on earth.

Lesson Outline

Topic 1: Jesus' Call to His Disciples

Topic 2: Jesus' Interaction with Two Others

- Nicodemus
- Zacchaeus

Topic 3: Signs of Discipleship

Topic 4: Remaining in Christ

Topic 5: An Eternal Relationship

Topic 6: Conclusion

Topic 1: Jesus' Call to His Disciples

At its heart, the Christian life is about having a personal relationship with Jesus Christ. Before we begin looking at Scripture, and to help you begin thinking about what is involved in a relationship, answer the following question.

QUESTION 1

What do you think are the necessary ingredients of a relationship? Write a paragraph in your Life Notebook describing what you believe is necessary. (You will have an opportunity later to further develop and modify this answer.)

The adventure of the Christian life begins when a person hears and responds positively to the invitation and call of Jesus. Responding to Christ's invitation requires that a person exercise faith. The invitation to salvation is an invitation to *trust* Christ. When we begin our relationship with Christ, we trust the sufficiency of Christ's sacrifice and the certainty of God's ability to forgive sin and to give us eternal life. The Christian life is a relationship to which faith is essential. It is essential when that relationship begins, and, as we will discover, it continues to be essential as the Christian lives out that relationship.

Relationships, of course, are dynamic things. Relationships deepen as trust deepens. For those who have been Christians for some time, it is not difficult to understand this process of a deepening relationship with Christ. Part of coming to know Him better is discovering that He is trustworthy. But for the person first considering the invitation of Christ, deciding to trust Him enough to begin a relationship can be a big decision that does not happen until the person begins to discover how much Christ already loves him.

Let's begin to explore this relationship by looking at how Jesus called His first disciples. Please read the article titled "The Call to Discipleship". Use the article and scriptures to respond to the questions that follow the article:

The Call to Discipleship

Have you ever wondered why Jesus spent so much time on earth? If His purpose was to redeem lost mankind and that redemption could be accomplished at Calvary, why not simply come as an adult, go directly to the cross, and get the business of salvation taken care of?

If the Lord's intent was to redeem robots, then that plan could have worked quite well. But His plan was far better—and more complex—than that. When God first created man, His obvious intention was to enjoy a relationship with His creation. The Garden of Eden was a place of fellowship where God communed with Adam and Eve. That relationship was broken by sin. After the fall the Lord was in the garden seeking Adam and Eve, but they were hiding, avoiding Him. Redemption makes possible a restored eternal relationship between the Creator and His creation, a relationship that God values and invites us to value as well. When a person accepts Christ as Savior, the relationship that the Lord intended becomes possible again. That God intends to call us into a relationship, and not merely into a set of mandated behaviors, can be seen in His calls to those who would become His disciples during His sojourn on earth.

The invitation to follow Him that Jesus gave to His disciples sometimes seems dramatic. Read, for example, the seemingly abrupt shift for Simon, Andrew, James, and John, as recorded in Mark 1:14-20. At the invitation of Jesus, they left their fishing nets and followed Him. Eventually, following Jesus would entail specific ministry responsibilities and challenges, but that was not the initial focus of Jesus' call. The practical outcome of Jesus' invitation and their decision was that they would begin to spend time—a lot of time—with Jesus. And they were not alone. Likewise, Matthew responded to the invitation of Jesus by leaving his relatively lucrative position as a tax collector for the economic uncertainty of following Jesus (Mt 9:9-10). The immediate result was spending time with Jesus, sharing a meal with Him, which resulted in the Pharisees' criticism of Jesus for socializing with a tax collector. Jesus valued a relationship with Matthew more than He valued the opinion of other people. Clearly Jesus' priority with those He called was relational.

When you spend time with another person, engaging in conversation and sharing activities, you begin to understand that person's values. What is important becomes apparent as it is expressed in both words and deeds. And if those values resonate with your own heart, the relational bond with that person becomes stronger. Over time, you come to really know the other person.

When Jesus began to call those who would become His disciples, it was not a call focused on specific ministry activity. He did not, for example, say to John, "Come and write an account of my life." Eventually, John would do so, but first he needed simply to get acquainted with Jesus, to know Him, to begin a relationship with Him.

This priority is even more obvious when Jesus began to identify those who would be His apostles. Consider Mark 3:13-15. Before they would ever be sent out, before they would ever be expected to exercise authority, they were called to be with Him. He did not miraculously and instantly fill them with all they would need to be His disciples; rather, He called them into a relationship with Himself in which they would begin to discover the Master's heart. The call to discipleship is always first and foremost a call to relationship.

Because Christ's invitation is an invitation to relationship, it is a very personal invitation. If His intention had been to recruit a team of workers, He could have done so with a broadly issued call to the masses and little or no personal interaction. But that is not what Jesus did. Instead, He came alongside individuals with a full awareness of both their unique personalities and individual circumstances. He invited them into a relationship of love in which they could experience total acceptance, total forgiveness, and total fulfillment. It is one thing to acknowledge the great truth that God loved the world, but what changes one's life is to discover that "God loves me as an individual and desires a relationship with me." One of the wonderful results of the incarnation is the reality of the Lord stepping into our sphere of experience and lovingly inviting us into relationship.

This relational priority does not mean that there is never a call to specific obedience or specific ministry; Scripture is clear that Jesus did indeed issue such calls. But the commitment to obey or the commitment to serve was intended to flow from a growing relationship of love that had been established. (See, for example, Jn 14:23 which states that obedience is both an expected outcome of a love relationship and a means of strengthening that relationship.) Without such a relationship obedience and service become burdens without lasting motivation. The priority Jesus expressed and the value He demonstrated was for a growing relationship that would become a foundation on which His followers could build a life of both obedience and service.

The good news is that Christians are much more than redeemed robots. Robots can be commanded to obey and programmed to serve. Disciples, on the other hand, are called into a relationship that fosters a growing desire to both obey and serve. Relationships take time. Jesus knew that; He invested the time necessary to build those relationships, and He invites His followers to do likewise.

QUESTION 2

From the beginning of creation God's intention for human beings was that they experience a mutually enjoyable relationship with Him. *True or False?*

QUESTION 3

Why did Jesus call His disciples at first?

A. To be with Him

B. To be sent out to minister

C. To exercise authority

D. To form an army

QUESTION 4

Ultimately what did Jesus want His disciples to do *(Select all that apply.)*

A. Be with Him

B. Be sent out to minister

C. Obey Him

D. Reject Him

Topic 2: Jesus' Interaction with Two Others

"The Call to Discipleship" article you read focuses on the priority of Jesus for a relationship with those He called as His disciples. But what about other people Jesus encountered who were not among the group of twelve disciples? Let's take a look at two individuals who, though they were not among the Twelve, faced a relational decision. They are two of the many people whom Jesus called into a relationship, even though they would have less opportunity to spend time physically with Him.

Nicodemus was a Pharisee and a member of the Sanhedrin, the highest Jewish legal authority. As such, he would have plenty of opportunity to dialog with other Pharisees who were irritated with Jesus and threatened by the idea that He could be the Messiah. But Nicodemus had honest questions, and so one night he sought out Jesus for a one-on-one conversation. Scripture does not tell us why he sought out Jesus under cover of darkness. Perhaps he was concerned about being seen with Him; perhaps it was a matter of convenient opportunity. Whatever the reason, the heart of the conversation is recorded in John 3. Read this conversation between Nicodemus and Jesus in John 3:1-21.

QUESTION 5

What questions did Nicodemus ask Jesus? *(Select all that apply.)*

A. How are you able to perform miracles?

B. How can a man be born when he is old?

C. How can these things be?

D. Why don't the Pharisees believe that you are the Messiah?

In responding to Nicodemus, Jesus used an interesting metaphor. He said that a person needed to be born from above or born again. The image of birth presupposes a relationship. In the normal course of events by the time a woman gives birth, she already senses a relationship with the newborn child. And the newborn child is utterly dependent on and trusting its mother to meet the needs that the baby could never meet by itself. It is normal and healthy for a baby to be loved by its parents. When separation occurs at birth and the parent-child relationship is interrupted, both parent and child suffer. Adoption becomes the human attempt to reestablish a parent-child relationship in which the child can thrive.

God's intention is not to spawn a host of spiritual orphans. When one is "born from above" into God's family and kingdom, no less a parent than God Himself is ready to lovingly meet every spiritual need of the utterly dependent newborn. What is the norm physically—being born into relationship—is also the norm spiritually, and God never abandons His newborns.

To talk or think about birth apart from relationship is difficult. While there are many other metaphors for the Christian life that Jesus might have used, He chose one in this conversation with Nicodemus that clearly implies a relationship of love and trust.

How Nicodemus responded is not clear from this initial conversation with Jesus. Later references to him in Scripture provide some insight. John 7 records a controversy about the identity of Jesus. Was He a prophet? Was He the Messiah? Should He be arrested? Nicodemus, as a member of the ruling council, urged caution by suggesting that the Jewish rulers would not be in a position to judge Jesus until they have listened to His teaching. Later, following His crucifixion, Nicodemus accompanied Joseph of Arimathea in taking the body of Jesus, preparing it for burial, and placing it in the garden tomb, acts that could have been both politically and monetarily costly. Read about these events in John 7:40-52 and John 19:38-42.

QUESTION 6

After reading all three of these passages (Jn 3:1-21; 7:40-52; 19:38-42) about Nicodemus, what would you conclude about his relationship with Jesus? Record your answer in your Life Notebook and be prepared to discuss your answer with other students.

While Nicodemus was a respected member of Jewish society, Zacchaeus was despised because of his occupation as a tax collector. But he, too, had a life-altering encounter with Jesus.

As a chief tax collector, Zacchaeus would have been one of the richest men in Jericho. He was curious about Jesus. Perhaps he had heard about the blind beggar whose sight He had miraculously restored. The miracle had taken place as Jesus was approaching Jericho, and Zacchaeus was eager to see this man.

Unfortunately, Zacchaeus, being a short man, was unable to see over the crowd. Being resourceful, he found a tree and climbed up so he could see. What happened next changed his life. Read Luke 19:1-10.

QUESTION 7

What reason did Jesus give to Zacchaeus for coming down out of the tree immediately?

A. He wanted Zacchaeus to accompany Him on His travels.

B. He wanted to pay the tax to Zacchaeus.

C. He wanted to stay at Zacchaeus' house.

D. He was afraid Zacchaeus would fall.

In spite of the criticism that would result from spending time with a despised tax collector, Jesus responded to Zacchaeus relationally. In fact, what Jesus did is very similar to His actions when He called Matthew, another tax collector, who became one of the twelve apostles. The encounter with Jesus apparently made a lasting impression on Zacchaeus. His public commitment to give half of his possessions to the poor and to repay fourfold those whom he had cheated must have been startling to those who knew this tax collector. Jesus had sought him, and Jesus had saved him.

QUESTION 8

Read Luke 19:10 again and consider the reason Jesus gave for His coming. Think about how that purpose has been fulfilled in your own life and spend some time thanking God for seeking and saving you. Write a paragraph in your Life Notebook reflecting on this experience.

Topic 3: Signs of Discipleship

When you spend time with someone in a relationship, that relationship will begin to look different. If you watch people for any length of time, you will soon begin to gain some insight into their relationships. Words, actions, and nonverbal communication will all give clues about the underlying relationships. If, for example, a couple say they are in love with each other, but their words and actions do not reflect that love, a reasonable observer might doubt the reality of their love.

The Christian life is about a relationship with Jesus Christ. If there is no evidence of that relationship, then one might wonder if in fact the relationship exists. When we enter into a relationship with Jesus, our lives will change. Other people may recognize that something is different about us; they are sensing the evidence of our relationship with Christ. That evidence should show up every day in various ways in the life of the disciple. In this topic we will look at three of the evidences that Jesus said should be present in the lives of His disciples.

Please read the article titled "How to Recognize a Disciple". Use the article and scriptures to respond to the questions that follow the article:

How to Recognize a Disciple

The flight was over, and the plane taxied to the gate. Howard was looking forward to meeting the people who had invited him to come and lecture at the university. He made his way off the plane, down the boarding ramp, and followed the crowd to immigration. After having his passport stamped and reclaiming his suitcase, he pulled out the note from the dean and read again that he would be met just outside security near a sign marked "Meeting Area." Howard had no trouble finding the sign, but there were hundreds of people milling around. "How on earth will I ever find the people I'm supposed to meet, and how will they ever find me?" he wondered to himself. A few people in the crowd held signs with names on them, but none of the signs had his name. He stopped and scanned the crowd again and glimpsed a small patch of red off to one side. As he looked in that direction he saw several people wearing shirts emblazoned with the name and logo of the university that had invited him to speak. Smiling, he headed in that direction, ready to meet his hosts.

Sometimes it seems that Christians blend into the crowd around them as easily as Howard and his hosts blended into the crowd at the airport. Christians do not necessarily wear shirts that identify them by color and logo as followers of Christ. But Jesus did say that His disciples should be recognizable. What sets them apart is not the color of their shirts or indeed anything about their physical appearance. There are, however, other recognizable qualities that identify them as followers of Christ. Let's look at three of those marks of discipleship that Jesus identified.

Obedience

In John 8, Jesus engaged in a conversation with Pharisees and as a result of the conversation, "many people believed in him" (Jn 8:30). To these believing Jews Jesus says, "If you continue to follow my teaching, you are really my disciples and you will know the truth, and the truth will set you free" (Jn 8:31-32).

Continuing to follow Jesus' teaching—doing what Jesus said—would mark them as His disciples. The idea here is not merely trying out the teaching of Jesus and then abandoning it when it seems inconvenient; rather it envisions a commitment to continue to follow His teaching. Jesus seems to have a lifestyle shift in mind.

Sometimes consistent obedience is imposed by a feared authority like a tyrant or slave-driver. That is not the case here. If it were, then the so-called disciple would likely abandon that pattern of obedience at the first convenient opportunity. Instead, this is an obedience that arises from a loving relationship. A little child obeys his parents not simply out of fear, but out of an implicit trust because he has sensed that his parents love him. While he may not consciously connect the boundaries they set with the love he has experienced, that love encourages him to trust. So it is with Christ and His disciples. We are called to consistently follow the teaching of Someone who loves us intensely, and our obedience is motivated by love rather than by fear. To choose some other alternative is to settle for less than the best.

This loving relationship makes sense of Jesus' next phrase: "you will know the truth, and the truth will set you free" (Jn 8:32). If consistent obedience were motivated only by fear, then it would be ludicrous to talk in the same breath about experiencing freedom. Jesus was implying that those who had become His disciples had formerly been in bondage. Now, as a result of this new relationship with Christ, they know the truth and are experiencing real freedom; later Jesus said that He is the truth. One who has been set free from bondage to sin rejoices in that freedom, and a commitment to consistently follow Christ's teaching simply illuminates this newfound freedom.

Christ's disciples follow His teaching. That is why in His final challenge to His followers after His resurrection and just before His ascension, He told them not only to make disciples, but He specifically told them how. "Go and make disciples…teaching them to obey everything I have commanded you" (Mt 28:19-20). Disciples today must follow Christ's teaching, just as did the original disciples in the upper room.

Love

Jesus identified a second mark of discipleship while meeting with His followers in the upper room shortly before His arrest and crucifixion: "I give you a new commandment—to love one another. Just as I have loved you, you also are to love one another. Everyone will know by this that you are my disciples—if you have love for one another" (Jn 13:34-35).

Since it is a "commandment," one could argue that this second evidence of discipleship is in a sense an extension of the first ("continue to follow My teaching"). Here too the motivation arises from a loving relationship with the Lord and not merely from a burdensome mandate. According to Jesus, visible loving relationships among Christians give evidence that those people have a loving relationship with Him. It is a statement that makes perfectly good sense, though at times it may be a challenge to live out. Fresh in the minds of the disciples would be the example of Jesus who that very evening had voluntarily taken the towel and washed their feet, not because He had to but because He loved them enough to want to serve them. It was an action that none of the disciples had chosen, leaving Jesus to take the role of a servant. And now Jesus told them to love one another "just as I have loved you."

Such love is intensely attractive. In the earliest days of the church such visible love was evident. The description given in Acts 2:42-47 focuses attention on the relational behavior of those early Christians—spending time together, sharing possessions, meeting needs, worshipping together, sharing meals, mutual humility, an apparently insatiable enjoyment of fellowship. The text indicates that they were well thought of by others, and then adds almost as an afterthought that the Lord added to their number daily those who were being saved. The quality of the obviously loving relationships within this early church became part of their evangelistic strategy. Unbelievers were drawn to the love they saw in this Christian community.

While such an evangelistic strategy still works, it is much less common than it should be. We do well to ask ourselves what unbelievers perceive when they look at our church. Do they see a stern and legalistic community, an ineffective and divided organization, or are they captivated by our love? How attractive to unbelievers are the relationships among Christians in your church? "Everyone will know by this that you are my disciples," Jesus said, "if you have love for one another."

Fruitfulness

Jesus identifies a third mark of His disciples in John 15. Jesus and the eleven disciples (Judas having previously departed) left the upper room, but the conversation continued as they walked. Jesus gave them a powerful visual image of the relationship between them and Him by using the metaphor of a vine and branches. Jesus identified Himself as the vine and His disciples as the branches. Read carefully through the first eight verses of this chapter (Jn 15:1-8).

Branches that are connected to the vine are supposed to bear fruit. In verse 8 Jesus says that producing fruit honors the Father (whom Jesus has likened to the gardener in this metaphor). Such fruit-bearing, in fact, demonstrates that the ones bearing fruit are disciples of Jesus Christ.

Since there is no record of the disciples questioning Jesus about the matter, they probably understood what He meant by bearing fruit. Scripture uses the image of fruit in a couple of ways. Reproductively it indicates that disciples are supposed to make more disciples as an apple tree produces apples or a grapevine produces grapes. It should not have surprised them much to later hear the resurrected Jesus command them to make disciples; after all, bearing fruit is what branches do. Fruit is also used as a metaphor for what God desires to produce in the lives of disciples (see Gal 5:22-23). Both interpretations make sense here, and it is helpful to understand the passage in the broad context of spiritual fruitfulness, including the expectation of reproductive fruit.

It may be obvious that only connected branches bear fruit, but it is worth noting since Jesus makes the point. A branch that has been severed from the vine will not produce. While it may continue to look alive for a time, it will soon wither and die. In order for a disciple to bear fruit (and so show himself to be a disciple), he must remain vitally connected to Jesus Christ, the vine. Exploring this concept of remaining in Christ in more depth is the subject for a different article. Suffice it to say here that bearing fruit requires a living relationship with Christ and arises from that relationship.

In the next paragraph Jesus again linked the importance of a vital relationship with Him to all three of these evidences of discipleship. Read John 15:9-17 and notice how all three marks of discipleship—obedience, love, fruitfulness—are woven into a relationship with Christ. In verse 10, obedience and remaining in Christ's love are irrevocably connected. In verse 12 (and again in verse 17), Jesus repeated the command to love one another, hinting at the supreme manifestation of love that He Himself was about to demonstrate. Then in verse 16, having called them friends, He reminded them that He chose them and appointed them to go and bear lasting fruit. Disciples do not have the luxury of choosing just one or two of these three marks of discipleship; all three evidences flow out of a growing relationship with Christ.

These three marks of discipleship are not intended to be burdensome or an impossible goal. They are the logical and expected result of a vital relationship with Jesus Christ. If I see a four-legged animal wagging its tail and barking, I might safely conclude that it is a dog. But it is not the barking, the wagging tail, or the four legs that make it a dog; it was born a dog, all of its cells have dog DNA, and therefore it acts like a dog. Obedience, love, and fruitfulness mark the life of a disciple simply because he IS a disciple, one who has joyfully committed to a lasting relationship with his loving Lord. A perceived weakness in one of these areas does not necessarily mean that one needs to work harder in that area to somehow squeeze out success. More likely, it means that he needs to grow in his relationship with Christ so that the evidence of that relationship will become more visible.

Disciples of Jesus Christ will be recognizable, not because they are wearing red shirts with heavenly logos, but because their lives reflect the visible evidence of a growing relationship with the Lord. Obedience, love, and fruitfulness, visible marks of discipleship identified by Jesus, will communicate to others that we are Christ's disciples.

QUESTION 9

Match each of these marks of discipleship with the Scripture passage in which Jesus talked about that mark.

Mark of Discipleship	*Scripture*
Loving One Another	John 8
Following Jesus' teaching	John 13
Bearing fruit	John 15

QUESTION 10

What is the underlying reason or basis for a Christian obeying the Lord and continuing to follow the Lord's teaching?

QUESTION 11

Read Acts 2:42-47. Make a list of the ways that these early Christians in Jerusalem showed their love for one another.

QUESTION 12

In applying Jesus' teaching about fruitfulness in John 15, on what should the Christian focus? *(Select all that apply.)*

A. Other Christians' fruitfulness

B. Reproductive fruit—making other disciples

C. Fruit of the Spirit like that listed in Galatians 5:22-23

D. Neither reproductive fruit nor fruit of the Spirit

QUESTION 13

Write a personal response in your Life Notebook to the article, "How to Recognize a Disciple." Identify what you believe to be the author's thesis or main point and evaluate how effectively that thesis was supported. Do you agree with the author's thesis; why or why not? Are there other marks of discipleship the author did not include?

Talking about evidence of a relationship with Jesus Christ in general terms can be helpful, but there is a more important and practical dimension to this topic. As we think about the various marks of a disciple, it is wise to think about one's relationship to Christ and how the evidence of that relationship can be seen. The next question gives you an opportunity to apply the truths from this section to your own life. Do not rush through this exercise; give yourself ample time for honest reflection prompted by God's Spirit.

QUESTION 14

Before moving ahead to the next topic, spend some time considering how each of these marks of discipleship is evident in your own life. If you sense a weakness in one or more of these three areas, ask the Lord to help you develop your relationship with Him in a way that will help you grow in that area. Include a note in your Life Notebook indicating that you have completed this exercise.

Topic 4: Remaining in Christ

When Jesus talked to His disciples using the image of the vine and branches (Jn 15), He carefully connected the result of fruitfulness to a command and condition that the branch remain in the vine. The disciples understood that if a branch, for whatever reason, became disconnected from the vine; it would cease to be fruitful. Branches that are broken off or cut off are functionally useless.

There is, of course, an important difference between branches and people. Branches lack the capacity to choose. The branch of a plant can become separated from its vine only if it is cut off, broken off, or falls off perhaps because it is diseased. Inanimate objects do not choose their associations. People, however, can and do make those choices, and Jesus recognized that important difference. In almost endless variety of ways people can choose to distance themselves from Christ. Choosing not to obey Him, choosing to avoid communication with Him (whether listening or responding), choosing to value what He does not value, choosing associations that become more important than Him—these are just some of the ways in which human branches can choose to wither. Jesus saw the danger, and that is why He made such an obvious point of the need for the branch to remain in the vine.

Read John 15:1-8.

QUESTION 15

Which of the following does Jesus say to the disciples in John 15:4? *(Select all that apply.)*

A. He commands them to remain in Him.

B. He promises that He will remain in them.

C. He reminds them that a branch must be connected to the vine to bear fruit.

D. He tells them they will not be able to bear fruit unless they remain in Him.

It may seem strange to think that a Christian would choose not to remain vitally connected to Christ. Since the Lord is our source, disconnecting does not make much sense. But it is clear both from what Jesus said and from what we see around us that not all Christians are enjoying such a relationship. That does not mean that they are not Christians, but it does mean that their lives will be spiritually unfruitful as long as they distance themselves from the Lord.

In Luke 15 Jesus told a story about a man with two sons, one of whom wanted to claim his inheritance early and leave home. While Jesus told the story to make a specific point to the Pharisees, it also serves well as an illustration of one who chose for a time not to remain connected. Read this parable in Luke 15:11-32.

While the younger son was out of touch with the father for significant period of time, he never ceased being a son. Even his resentful older brother recognized that. His father consistently acted like a father, longing for the relationship to be restored. The young man was his father's son, and while no one in the distant country to which he had gone would have known that, his behavior did not change his DNA.

QUESTION 16

Both brothers in Luke 15 were related to the father. At the end of the story, which brother do you think is more likely to have the kind of relationship with the father that will enable him to live a life that bears fruit? Why? Record your answer in your Life Notebook and be prepared to discuss it.

Scripture passages that focus on what the believer has in Christ underline the necessity of that younger relationship and help us understand the importance of maintaining a vital relationship with Christ. When Paul wrote to the Christians at Ephesus, he addressed them as "the faithful in Christ Jesus." Read Ephesians 1:1-14, meditating on what Scripture says flows out of this "in Christ" relationship.

QUESTION 17

Match these outcomes of being in Christ with the verse that refers to it.

Verse	*Outcomes*
Ephesians 1:3	Chosen by God
Ephesians 1:4	Grace
Ephesians 1:6	Redemption and forgiveness
Ephesians 1:7	Every spiritual blessing

Remaining in Christ means that one's life reflects an ongoing submission to the lordship of Jesus Christ. We call Him Lord sometimes without thinking much about what that title implies. Please read the article titled "Jesus Christ is Lord". and consider the Scripture passages in the article. Then respond to the questions that follow the article.

Jesus Christ Is Lord

I taught for several years at the university. Each spring a new set of students would graduate and move into life beyond academics. One spring, when graduation was a few days away, the academic work had been completed, and I was enjoying some time at the beach with some of my students. For the last four years I had been their teacher and advisor. In the classroom my word had been the law, and in recognition of that authority, they were used to addressing me using the title Mr. or Dr. Now they were testing what for them was a new experience, calling me by my given name because we had become friends. For some of them, it was a difficult experiment; the title Mr. or Dr. would always be prefixed to my surname. Others freely enjoyed the newfound emphasis on friendship, yet without any diminishing of the authority inherent in the teacher-student relationship. One or two thought that using my given name somehow erased the teacher-student relationship and the need to submit to authority; they needed to be quickly, gently, and effectively corrected.

When a person comes to Christ, accepts the gift of salvation, and begins the adventure of the Christian life, the new believer will realize that Jesus Christ is Lord. Paul, writing to the Romans, indicates that the believer confesses with his mouth that Jesus is Lord (Rom 10:9); that recognition is inseparably woven into the salvation experience. But as the believer begins to experience and enjoy a relationship with the Lord, sometimes the practical effects of Jesus being Lord go unnoticed. The Christian has no difficulty in referring to Jesus as his Savior or Friend, but His role as Lord can become little more than an empty title devoid of meaning.

The problem with avoiding the lordship of Jesus is that "Lord" is part of who He is. The miracle of the incarnation is not only that God became man in the person of Jesus, but also that He never ceased to be God. He is, thankfully, our Savior and our Friend. Having died for us and risen again, He is also our Lord (Rom 14:9), and that fact should continually be evident in our relationship with Him.

Jesus identified the problem as He was speaking to His disciples and the crowd that had gathered to hear Him. "Why do you call me 'Lord, Lord,' and don't do what I tell you?" (Lk 6:46). To call Jesus Lord and fail to do what He says is an inherent contradiction. Jesus illustrated the point by likening the one who hears and obeys to a man building a house with a solid and safe foundation. The man who hears but does not obey Him likens to a man who builds a house with no foundation that will collapse when the storm comes.

Obedience in recognition of the fact that Jesus is Lord is an ongoing issue in the life of the believer. God has created us with the ability to make decisions and to exercise our will. To voluntarily subject that ability to the lordship of someone else does not come easily to us. Repeatedly, in fact almost constantly, Christians have the ability to choose not to obey the Lord. When a believer makes that choice, he or she is saying in effect that Jesus is not the sovereign Lord over that particular decision.

Scripture encourages us to continue in our relationship with Christ the way we began, and we have seen that the recognition that Jesus is Lord is a central part of our initial confession (Rom 10:9). Colossians 2:6 says, "Therefore, just as you received Christ Jesus as Lord, continue to live your lives in him." We began a relationship with Jesus Christ acknowledging Him to be Lord and Savior. As that relationship continues, Jesus does not change. He still desires to be Lord and Savior; He still loves us unconditionally; He still values a relationship with us.

If a Christian is to continue recognizing Jesus as Lord, then he will continue to let what Christ says shape what he does. The discovery of what it means to submit to the lordship of Christ is progressive, unfolding as a believer encounters new and different situations and circumstances. With each new situation comes a fresh opportunity to recognize Jesus Christ is Lord and to continue voluntarily surrendering to Him as we recognize who He is. To call Him Lord should be more than a title—it is a reflection of a relationship.

Ultimately, Jesus Christ will be acknowledged as Lord. Philippians 2:9-11 indicates that Jesus, having died for our sins, has been given by the Father the highest place and the highest name, "so that at the name of Jesus every knee should bow—in heaven and on earth and under the earth, and every tongue confess to the glory of God the Father that Jesus Christ is Lord." The good news is that we who are believers do not have to wait. We have the immense privilege of daily demonstrating by our lives and our choices the truth that Jesus Christ is Lord of our lives.

QUESTION 18

Match the following Scripture references with what they say about Jesus being Lord.

Scripture	*Jesus being Lord*
Romans 10:9	Eventually everyone will confess that Jesus Christ is Lord.
Philippians 2:9-11	Christians should acknowledge that Jesus Christ is Lord
Colossians 2:6	A new believer needs to confess that Jesus Christ is Lord.

QUESTION 19

Can you imagine situations where it might be difficult to surrender to Christ's lordship? Most Christians have experienced such circumstances. In what kind of situations might it be difficult for you to submit to Jesus as your Lord? What would help you in those circumstances to maintain your relationship with Christ (to "remain" in Him)? Record your response in your Life Notebook and take some time in worship to acknowledge Jesus Christ as Lord.

Topic 5: An Eternal Relationship

Your relationship with Jesus Christ began when you invited Him to be your Savior by accepting His forgiveness from sin and eternal life. You will continue to grow in that relationship as you discover more about Christ and what He intends. Salvation is more than a life-long relationship since it is designed not only for this life but also for all of eternity. In this section we will look at some of what the Bible says about this relationship as it extends into our eternal future.

Let's begin with Jesus and the disciples in the upper room, hours before His arrest and crucifixion, as He prepares His followers for His departure and what lies ahead. Read John 14:1-3.

QUESTION 20

When Jesus told the disciples that He will come again, what reason does He give them for His return?

The dwelling places Jesus is preparing for them are in His Father's house, and Jesus anticipates that after His return, His disciples will again be in the same place as He is. His desire is that they be with Him in heaven.

This unity that Jesus seemed to anticipate is much more than mere geographic proximity. This is not just a matter of Jesus and His followers being in the same place because they will all be in heaven. This is a continuity of relationship. Consider what Paul says about our experience after death as he writes to the church at Corinth. Read 2 Corinthians 5:1-9.

Paul envisions just two possibilities for the believer in this passage. Either he is alive in the body (physically alive) or he is at home with the Lord (physically dead but alive in the presence of the Lord). In spite of the obvious differences between these two states (for example, now we live by faith since we cannot physically see the Lord, but then we will be in His presence), the continuity of the relationship beyond physical death is clear. Notice particularly how that continuity of purpose is expressed in verse 9: "So then whether we are alive [in the body] or away [after death] we make it our ambition to please him." In this life we have been brought into a relationship with Christ and we want to please Him. After death, our continuing ambition will be to please the One who has brought us into an eternal love relationship with Himself.

The apostle reflected on that future relationship when he wrote to the Philippians. At the time, Paul was imprisoned in Rome, and he had thought realistically of the possibility of his own death. Read Philippians 1 and notice what Paul said about his relationship with Christ both present and future. His perspective was that "to live is Christ, and to die is gain" (Phil 1:21). His relationship with Christ was so integral to his life on this earth that he could say, "to live is Christ." And yet his anticipation of what lay ahead led him to the conviction that his relationship with Christ beyond the grave would be even better—"gain"! He describes his feeling of being torn between the two. "I have a desire," he says, "to depart and be *with Christ, which is better by far…*" (Phil 1:23, emphasis added).

QUESTION 21

Paul expresses his confidence that his death is not imminent, and he will remain alive in the body for a time yet. Since it is "better by far" to depart and be with Christ, why is staying in the flesh an acceptable alternative? What is the value to staying?

Interestingly, Paul then applied the same idea of continuity to the Philippians in their relationship with him. He encourages them to a life of faithfulness regardless of whether he was physically present with them. They were to stand firm "whether I come and see you or whether I remain absent" (Phil 1:27).

Our relationship with Christ here in this life prepares us for an even better relationship with Him that will endure for all eternity. This relationship is not interrupted by death; if anything, it is fulfilled as we are in the presence of the Lord—*with* Him.

QUESTION 22

Read the following Scriptures and match each reference with the truth taught in that passage.

Scripture	*Truth Taught*
John 14:1-3	When a believer dies and is absent from the body, he is present with the Lord
2 Corinthians 5:1-9	Being with Christ is better by far than remaining in the flesh.
1 Thessalonians 4:13-14	When Christ returns, He will bring with Him believers who have died.
Philippians 1:21-23	Jesus promises to take His followers to be with Him in a place He has prepared.
Revelation 21:1-3	God's purpose is that we dwell with Him for all eternity.

Topic 6: Conclusion

The Christian life is centered on a relationship with Jesus Christ. That relationship begins when a person receives Christ and continues for all eternity. The life of the Christian should show evidence of that relationship in obedience to the Lord, love for other believers, and fruitfulness. God has made it possible for you to enjoy a growing relationship with Him. In the next lesson we will continue to look at the nature of this relationship and what it makes possible for us. But before we move on, let's review something you wrote earlier. When you began this lesson, you identified what was necessary for a relationship in your answer to question one in your Life Notebook. Open your Life Notebook and review what you wrote.

QUESTION 23

Taking into consideration what you have studied in this lesson, rewrite your answer to Question 1, making whatever changes and additions you deem appropriate.

Lesson 1 Self Check: The Christian Life

QUESTION 1

The call to discipleship is a call to relationship. *True or False?*

QUESTION 2

Why should Christ's followers obey Him?

A. They are afraid of the consequences

B. They know that Christ loves them

C. Other disciples expect them to obey

D. To make a good impression on unbelievers

QUESTION 3

When Jesus began to call His disciples, it was a call focused on specific ministry activity. *True or False?*

QUESTION 4

In His nighttime conversation with Nicodemus, what metaphor did Jesus use?

A. The potter and the clay

B. The new birth

C. The shepherd and the sheep

D. The vine and the branches

QUESTION 5

In Luke 19:10 what did Jesus say that He came to do?

A. Save lost people

B. Heal sick people

C. Establish His kingdom

D. Train disciples

QUESTION 6

Which of the following is *not* a mark of a disciple?

A. Obedience

B. Love

C. Fruitfulness

D. Attending church

QUESTION 7

In order for a Christian to bear fruit, he must remain in Christ. *True or False?*

QUESTION 8

In the metaphor of the vine and branches, what does the vine represent?

A. The church

B. The disciples

C. Jesus

D. Pharisees

QUESTION 9

How does the believer's relationship with Christ change at death?

A. It is temporarily interrupted until after Christ's return.

B. It permanently ceases since the believer is absent from the body.

C. The relationship begins after death.

D. The relationship continues uninterrupted.

QUESTION 10

According to 2 Corinthians 5, what is always the believer's ambition?

A. Different; his ambition changes at death

B. To make disciples

C. To please the Lord

D. To reign over the nations

Lesson 1 Answers to Questions

QUESTION 1: *Your answer*
QUESTION 2: True
QUESTION 3
A. To be with Him
QUESTION 4
A. Be with Him
B. Be sent out to minister
C. Obey Him
QUESTION 5
B. How can a man be born when he is old?
C. How can these things be?
QUESTION 6: *Your answer*
QUESTION 7
C. He wanted to stay at Zacchaeus' house.
QUESTION 8: *Your answer*
QUESTION 9

Mark of Discipleship	*Scripture*
Loving One Another	John 13
Following Jesus' teaching	John 8
Bearing fruit	John 15

QUESTION 10: *Your answer should be similar to the following:*
Love, a loving relationship with the Lord, his relationship with Christ
QUESTION 11: *Your answer should be similar to the following:*
Spending time together; sharing their possessions; sacrificially meeting one another's needs; sharing meals; worshipping together.
QUESTION 12
B. Reproductive fruit—making other disciples
C. Fruit of the Spirit like that listed in Galatians 5:22-23
QUESTION 13: *Your answer*
QUESTION 14: *Your answer*
QUESTION 15
A. He commands them to remain in Him.
B. He promises that He will remain in them.
C. He reminds them that a branch must be connected to the vine to bear fruit.
D. He tells them they will not be able to bear fruit unless they remain in Him.
QUESTION 16: *Your answer*
QUESTION 17

Verse	*Outcomes*
Ephesians 1:3	Every spiritual blessing
Ephesians 1:4	Chosen by God
Ephesians 1:6	Grace
Ephesians 1:7	Redemption and forgiveness

QUESTION 18

Scripture	*Jesus being Lord*
Romans 10:9	A new believer needs to confess that Jesus Christ is Lord.
Philippians 2:9-11	Eventually everyone will confess that Jesus Christ is Lord.
Colossians 2:6	Christians should acknowledge that Jesus Christ is Lord

QUESTION 19: *Your answer*

QUESTION 20: *Your answer should be similar to the following:*

So they will be with Him; so that they will be where He is

QUESTION 21: *Your answer should be similar to the following:*

His ministry in this life is not yet finished; the Philippians (and others to whom he ministers) will be better off if he stays (see Phil 1:22, 24-26).

QUESTION 22

Scripture	*Truth Taught*
John 14:1-3	Jesus promises to take His followers to be with Him in a place He has prepared.
2 Corinthians 5:1-9	When a believer dies and is absent from the body, he is present with the Lord
1 Thessalonians 4:13-14	When Christ returns, He will bring with Him believers who have died.
Philippians 1:21-23	Being with Christ is better by far than remaining in the flesh.
Revelation 21:1-3	God's purpose is that we dwell with Him for all eternity.

QUESTION 23: *Your answer*

Lesson 1 Self Check Answers

QUESTION 1: True

QUESTION 2

B. They know that Christ loves them

QUESTION 3: False

QUESTION 4

B. The new birth

QUESTION 5

A. Save lost people

QUESTION 6

D. Attending church

QUESTION 7: True

QUESTION 8

C. Jesus

QUESTION 9

D. The relationship continues uninterrupted.

QUESTION 10

C. To please the Lord

Lesson 2: My Identity in Christ

Lesson Introduction

The Christian's life is significantly different from the lives of unbelievers around him. Having been brought into a new relationship with Christ, his life is no longer tied to the false philosophies of the fallen world in which he lives. The new Christian has a new identity; he has been born again. His outlook and values will be shaped by his relationship with the Lord. As his actions reflect those new values, his behavior will be different from the non-Christians around him as well. In order to live this new life to its full potential, the believer needs to understand just how radical this change is that was initiated in his life when he began his relationship with Jesus Christ.

This lesson will focus on the nature of the Christian's relationship with Christ. Topic 1 will review the condition of the person who has not received Christ. Topic 2 focuses on the change that takes place when a person becomes a Christian and will look at some additional metaphors of the Christian life. Topic 3 addresses some of the old things that should pass away for new believers. In Topic 4, we will see how all things become new for believers.

Lesson Outline

Topic 1: Dead in Sin

Topic 2: Alive in Christ

Topic 3: Old Things

- Behaviors
- Values
- What is Central

Topic 4: New Things

Topic 5: Conclusion

Topic 1: Dead in Sin

When you became a Christian, you began an adventure that would involve several important changes. One such example might be returning the extra money—which would be different from what your behavior would have been before becoming a Christian. Your attitudes and values have changed. At the heart of these changes is the issue of who ultimately has the right to determine the course of one's life. For unbelievers it is self; for Christians it is Christ. So profound is the difference between a believer and an unbeliever that the Bible describes the unbelievers as dead and Christians as born again.

Obviously, unbelievers are not yet *physically* dead. They walk, talk, eat, breathe, and carry on normal lives. The Bible calls them dead because they are separated from God. Separation is at the heart of what the Bible means when it talks about death. Christians, on the other hand, are alive in Christ. They are not separated; they have been brought into a relationship with Christ and are vitally and eternally connected to Him.

Let's begin to explore this difference. Read Ephesians 2:1-3 and notice how Paul describes a person who has not received Christ.

QUESTION 1

What characterized the lives of the Ephesians (and other unbelievers) before they became Christians? *(Select all that apply.)*

A. They were dead in their sins.

B. Their lives followed a worldly course.

C. They indulged their physical and mental cravings.

D. They were good citizens of Rome.

The article below entitled, "Once I Was Dead" was written from the perspective of someone who has become a Christian and is now reflecting on the magnitude of the change that has taken place in his life. Most spiritually dead people do not know that they are spiritually dead. It is the experience of a Christian's new life in Christ that reveals the depth of his former deadness. Having experienced that new life in Christ, the author now can recognize his former condition and identify it for what it is: spiritual death.

Read "Once I Was Dead"," and then answer the questions that appear after the article.

Once I Was Dead

I used to be dead, but I did not know it. You would not have thought I was dead because I functioned much like any other person you know. I walked and talked, slept and ate, worked and played; my life looked normal. I just did not know that I was dead.

Dead people are unresponsive and disconnected. They cannot do anything to transform their deadness into life. That was my condition. I was dead—not physically dead, but spiritually dead. I was dead spiritually, separated from God, and unable to do anything on my own to change that condition.

My problem was not God's holiness; it was my sin. My sinfulness was incompatible with God's holiness. Any action, attitude, or thought that goes against God is sin. Ever since Adam and Eve's fateful decision in the Garden of Eden to disobey God, all of humanity has been subject to both physical and spiritual death. It might be tempting to blame my problems on God, instead of my sin. That approach would be a dead end. Would I really want a god who is unholy? Since God is holy and I am not, it was not possible for me to be both sinful and vitally related to God. At its fundamental meaning, death is separation, and I was separated from God. For me to try to initiate a relationship with the Lord without addressing the problem of sin would be futile.

The Old Testament prophet Isaiah understood the problem of sin. He found himself in the presence of the Lord, hearing the angels proclaiming God's majesty and holiness (Isa 6:1-5). Isaiah's initial response was to assume that he would be destroyed because of his sin. He was helpless to do anything about it. That is the problem with sin. Its consequence is spiritual death (Rom 6:23). It took divine intervention to rescue Isaiah.

The problem of sin, of course, was not unique to me. In fact, it is universal. When Paul wrote to the Ephesian Christians, he said that they had been dead in trespasses and sins (Eph 2:1). Then he included himself and others by using the phrase "all of us" (Eph 2:3). Were it not for the grace of

God, I—along with the Ephesians and Paul himself—would have remained spiritually dead and eternally separated from God.

But God is gracious, and He was not content with the irrevocable separation caused by sin. While a dead sinner could do nothing about the problem, the living Lord provided a solution that was shockingly costly. Jesus Himself would atone for sin, satisfying the holiness of God and making possible reconciliation. When Jesus Christ was crucified, He bore the penalty not for His own sin (He had none) but for ours. God in His great love chose the only way to both satisfy His holiness and pay for our sin. It is in accepting the gift of His sacrifice that spiritually dead people like me are made alive and brought into a relationship with the Lord. Though I was once dead, by the grace of God I have been given new life and an eternal relationship with my redeemer. That life and relationship are forever.

QUESTION 2

Sin always involves actions, but not attitudes, that go against God. *True or False?*

QUESTION 3

Spiritual death is separation from God. *True or False?*

QUESTION 4

What was Isaiah's initial reaction when he found himself in the presence of a holy God?

A. He was joyful; he thought he was in heaven.
B. He was fascinated at the sight of angels.
C. He was confused; he did not understand where he was.
D. He was overwhelmed with his sin and expected to be destroyed.

QUESTION 5

Before you go on to the next topic, open your Life Notebook and take some time to reflect on what your life might have been like if you had never become a Christian and had remained spiritually dead. Give God thanks for making you spiritually alive.

Topic 2: Alive in Christ

What does it mean to be alive in Christ? How do we explain this concept to other people, especially those who are not yet Christians? There are several passages of Scripture that describe the change that takes place when one becomes a Christian.

Read Ephesians 2:4-10.

QUESTION 6

What does this passage (Eph 2:4-10) say that God has done? *(Select all that apply.)*

A. Made us alive with Christ

B. Saved us

C. Prepared good works for us so we could earn our salvation

D. Seated us with Christ in the heavenly realms

This passage teaches us that Christians are spiritually alive. Becoming a Christian gives us a new sensitivity to God and his purposes.

Read Colossians 1:9-14

QUESTION 7

According to Colossians 1:9-14, what has the Lord accomplished in our salvation? *(Select all that apply.)*

A. Rescued us from the domain of darkness

B. Redeemed us

C. Brought us into his kingdom

D. Forgiven us

E. Qualified us for an inheritance

This passage in Colossians not only clarifies God's intent for Christians, it also includes several phrases that describe what God has done in saving an individual.

These passages in Ephesians and Colossians are certainly not the only ones that describe the change that takes place when a person is born again. But the description of what God has done is sufficiently broad that it is worth taking some time to consider and respond to what God has done in saving you.

QUESTION 8

Open your Life Notebook and consider again the list of things from Ephesians 2 and Colossians 1 that God has done. What things are most meaningful to you? Why?

Jesus must have known how challenging it would be for people to grasp the difference that He would make in their lives. He used a number of word pictures to help people understand what a relationship with Him would look like and what it would mean to be "alive in Christ." The following article discusses some of these word pictures that Jesus used. Please read "Pictures of the Christian Life", and then answer the questions that appear after the article.

Pictures of The Christian Life

Good pictures are priceless. I was reminded of that truth while sorting through a box of old family photos and memoirs that had been created by my parents and grandparents. Looking though pictures of places they had lived or visited and people they had known, I deepened my understanding of the lives they had lived. Reading their graphic accounts of surviving World War II created pictures in my own mind of the reality of their struggles far more vividly than if they had simply said that they lived through the war. Good pictures, whether they are photographs or word pictures, are valuable tools that help us understand what is real.

Jesus was a great visual communicator. He had a way of painting word pictures and telling stories that was remarkably effective. Both to His closest disciples and to the larger crowd of curious people, He used word pictures and images that would help them grasp what a relationship with Him was all about. Looking at some of those pictures will help us, too, grasp more deeply what the Christian life is meant to be.

Sheep under a Shepherd's Care

One of the images Jesus liked to use was that of a shepherd with his sheep. In the agrarian society in which Jesus lived and ministered, it was a readily understood metaphor. In John 10:1-15, for example, He describes Himself as both the door of the sheepfold and the shepherd of the sheep. He identified Himself as the one through whom salvation comes. The sheep recognize Him as their shepherd, and in dependence on the shepherd, they readily follow Him. He said that His desire for the sheep is that they will enjoy life abundantly. The very existence of the sheep depends on the wise decisions and actions of the shepherd. They depend on Him for nourishment and safety.

So concerned is the shepherd for the welfare of the sheep that he is willing to lay down his life for them. The shepherd that Jesus describes is not merely the employee of an absentee owner-farmer; he has accepted responsibility for the sheep to the point that he is willing to risk his own life for the sake of the sheep. In other Scripture passages Jesus described the shepherd going out of his way to bring back a lost sheep and to carry a wounded sheep.

The emphasis in this picture is on the shepherd-sheep relationship. While there are certainly applications to be made from the idea of a Christian being part of a flock that stays together, the primary message that Jesus communicates here is a picture of His relationship with the Christian. We who have been given new life in Christ have a Shepherd who is a guide, protector, and provider. We have been transformed from wandering and independent sheep to those who live under the protective leadership of a shepherd's care.

Good Neighbors

In a well-known response to a question posed to Him, Jesus acknowledged that all the Law rested on the commandment to love God and love one's neighbor. The Jewish legal expert who had asked the question pushed for more detail by asking who his neighbor was (Lk 10:25-37). The story that Jesus told in answering that question clarified what it is like to live as one of His followers in an imperfect world.

A man who was traveling from Jerusalem to Jericho was robbed, stripped, beaten, and left lying by the road half dead. The first two people to come by were Jews in good standing. First a priest and then a Levite passed the crime victim. Each of them saw him but took no action to help. By saying that they passed on the other side, Jesus made clear that both of them not only chose not to help but went out of their way to avoid the man. Like the man whose question sparked the story, both were well acquainted with Jewish law that Jesus and the questioner agreed was summed up in the commands to love God and love one's neighbor.

The third man to pass was a Samaritan. Since the Jews and the Samaritans disliked each other, one can easily imagine Jesus smiling as He told the story. Unlike the previous two religious experts, the Samaritan stopped, went to the victim, and tended to his wounds. He then transported this wounded stranger to an inn where he further cared for him. The next day he paid the innkeeper to continue looking after the man, promising to return and reimburse any additional expenses the innkeeper had.

When Jesus concluded by asking which of the three men became a neighbor to the man, there could only be one answer. The model to which Jesus pointed was not the priest or the Levite in spite of their religious knowledge. The model was the Samaritan who, though despised by the religious establishment, demonstrated love for a man in need. Living as a follower of Jesus is less about how much one knows than it is about how much one loves.

Wise Managers

At other times Jesus told stories about servants who were responsible for managing their master's assets to illustrate the responsibility of His followers. You can read one of those stories in Matthew 25:14-30. In this story, a rich owner entrusted varying amounts of money to three different servants. Two of the three used the money to earn more money, effectively doubling what they were initially given. The third buried the money he had been given. When the rich owner returned, he praised and rewarded the first two but he punished the third.

Jesus dramatically made the point that His followers are stewards or managers rather than owners. They are responsible for what has been entrusted to them and will be held accountable for their actions (or lack of action). Everything a believer has, whether material assets or immaterial things such as abilities, is a gift from God that is held in trust. Since the Lord remains the owner, what He has entrusted should be used in ways that benefit His kingdom and further His purposes. Because Christ's followers are managers rather than owners, it is both appropriate and expected that they will be asked to account for their use of what has been entrusted.

This stewardship principle applies to material things like money; what may be less obvious is that it also applies to the gospel itself. Read 1 Thessalonians 2:4 and notice how the apostle Paul described himself. Followers of Christ are entrusted with the good news of the gospel, and burying it is obviously not the Lord's intent. Just as Christians are accountable for what they do with material things entrusted to them, so they are accountable for what they do with the gospel.

An Eternal Focus

Several of the word pictures Jesus used include hints that His followers are focused on more than this present life and are anticipating an eternal future. That characteristic is another way in which Christians differ from other people in the culture around them. Consider two stories Jesus told in Luke 12. Read Luke 12:16-40.

The first story focuses on a man who is rich, but foolish. Like some people today, his primary goal was accumulating wealth for himself in this world. He was unaware that his life was about to end, and he was mindless of eternity. God called him a fool; death would separate him from everything he had accumulated. Jesus then encouraged His disciples not to worry about the physical and material needs, but rather to set God's kingdom as a priority.

The second story likens Christ's followers to the servants of a man attending a wedding banquet. As faithful servants they were prepared for the return of their master even though they do not know exactly when he would return. Jesus made the point very clear as He told His disciples they too must be ready because they do not know when He will return.

The Christian can and should live with an eternal perspective, anticipating and ready for Christ's return. Having that kind of perspective provides some freedom from temporal and earthbound ambitions. Instead of devoting all one's time and energy to what will not last beyond death, the believer lives with a view to eternity.

These pictures are a few of those Jesus used to communicate the kind of people His followers should be and the kind of life they should live. Christians are valued sheep under the care of a loving shepherd. They are good neighbors ready to meet people's needs. They are wise managers who are always accountable to their Lord. And they are people who are living beyond the present with eternity in view. Good pictures are priceless, and the pictures Jesus created help us see what the Christian life is meant to be.

QUESTION 9

Match the Scripture reference with the word picture Jesus used.

Scripture reference	*Word picture*
John 10	Sheep and shepherd
Luke 10	Good neighbor
Matthew 25	Wise manager
Luke 12	Eternal focus

QUESTION 10

In 1 Thessalonians 2, with what does Paul say he has been entrusted?

A. Money
B. Time
C. Abilities
D. The gospel

QUESTION 11

In the story Jesus told in Luke 10:25-37, who was the good neighbor?

A. A priest
B. A Samaritan
C. A Levite
D. An innkeeper
E. A Pharisee

QUESTION 12

What is the point of the story of the good neighbor in Luke 10?

A. Samaritans are more godly than Levites.
B. Religious people should avoid other people's wounds.
C. Christians are expected to show love for other people.
D. Helping strangers might interfere with other important responsibilities.
E. Traveling alone is dangerous and should be avoided when possible.

QUESTION 13

Open your Life Notebook and write a personal response to the article "Pictures of the Christian Life." Include a summary description of the Christian life based on the stories Jesus told that are referred to in the article. Are there other word pictures or parables that Jesus used to describe the Christian life that were not included in the article?

Topic 3: Old Things

The Bible teaches us that when we come to faith in Christ, our old lifestyle passes away. Our old desires, such as keeping extra change from the store, are replaced with new desires that are Christ-like.

We see this explained in 2 Corinthians 5:17: "So then, if anyone is in Christ, he is a new creation; what is old has passed away - look, what is new has come!"

For Christians, the old things die. What was once true of us will no longer be true. Part of becoming a new creation in Christ involves letting go of some old things that should be considered dead. In this topic we will look at some of those old things that the believer should recognize as having passed away.

Behaviors

There are several places in the Bible that talk about some of these old things that should pass away. A very visible area of change has to do with behaviors—the things we do (or do not do) and the way we act. In his letter to the Ephesian believers, Paul encourages Christians to let go of some old behaviors. Read Ephesians 4:17-32.

QUESTION 14

According to Ephesians 4:25-31, what are some of the behaviors that Christians should lay aside?

QUESTION 15

Open your Life Notebook and reflect on the behaviors in Ephesians 4:25-31 that Christians should lay aside. Are there any behaviors in this list with which you struggle? Take some time to ask God to help you lay aside those areas of struggle and thank him for bringing change to your life.

Values

It is not only old behaviors that pass away; Christians may need to release old values as well. When a person becomes a Christian, he is acting on the truth in which he believes. When those beliefs shape behavior, they become values. In other words, usually our behaviors—what we do and say—are shaped by our values. Our values are those truths we deem sufficiently important to act on. If, for example, I *value* fellowship with other believers (rather than simply believe it is important), I will schedule fellowship opportunities into my life. If I value my own comfort over the good of others, that value will shape my actions. Values have to do with what is most important to us. It is almost certain that when a person becomes a Christian, some values—the things he considers most important—will need to change.

In a very personal passage in his letter to the Philippians, Paul talked about this shift in values in his own life. He valued his background and position as a respected Jew, and not without cause. Paul had good reason to value and be proud of his credentials as a Jew. Read Philippians 3:1-11 where Paul outlines some of things about his background that he had treasured and puts them in new perspective.

QUESTION 16

Which of the following items did Paul list as among his valued human credentials? *(Select all that apply.)*

A. Circumcised on the eighth day

B. Living as a Pharisee

C. Persecuting Christians

D. Serving as a priest

E. Knowing his heritage as belonging to the tribe of Benjamin

Paul considered these things that he had once highly valued to now be the equivalent of worthless dung. His Jewish background still existed, but it ceased to be a value in his life that controlled what he did. What mattered to him now was knowing Christ, and that had turned his values upside down.

What is Central

Paul's shift in values raises a more basic "old thing" that for the believer needs to pass away. Underlying behaviors and values are the way we view ourselves. Human beings are by nature self-centered. We easily become our own highest priority, and when that is true, then what we have, who we are, or what we do can get in the way of a relationship with Jesus Christ. A focus on self, whether evidenced in behaviors or values, is incompatible with a relationship in which Jesus Christ is Lord.

Consider the sad case of the rich young man who seems to want to follow Christ until he is faced with the cost. Read Mark 10:17-25.

QUESTION 17

What do we learn from this conversation between the young man and Jesus? *(Select all that apply.)*

A. It is not possible to be both rich in possessions and spiritually rich.

B. The young man had tried to live according to God's law.

C. Jesus loved the rich young man.

D. The man was sad because Jesus told him to get rid of his wealth.

E. Material wealth can keep a person from Christ.

Anything that is more important to a believer than his relationship with Christ needs to be released. There was nothing inherently wrong with the rich young man's wealth; the problem was that it got in the way of a relationship with Jesus. For the Christian, Christ is central. To try to live as an ego-centric Christian is to try to live a contradiction. Though many people try to live that kind of life, it is not what God intended.

What the ego-centric Christian life looks like will vary from one person to another, but what they have in common is giving priority to someone or something that takes the place that Christ should have in their lives. For one person it may be the material possessions they own, as it was for the rich young man that Jesus encountered. For another, it might be ambition or a desire to excel in a chosen career. For someone else, some practice or habit that has been a part of one's pre-conversion life may be given a place that belongs to Christ. Even something as good as family can usurp the central position that should be given to the Lord. The problem is not that these things are intrinsically bad; in fact, many of them are good. The issue is who or what is central in the life of the believer.

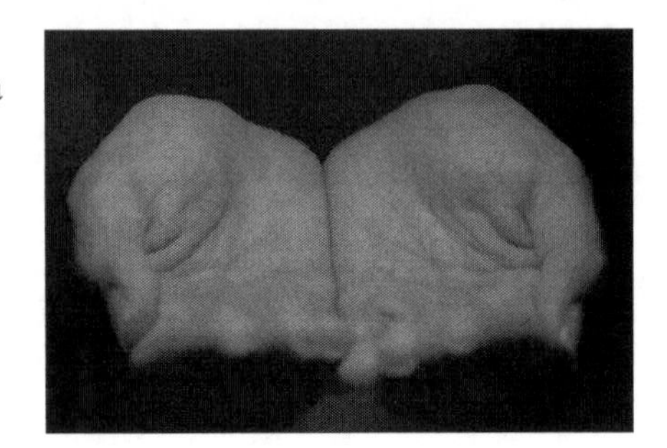

Whether it is personal desires, a particular habit or sin, an accomplishment, an ambition, or a possession, whatever obstructs a relationship with Christ must be released so that the Christian can enjoy his new life in Christ.

Before you move on to the next section, take some time in quiet prayer to reflect on who or what is central in your life. Thank God for His desire to be central in your life, and, letting go of anything that you need to, willingly give Him that place again.

Topic 4: New Things

As shown in Topic 3, 2 Corinthians 5:17 teaches us that old things have passed away. This explains why we do not kept the extra change from the store. But notice that this same verse also teaches us that "what is new has come!" That's important! The Christian life isn't just a collection of *don'ts*! Christianity is not a giant collection of negatives—things to give up. There's far more to it than that. Our new relationship with Jesus is at the top of the list of new things in our lives.

This means we are no longer separated from God. And because of that, we experience many other new things as well. As we grow in our relationship with Christ, what is important to Him becomes important to us. In other words, we have new values. And out of those new values come new behaviors. We say and do things differently—like returning that extra change. What is new far outweighs the old that is gone.

For the believer what is new far overshadows what is old; what has come is far better than what has passed away. In this topic, we will explore some of the new things that may come into our lives.

QUESTION 18

Memorize 2 Corinthians 5:17. Write it from memory below.

The Christian life begins with a transition. Like most transitions it involves not only leaving some things behind, it also means taking hold of some things that are new. The article entitled, "New Things Have

Come" is about the positive side of this transition. Read this article "New Things Have Come" below, and then answer the questions that follow it.

New Things Have Come

Hannah was not at all sure that she would like her new home. Her father had taken a job in a distant town, and now she and her family were traveling to begin their new life. Her parents were excited about the move, and while some of that excitement rubbed off on Hannah, she could not help thinking about what she was leaving behind. All her friends lived in the town they were leaving. Hannah had been born in that town, and it was the only place she knew. In preparation for the move, her family had discarded some of their belongings, thinking that some things would be easier to replace than to move, but already Hannah missed some of those things. Hannah sensed that she was being separated from much of what had been important to her. Sensing her anxiety, her mother reached out to her. Speaking softly and with a gentle smile, she said, "A world of new opportunities is waiting for you, and we'll discover them together."

Becoming a Christian involves significant change. When a person focuses only on the old things that fall away, one can begin to think of Christianity in terms that are only negative and fail to recognize the wonder of what Christ has done. For these few minutes let's focus our attention on some of the wonderful new things that are the believer's to experience and enjoy.

At the heart of Christianity is a new relationship with Jesus Christ. He is our Savior, Friend, Teacher, Lord, and Shepherd. Christians live a daily adventure of ongoing discovery of His character and experience of His love. Christians are able to experience a new relationship that reflects the reality of which David wrote in Psalm 23. When a believer reads that psalm, he can recognize that the multiple roles of the shepherd reflect the richness of the ways in which the Lord relates to His people. We Christians have been brought into a new relationship that is sensationally wonderful.

Along with this new relationship come new values. The Christian is no longer a slave to the things of this world; instead he is invited to make God's kingdom his primary priority. Before continuing with the rest of this article, read Matthew 6:24-34 for a sense of the difference that this new priority can make in the life of the believer and the liberty it brings. Because the Lord is his shepherd and provider, the Christian does not need to gain the things of this world as his first priority.

The Christian has a new and deep commitment to truth. In today's world many people lack an awareness of the reality of unchanging truth. They wrongly think of truth as though it were relative. But what changes is hard to trust. Believers are encouraged not only to trust what is true but also to let their minds focus on what is true and to speak that which is true (see, for example, Phil 4:8 and Eph 4:14-15). Truth becomes an integral characteristic of their new life in Christ.

Part of that truth is the reality of the believer's immortality—the wonderful truth that they are created for eternity. Unlike other people whose hope is limited to what they can experience here and now, the Christian's hope is focused on an eternal future and anchored in the person and work of Jesus Christ. That reality impacts not only their attitude toward day-to-day life, but their response to physical death as well. Their hope even shapes their grief. Paul explains this outworking of hope in 1 Thessalonians 4:13-18, expressing his desire that the Thessalonian Christians not "grieve like the rest who have no hope." Their expectation of an eternal future with the Lord is to be an encouragement to them that is a response strikingly different from the grief of unbelievers.

But what about the Christian who fails to enjoy the new things that are his in Christ? It may seem strange that a believer would choose to live life as he always had as though no new things had come. However, it is clear from both experience and Scripture that some Christians do make that choice. Whether the choice is made consciously or not, the result is that they live as though Christ had made no difference in their lives. The Bible refers to such people as "worldly" or "people of the flesh." They are Christians; they belong to Christ, but they live as though Christ had not saved them. Paul points out that some of the Corinthian Christians were worldly because of their behavior—jealousy, quarreling, factions among them, and other kinds of sinful behavior (1 Cor 3:1-4).

Such worldly Christians are like Hannah. They are so tied to the habits of the past or fearful of the future that they fail to enjoy the new things they have been given. They try to live life as they have always lived it. Just as Hannah heard her mother inviting her to discover new opportunities, so they need to hear the Lord who has redeemed them and invited them to discover the new things that have come.

QUESTION 19

Match the Scripture passage to the new thing that it describes.

Scripture Passage	*New Thing*
Psalm 23	Truth
Matthew 6	New relationship with the Lord
Ephesians 4:14-15	New values
1 Thessalonians 4	Hope

Because human beings are finite creatures, they have to make choices, and those choices reflect their values. A believer who has adopted Christ's values has different priorities. In the Matthew 6 passage you read, Jesus sums up these new priorities as seeking first God's kingdom.

QUESTION 20

Read Matthew 6:24-34 again. If someone in your church asked what it meant to seek first God's kingdom and righteousness, how would you respond? Write your answer in your Life Notebook and be prepared to discuss it.

The new things that come into the life of the believer arise from the new relationship he has with the Lord. The psalmist creates a vivid word picture of that relationship by describing the Lord as a Shepherd. The role of a Shepherd is anything but passive; he must relate to the sheep in a variety of ways.

QUESTION 21

Which of the following does the shepherd do in Psalm 23? *(Select all that apply.)*

A. Provides nourishing food and refreshing water

B. Restores strength

C. Avoids dark and dangerous places

D. Leads and directs

E. Remains faithful

F. Provides a home

The Christian life is much more than a collection of old things to be put off. It involves a host of new things that become part of the Christian's life. Earlier in this lesson you looked at a list of old behaviors in Ephesians 4. Now let's look at the other side—the new things that come.

QUESTION 22

Open your Life Notebook and review the list of "old things" that you wrote in response to Question 14. Reread Ephesians 4:25-32 and make a new list of new behaviors that should replace the old ones.

Some Christians have difficulty with this transition. For a variety of reasons, they get stuck in the "old" and so have difficulty taking hold of the "new." The Bible calls such worldly Christians *people of the flesh*. It is possible—and even likely—that you know people like that, Christians who are having difficulty with the transition from the old to the new.

QUESTION 23

How would you help a person who is a worldly Christian or person of the flesh? Record your answer in your Life Notebook.

Topic 5: Conclusion

Understanding our new life in Christ can sometimes be frustrating, but it can also be a rich source of blessing. We need to remind ourselves of the magnitude of our salvation. We used to be spiritually dead, so dead that we were unaware of our own deadness; now we are alive in Christ. Old behaviors and values have shifted and are being replaced by new ones. Just thinking about what God has made possible in our lives should prompt us to be deeply grateful.

The next lesson will focus on God's role in the believer's life through the indwelling Holy Spirit. Before we get there, let's take some time to reflect on the greatness of what God has done.

QUESTION 24

In Question 22 you listed some of the new behaviors that replace old ones. Now think beyond behaviors. Open your Life Notebook and list some of the new things that have come into your life since you became a Christian. Take some time to specifically thank God for each of these new things that he has made possible for you through your new life in Jesus Christ.

Lesson 2 Self Check: The Christian Life

QUESTION 1

To be spiritually dead is to be separated from God. *True or False?*

QUESTION 2

In John 10, how does Jesus describe himself?

A. As the good shepherd and as the hired hand
B. As the good shepherd and as the door
C. As the good shepherd but not the door
D. As the door but not as the shepherd or the hired hand

QUESTION 3

Which of the following is not used by the shepherd in Psalm 23?

A. Rod
B. Oil
C. Table
D. Knife

QUESTION 4

What question did Jesus answer by telling the story of the good neighbor?

A. How can a man be born again?
B. What is the greatest law?
C. Who is my neighbor?
D. Why are you worried?

QUESTION 5

In the story of the wise managers, who does the owner punish?

A. All three servants
B. The servant to whom he entrusted the most
C. The servant who returned exactly what was entrusted to him
D. None of the servants

QUESTION 6

What are the old things that pass away when a person becomes a Christian?

A. Both values and behaviors
B. Values but not behaviors
C. Behaviors but not values
D. Neither values nor behaviors

QUESTION 7

Why did Paul consider his human credentials to be worthless dung?

A. They did not impress his Gentile converts.

B. Nothing was as important as knowing Christ.

C. Jewish leaders persecuted him.

D. They did not seem to help him win people to Christ.

QUESTION 8

What new value replaces concern for material needs as a priority in Matthew 6?

A. Truth

B. Hope

C. Family

D. God's kingdom

QUESTION 9

The Christian's hope is focused on his relationships with other believers in this life. *True or False?*

QUESTION 10

In the context of this lesson, who is described by the term "people of the flesh"?

A. Non-Christians

B. All Christians who have not yet died

C. Christians who live as though Christ has not saved them

D. Christian martyrs

Lesson 2 Answers to Questions

QUESTION 1

A. They were dead in their sins.
B. Their lives followed a worldly course.
C. They indulged their physical and mental cravings.

QUESTION 2: False

QUESTION 3: True

QUESTION 4

D. He was overwhelmed with his sin and expected to be destroyed.

QUESTION 5: *Your answer*

QUESTION 6

A. Made us alive with Christ
B. Saved us
D. Prepared good works for us so we could earn our salvation

QUESTION 7

A. Rescued us from the domain of darkness
B. Redeemed us
C. Brought us into his kingdom
D. Forgiven us
E. Qualified us for an inheritance

QUESTION 8: *Your answer*

QUESTION 9

Scripture reference	*Word picture*
John 10	Sheep and shepherd
Luke 10	Good neighbor
Matthew 25	Wise manager
Luke 12	Eternal focus

QUESTION 10

D. The gospel

QUESTION 11

B. A Samaritan

QUESTION 12

C. Christians are expected to show love for other people.

QUESTION 13: *Your answer*

QUESTION 14: *Your answer should be similar to the following:*

Falsehood, letting anger lead to sin, stealing, unwholesome talk, bitterness, anger, wrath, quarreling, evil.

QUESTION 15: *Your answer*

QUESTION 16

A. Circumcised on the eighth day
B. Living as a Pharisee
C. Persecuting Christians
E. Knowing his heritage as belonging to the tribe of Benjamin

QUESTION 17

B. The young man had tried to live according to God's law.
C. Jesus loved the rich young man.
D. The man was sad because Jesus told him to get rid of his wealth.
E. Material wealth can keep a person from Christ.

QUESTION 18: *Your answer should be similar to the following:*
So then, if anyone is in Christ, he is a new creation; what is old has passed away, see, what is new has come!

QUESTION 19

Scripture Passage	*New Thing*
Psalm 23	New relationship with the Lord
Matthew 6	New values
Ephesians 4:14-15	Truth
1 Thessalonians 4	Hope

QUESTION 20: *Your answer*

QUESTION 21

A. Provides nourishing food and refreshing water
B. Restores strength
D. Leads and directs
E. Remains faithful
F. Provides a home

QUESTION 22: *Your answer*

QUESTION 23: *Your answer*

QUESTION 24: *Your answer*

Lesson 2 Self Check Answers

QUESTION 1: True

QUESTION 2

B. As the good shepherd and as the door

QUESTION 3

D. Knife

QUESTION 4

C. Who is my neighbor?

QUESTION 5

C. The servant who returned exactly what was entrusted to him

QUESTION 6

A. Both values and behaviors

QUESTION 7

B. Nothing was as important as knowing Christ.

QUESTION 8

D. God's kingdom

QUESTION 9: False

QUESTION 10

C. Christians who live as though Christ has not saved them

Lesson 3: The Holy Spirit—How God Lives in Me

Lesson Introduction

In the Christian's relationship with the Lord, both parties are committed to an irrevocable and ongoing relationship. Not only is the Christian described as being "in Christ," but also God in the person of the Holy Spirit indwells the believer. This lesson will focus on the important role of the Holy Spirit in the life of the Christian.

It is crucial to understand that the Holy Spirit is fully God. God is triune, that is, He exists as three distinct persons, each of whom is fully God. Explaining the doctrine of the Trinity is beyond the scope of this course, but the reality of the Trinity is essential to the Christian life. The Holy Spirit, who is no less God than the Father or the Son, lives within the Christian, and His presence should make a difference.

The first topic explores the promise of another helper Jesus gave to the disciples as the time of His departure drew near. The second topic looks at the implications for the believer of the Holy Spirit dwelling in him. The third topic provides a few principles relating to the gifts of the Spirit. Topic 4 discusses with the fruit of the Spirit, which are the visible evidences of the Spirit's presence in the believer's life. Topic five focuses on several specific ministries of the Holy Spirit in the life of the Christian.

Lesson Outline

Topic 1: The Promised Helper

Topic 2: Spiritual Temples

Topic 3: The Gifts of the Spirit

Topic 4: The Fruit of the Spirit

Topic 5: The Holy Spirit's Work in Me

Topic 6: Conclusion

Topic 1: The Promised Helper

The Holy Spirit indwelling the life of the believer *ought to* and *does* make a difference in our lives. Jesus explained to His disciples that the indwelling Holy Spirit would be active in their lives. The Spirit would teach, remind, encourage, empower, and convict. Not only would the Holy Spirit interact with them in ways similar to Jesus, but Jesus said they would actually be better off with the Holy Spirit than they had been with the physical presence of Jesus.

If you are a Christian, the Holy Spirit has been active in your life. Before exploring what the Bible has to say about the Holy Spirit's work in the Christian, take a few minutes to think about how the Spirit has worked in your life.

QUESTION 1

In your Life Notebook, write down one or two ways that the Holy Spirit has worked in your life. How do you know that it is the work of the Holy Spirit?

It was in the hours leading up to His arrest and crucifixion that Jesus explained to the disciples that the Holy Spirit would come to be with them and in them. Read John 14-16 first. Then read the following article "The Promised Helper" before answering the questions below that follow.

The Promised Helper

It had been a long day, and Jesus was talking about leaving them. For the disciples it was a disquieting conversation. In a matter of hours Jesus would be arrested and soon after that crucified, and now He was preparing them for what lay ahead. The idea of Jesus leaving them to go to the Father was no more appealing to the disciples than the idea of losing any valued friend to death. But in the middle of the conversation, Jesus made it clear that they would not be left alone. The Father, He said, would give them another Advocate who would live with them and be in them.

The word Jesus used to describe the Holy Spirit has been translated as counselor, comforter, advocate, or helper. It literally means someone who has been called alongside a person in need to help them. Exactly what needs the disciples had and exactly how the Spirit would help them may not have been clear to the disciples; they were preoccupied with their own welfare in light of the thought of Jesus leaving them. As He spoke of the promised Helper, Jesus began to open their understanding of what the Spirit would mean to them.

While they were still in the upper room, Jesus began to describe the relationship they would have with the Holy Spirit. In John 14:15-17 He made two important points. First, the Spirit would come to be with them and in them permanently. While they had experienced the enablement of the Spirit in particular instances, after Jesus departed, the Spirit would come to stay, indwelling every believer. This truth is repeated elsewhere in passages such as Romans 8:9 that indicate that the Spirit is present in everyone who belongs to Christ. The idea of the Spirit indwelling only some Christians or departing for one reason or another is foreign to what Jesus said. The Son asks the Father, and the Father sends the Spirit "to be with you forever." The Christian is never in a position where he can honestly complain, "Where is the Spirit when you need Him?"

The second point Jesus made is to identify the helper as "the Spirit of truth," a phrase He used several times. An important part of the Spirit's work in believers is linking them to the truth of God. Truth is an inseparable part of who God is, and moments earlier Jesus had told them, "I am the truth" (Jn 14:6). The Spirit opens one's understanding of who God is. Jesus told them that the Spirit would teach them everything and bring to mind everything that Jesus had said (Jn 14:25-26). Without communication, relationships wither. Since part of the Spirit's ministry in the life of the believer is bringing to mind what Jesus had said, the Spirit is essential to an ongoing healthy relationship with the Lord.

If Jesus had said no more about the Holy Spirit, He would have said enough to ease the disciples' minds. But He was not finished. In John 15:26-27 He said that the Spirit of truth will testify about Him and that the disciples, indwelt with the Holy Spirit, will testify about Jesus. The Spirit's work of exposing people to the truth of Jesus Christ is often carried out through believers who are empowered by the Spirit.

In the next chapter Jesus developed this thought further (Jn 16:7-11). The Spirit will come to *believers*, and when He comes He will convict (prove them wrong) *the world* concerning sin, righteousness, and judgment. Once again, more often than not, unbelievers come in contact with the convicting work of the Spirit through believers. One of the reasons that can happen is that believers have experienced that convicting work of the Spirit for themselves. Most people in holding to a typical view of the world are wrong about sin, righteousness, and judgment, and it takes the work of the Spirit of truth to open their eyes to the reality of their own plight and the good news of Christ's provision of salvation.

The emphasis on the truth-disclosing nature of the Spirit's work continues in the following verses (Jn 16:12-15) as Jesus assured them that the Spirit will guide them into all truth and will glorify Jesus.

After His resurrection and just before His ascension to heaven, Jesus again reminded His followers that the Holy Spirit would empower them to be His witnesses in the world. In Acts 1:4-9 He told them to wait for the Spirit, and that when the Spirit came, they would receive spiritual power and be His witnesses. In a matter of days they would see the Spirit's power demonstrated in their lives as thousands were convicted and turned to Christ on the Day of Pentecost as the Spirit of truth did His work.

At first glance this may seem like a poor plan for Jesus to leave and give His followers the massive responsibility to take the gospel to the world. Apart from the Holy Spirit, it *would* be insane. But Jesus promised that a Helper, the Holy Spirit, would be with them forever. The Spirit of truth would testify of Jesus and empower His followers to do likewise. And with the Spirit's help the gospel is reaching every part of the world.

Once the Spirit was given, the disciples would discover that His help and influence extended into every area of their lives. They would discover the truth of what Jesus had told them, that it was to their advantage that Jesus leave them so that the Spirit could come. In His earthly body, Jesus was limited by time and space; there were times He could not physically be present with His disciples. The Holy Spirit, who comes to permanently reside in every believer, is a helper whose influence can be even greater than that of Jesus whose physical presence was limited.

Jesus kept His promise. From the first day the Spirit was given, Christ's followers began to experience His help, guidance, empowerment, and resources as they lived in the fulfillment of Christ's promise.

QUESTION 2

What phrase did Jesus repeatedly use to describe the Holy Spirit to His disciples?

A. Spirit of power

B. Source of comfort

C. Spirit of truth

D. Blessed hope

E. Spirit of love

QUESTION 3

Match the Scripture references with the truth it teaches about the Holy Spirit.

Scripture	*Truth about the Holy Spirit*
Romans 8:9	The Holy Spirit empowers believers for witness.
John 15:26	Every Christian is indwelt by the Holy Spirit.
John 14:16	The Holy Spirit testifies about Jesus.
Acts 1:8	The Holy Spirit indwells believers permanently.
John 14:26	The Holy Spirit brings to mind what Jesus said.
John 16:8	The Holy Spirit convicts of sin.

Topic 2: Spiritual Temples

Sometimes we may struggle to understand the idea of God's Spirit indwelling Christians. Many other religions have temples or special places where they believe God resides, and those places become the focal points for worship and religious activity. However, for Christians, we are the temple. That does not mean that church buildings are unimportant; it means that God's Spirit comes to reside in us. Of course, there are implications for how we live that go along with the presence of God's Spirit since we are spiritual temples.

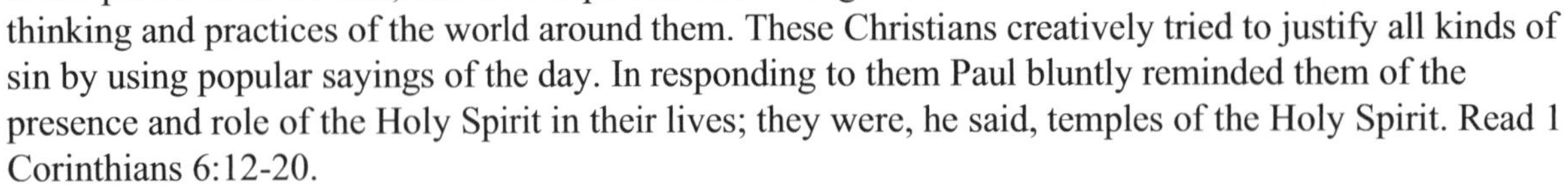

The idea that God in the person of the Holy Spirit comes to reside in the Christian is a radical concept. It does not mean, as some believe, that we become gods and it does not mean that we are somehow superhuman. But it does mean that God is our constant companion, going where we go, witnessing everything we do, and hearing everything we say. Because we are Christians in whom He dwells, we are irrevocably identified with Him. In this topic we explore the implications of the Holy Spirit residing in the Christian.

The Christians at Corinth to whom Paul wrote were not much different from contemporary Christians. They lived in a world that accepted many sinful practices as normal, and the temptation was strong to follow the thinking and practices of the world around them. These Christians creatively tried to justify all kinds of sin by using popular sayings of the day. In responding to them Paul bluntly reminded them of the presence and role of the Holy Spirit in their lives; they were, he said, temples of the Holy Spirit. Read 1 Corinthians 6:12-20.

QUESTION 4

To what specific sinful practice was Paul responding when he said that the Christian's body was the temple of the Holy Spirit?

A. Dishonesty

B. Sexual immorality

C. Murder

D. Idolatry

E. Coveting

QUESTION 5

In your Life Notebook write a paragraph or two explaining why sexual purity is an important issue for Christians.

In Old Testament times God's people were given strict instructions regarding the temple. It was to be considered holy because God dwelt there. It is no less true today that Christians, whose bodies Scripture describes as temples for God's Spirit, should treat their bodies as the holy temple of God.

In the last lesson we looked at a passage in Ephesians 4 that focused on the behavioral changes that should take place in the life of a Christian. The verses cited in that lesson are part of a larger passage providing very practical teaching about the way Christians should live. In the context of that teaching comes a specific exhortation regarding the Holy Spirit. Read once again Ephesians 4:17–5:2.

QUESTION 6

In this passage, what are Christians specifically commanded not to do regarding the Holy Spirit?

A. Grieve him

B. Imitate him

C. Ignore him

D. Talk to him

QUESTION 7

The immediate context of the command indicates that what we say, as well as what we do, can displease the Holy Spirit. *True or False?*

It is abundantly clear in this section of Ephesians that sin in any form will displease the Holy Spirit. Christians are encouraged to live a life of love (Eph 5:2) and live as children of the light (Eph 5:8). Love and light reflect the character of God; sin, of course, does not. Christ was crucified to pay for our sin, so it is not hard to understand why sin would cause the Holy Spirit to grieve.

A similar exhortation occurs in the closing verses of Paul's first letter to the Thessalonians. Read 1 Thessalonians 5:12-24.

The command here uses a different kind of language and imagery from the command in Ephesians 4. Here Christians are told to not extinguish or quench the Holy Spirit. The image of the Holy Spirit being like fire is one that is repeated several times in Scripture. John the Baptist, speaking of Jesus, said that He would baptize with the Holy Spirit and fire (Mt 3:11). When the Spirit was given on the Day of Pentecost, the visible representation of the Spirit was like flames (Acts 2:3-4). If the Holy Spirit is like fire, then to extinguish Him is to make Him ineffective. The context of the command in 1 Thessalonians 5 gives us some hints as to how that quenching might happen.

QUESTION 8

Which of the following does Paul say are to be avoided along with extinguishing the Spirit (1 Thess 5:12-24)? *(Select all that apply.)*

A. Indulging evil

B. Neglecting prayer

C. Ingratitude

D. Disrespect for spiritual leaders

E. Devaluing God's prophetic word

The image of extinguishing or quenching the Holy Spirit does not mean that the Christian is in danger of losing the indwelling Holy Spirit. When Jesus promised His disciples another helper, remember that the Spirit would be with them forever. It is not the presence of the Spirit that is at stake; it is the Christian's willingness to let the Holy Spirit work in and through him.

QUESTION 9

Open your Life Notebook and consider the metaphor of the Holy Spirit as fire. How is the Holy Spirit's activity in your life like fire? What might be the effects of extinguishing or cooling that fire?

Topic 3: The Gifts of the Spirit

One of the important ways in which the Holy Spirit enables us to function as God intends is by equipping us for whatever ministry God gives us. Scripture calls these equipping *gifts*, and the term fits since Christians do nothing to earn or even choose their gifts. The Bible includes several lists of these gifts, and no two are identical. Some writers have identified as many as twenty-five or more different spiritual gifts in Scripture. The gifts include things like prophecy (proclaiming God's Word), teaching, helping, giving, and leading. Our purpose here is not to examine each gift in detail, but to look at some principles that will help us understand how spiritual gifts fit into the life of the Christian.

Read 1 Corinthians 12-13 and then read the following article "The Gifts of the Spirit" These two chapters in 1 Corinthians provide not only a list of some of the gifts, but also a discussion of how those gifts should be perceived within the context of the church. The article focuses not on the individual gifts themselves, but on several important principles that Christians need to understand if they are to use the gifts effectively. Understanding the source and purpose of spiritual gifts as well as the nature of the giver and the attitude of the recipient help equip us to use these gifts as God intended. After you have read the article, answer the questions that follow.

The Gifts of the Spirit

One of the important functions of the indwelling Holy Spirit is equipping Christians to become effective servants of Jesus Christ. Every believer is unique, and the ways in which a particular believer is called to serve Christ will differ from the ministries entrusted to other believers. The Holy Spirit is the one who endows each believer with whatever gifts that Christian will need for the ministry to which he has been called. In writing to the Corinthians Paul said he wanted them to be informed and not ignorant regarding spiritual gifts. Christians today are also wise to be informed and not ignorant when it comes to the matter of spiritual gifts.

There are several lists of gifts in the Bible, but none of them lists all of the gifts. Because these are gifts from an infinite and unlimited God, it is likely that no list, no matter how carefully compiled, will exhaust the possible gifts the Spirit might give. Read for yourself the lists in the following three passages and notice both the variety of gifts within each list and the differences among the lists: Romans 12:4-8; 1 Corinthians 12:7-11; Ephesians 4:11-13. The variety within these lists is easy to see. Some of the gifts are prominent and public; others are less likely to be seen. Some are exercised in group settings, others in person-to-person encounters. Some are special enablements of qualities expected of all believers. Probably no one possesses every gift, but mostly likely every believer has at least one gift and some have two or more.

While the three passages cited above are the ones most often used in discussing and studying the gifts, they are not the only places that refer to spiritual gifting. Even in Old Testament times, God gifted certain individuals in special ways for the ministry to which He called them. When God commanded the building of the tabernacle, He gave those who would be in charge of the project the gift of craftsmanship, a gift not specifically mentioned in any of the New Testament passages above. Exodus 35:30-35 makes clear that Bezalel and Oholiab were not just talented craftsmen; they were gifted by God to enable their service and for the good of God's people in the same way God enables believers in the New Testament with spiritual gifts.

In 1 Corinthians 12, Paul specifically addressed the matter of spiritual gifts and made several important principles clear. First, he emphasized that the Holy Spirit is the source of the gifts. Spiritual gifts are not a matter of one's own ability, cleverness, or spirituality; they are *gifts* that originate from God, who is sovereign. This fact is true of all spiritual gifts, including those that may be less valued or less noticeable by other people. Virtually any group of Christians will exhibit a wide variety of gifts, but all those gifts are given by the same Spirit. The Spirit enables a person to acknowledge Jesus Christ as Lord, and the use of one's spiritual gifts, whatever they may be, should point to Christ's lordship.

Second, Paul emphasized that gifts are given for the common good rather than only for an individual's good. If, for example, God has gifted someone as a teacher, He has done so not so much for the person's good as for the good of the larger body of believers. Understanding that principle is important in maintaining a healthy attitude toward gifts. At the same time each believer should recognize that if God has gifted him in a particular way, he will not be fulfilled as a Christian unless he chooses to exercise that gift for the good of the body of believers.

Since gifts are intended for the good of other believers and not merely for the good of the individual, gifts are best identified within the context of Christian fellowship. If someone thinks he has the gift of prophecy and no one else in his church thinks he has that gift, probably they are right, and he is wrong. Likewise, if the believers, and particularly spiritual leaders, in his church see that God has gifted him as a teacher, then he should probably seek to develop and exercise that gift in spite of any reluctance he may feel about his teaching ability. Usually the most reliable indicator of a person's spiritual gifting is the feedback from other spiritually minded Christians who know that person well. This principle is illustrated in Acts 6:1-7 with the recognition of the first deacons and in Acts 13:1-3 when the Christians at Antioch sent out Saul and Barnabas on their first missionary journey. In both instances other believers identified those they saw as gifted and qualified for the ministry at hand.

Third, Paul emphasized spiritual gifts should never become an excuse for disunity among believers. Beginning in 1 Corinthians 12:12, he stressed that though believers may be quite varied in their gifting, they are parts of one body. He continued the metaphor of the body to the point of being grotesquely comical: What if the entire body were one giant eye? Or what if the hand sought to eliminate every part of the body that was not a hand? What if the body consisted only of those parts that are usually visible? The images these questions evoke are in sharp contrast to a healthy body. The same kind of variety that exists among the various parts of the human body should also exist in the gifts of a group of Christians. Clearly homogeneity of giftedness is not a biblical value.

Because of this intentional variety of giftedness, it is a mistake to consider any gift or group of gifts as a mark of spiritual achievement. A believer or church that makes that mistake virtually guarantees disunity. Gifts are related to a Christian's calling, not to his level of spirituality.

Fourth, Paul reminded the Corinthians of God's sovereignty. Fundamental to understanding and accepting the concept of diverse gifts within an undivided body is the reality of God's sovereignty. God is the one who has determined how the gifts should be distributed and arranged. They are *spiritual*—from God—and they are *gifts*—the giver, not the recipient, determines the content. To be uncomfortable with the arrangement of gifts is to be uncomfortable with the sovereignty of God. In any body of believers, the proper exercise of gifts requires submission to the sovereignty of a wise and loving Lord.

Fifth, Paul pointed out that no matter how powerful or dramatic a gift may seem to be, to exercise it apart from love is to be utterly ineffective. 1 Corinthians 13 is a beautiful passage about love, but its context is the proper exercise of spiritual gifts. Paul mentioned several specific gifts in 1 Corinthians 13:1-3 and pointed out the futility of using those gifts without love. How ironic that a Christian would take a gift from God and use that gift in an unloving manner, but sadly, that sometimes happens. Jesus summed up all of the law in the commands to love God and love one's neighbor. That love should be the context in which believers exercise their gifts.

God's Spirit gives gifts to believers to enable them to serve the Lord, and His gifts are never useless. As Christians become aware of the ways in which God has gifted them, the appropriate response is to use those gifts with an attitude of thankfulness for the good of the church and the glory of the Lord.

QUESTION 10

Open your Life Notebook and make a chart with four columns, one column for each of the following Scripture passages: Romans 12:4-8; 1 Corinthians 12:7-11; 1 Corinthians 12:27-30; Ephesians 4:11-13. List the gifts that are mentioned in each passage. What spiritual gifts, if any, are mentioned in all four lists?

QUESTION 11

Spiritual gifts originate with a person's natural abilities. *True or False?*

QUESTION 12

Which of the following is usually a reliable way of identifying one's spiritual gift(s)?

A. Reading one of the lists in the Bible and noting which gifts appeal to me
B. Listening to spiritually minded Christians who know me
C. Praying for a gift that I want
D. Isolating myself and studying the gifts
E. Completing this lesson

QUESTION 13

What is the necessary context for the effective use of spiritual gifts?

A. Love
B. Faith
C. Hope
D. Patience
E. Self-control

QUESTION 14

Open your Life Notebook and look at the chart you created in Question 10. For any five of the gifts on your chart, explain how that gift can be used for the common good of a group of Christians and describe how you would recognize that gift in another Christian.

Topic 4: The Fruit of the Spirit

How do we really know God's Spirit is in us? And does His Presence in us really make a difference? The answer is that He does make a very significant difference in our lives. Not only does God's Spirit impact what we do, He also shapes the kind of person we are. It's not just a case of the Holy Spirit being a resource so that we can *do* what God wants; even more basic than that, He develops the kind of qualities in our lives that are honoring to God and that we would not develop on our own.

The Bible calls this the fruit of the Spirit. God's Spirit indwelling the Christian produces characteristics that are at odds with sinful human nature. Read Galatians 5:16-26.

QUESTION 15

Which of the following are included in the list of the works of the flesh? *(Select all that apply.)*

A. Sexual immorality
B. Murder
C. Jealousy
D. Heresy
E. Drunkenness
F. Sorcery

QUESTION 16

The list of the works of the flesh in Galatians 5 is exhaustive and complete. *True or False?*

Twice in this passage (verses 16 and 25) Paul encouraged the Galatian Christians to live by the Spirit. Earlier in this letter to the Galatians Paul described his life as a Christian by saying that he has been crucified with Christ so that it is no longer he who lives, but Christ living in him (see Gal 2:20). Obviously, Paul was not physically dead when he wrote these words; he was describing his new life in Christ. Not only is this new life initiated by the Holy Spirit (Tit 3:4-7), but the Spirit enables the Christian to live day-by-day as God intends. The kind of change Paul envisioned in Galatians 5 impacts both behavior and attitudes and becomes possible because of the Holy Spirit indwelling the believer. Using the metaphor of fruit, Paul described the qualities that the Spirit produces in the life of the believer.

QUESTION 17

What are the nine qualities identified as the Spirit's fruit in Galatians 5?

Two things are obvious about the items in this list. First, they are in sharp contrast to the works of the flesh. Left to his own resources, a person is much more likely to live a life that looks like the works of the flesh list than the fruit of the Spirit list. The Spirit produces His fruit in a believer's life only as he yields to His control. Even a believer, if he chooses not to live in submission to the Lord, will tend toward sin rather than spiritual fruit. The fruit of the Spirit is an expected outcome of a healthy relationship with the Lord.

Second, these qualities that Paul called fruit of the Spirit reflect God's desire and intention for the Christian's life. For example, Jesus told His disciples in the upper room that love would mark them as His disciples. Both before and after His crucifixion, Jesus was their peace-giver. He promised them joy. The characteristics listed as spiritual fruit describe what the Christian life ought to look like as Christians live in submission to the Lord.

While these qualities can be individually defined and described, it is difficult to imagine a life that evidences only one or two of the items on the list. The qualities that comprise the fruit of the Spirit are related so that some believe they should be thought of as singular (one unified fruit) and not plural (an assortment of characteristics).

QUESTION 18

Some have suggested that rather than nine individual qualities, the fruit of the Spirit is love, and the other eight characteristics describe love. Open your Life Notebook and write a personal response to this suggestion. Do you agree or disagree? Why?

It is one thing to gain knowledge of Spirit's work, gifts, and fruit; it is something else entirely to recognize and display that work in one's own life. Before moving on to the next topic, take some time to consider the fruit of the Spirit in your own life.

QUESTION 19

Open your Life Notebook and reflect on the fruit of the Spirit in your life. In what areas are you strong? In what areas do you sense a need to grow? Take some time and thank God for the work of His Spirit in your life in developing spiritual fruit and ask Him to help you grow in those areas where you sense growth is needed.

Topic 5: The Holy Spirit's Work in Me

Think for a few minutes about the role of the Holy Spirit in your life. *If the Holy Spirit lives in us, then His impact on our life is pervasive. It's greater than we may have realized!*

Often when Christians talk about the Holy Spirit and His role in the Christian life, the discussion focuses on His empowerment and the gifts He gives, or it focuses on the fruit the Spirit produces in the believer. However, the work of the Spirit is greater than we often perceive. In this topic we will take a look at some of the ways the Spirit works in the lives of believers. Read the following article "The Holy Spirit in Me" and then answer the questions that follow the article.

The Holy Spirit in Me

When Jesus told His disciples that He would send them another helper or advocate to be with them forever, it took the disciples some time to understand all that that would involve. Most Christians today do not differ much from the disciples; it takes us some time as well to discover the wonderful benefits of the Spirit's presence in our lives. Some of those benefits are fairly obvious and well-known; most Christians have some awareness, for example, of the gifts of the Spirit and the fruit of the Spirit. They may, however, be less focused on some other equally important results of the Spirit's indwelling. Let us look at five of these ways in which the Spirit works in the believer.

Scripture is clear that the Holy Spirit comes to indwell believers at the moment of their salvation. Ephesians 1:13-14 says the believer is marked with the seal of the Holy Spirit and describes the Spirit as the down payment or initial installment of our inheritance. Later, in Ephesians 4:30, Paul again said that believers are sealed by the Holy Spirit for the day of redemption. In a passage that focuses on our eternal destiny, 2 Corinthians 5:5, he describes the Holy Spirit as the down payment or deposit. Our guarantee of eternal life in Christ is no less than the Holy Spirit Himself. Our salvation is secured not by our own effort or faithfulness but by God in the person of the Holy Spirit. The Spirit is both our seal and guarantee. As a result the believer can be confidently assured of his salvation because of the witness of the indwelling Holy Spirit (see Rom 8:16-17).

Second, the Holy Spirit enlightens the understanding of believers regarding spiritual matters. When Jesus gave His disciples the promise of the Holy Spirit, He told them that the Spirit would guide them into all truth (Jn 16:12-14). When Paul wrote to the Corinthian church, he reminded them of this truth (1 Cor 2:9-13). He pointed out that the Spirit of God knows the things of God, and believers have received the Spirit so that they can know the things God has given them. The wise believer will approach Scripture with an invitation to God's Spirit to open his understanding. Spiritual discernment is made possible by the indwelling Holy Spirit and is not possible without Him.

A third way in which the Holy Spirit works in the life of the Christian focuses on His leading and encouraging. Romans 8:14 says that those who are led by the Spirit of God are sons of God. Those who have been born again can expect to be led by the Spirit. In order for such leading to be effective, the believer must be willing to submit and follow. The Bible frequently encourages Christians to be filled with the Spirit. Since the Spirit indwells the believer from the moment of salvation, what is in view here is obviously something more than that. When a believer is filled with the Spirit, he is under the Spirit's control and ready to be led.

Sometimes such leading can bring surprises. In Acts 16:6-10 Paul and his companions thought they knew where they were going, but the Holy Spirit redirected them. They probably experienced some temporary frustration until they discovered that God had a different opportunity prepared for them. Once we understand it and get beyond those temporary frustrations, the leading of the Spirit is always encouraging. One of the brief but appealing pictures of the church in Acts 9:31 describes them as living in the fear of the Lord and in the encouragement of the Holy Spirit. That description ought to fit the life of every believer.

A fourth way in which the Holy Spirit ministers to believers is by intercession. When Jesus promised the Spirit, He called Him another paraklete, a word often translated as advocate or helper. In a very practical and encouraging fulfillment of that role, the Spirit intercedes for believers before the Father. Romans 8:26-27 describes this ministry. Most Christians have experienced times when they did not know how to pray. What great comfort there is in knowing that there is always one who knows exactly how to pray on our behalf. The Spirit knows the will of God and prays in accord with that will. To agree with such a prayer takes submission and faith. In effect, believers say, "I want your will, even though I don't yet know what that is. Your Spirit knows, and that is enough." The Spirit who indwells believers intercedes and leads in accord with God's will.

Another way the Spirit works in believers is to give them hope. In a sense this hope results from the Spirit's other ministry in our lives. Romans 15:13 refers to the Holy Spirit as an agent of hope in our lives. This hope is related to other ministries of the Spirit who indwells believers. They are filled with joy and peace, part of the fruit of the Spirit, and abound in hope by the power of the Spirit. It is not difficult to see how hope flows from the other four works of the Spirit discussed here. We experience hope in the assurance that comes from the Spirit's seal and guarantee. We experience hope as we understand of the Lord and His Word. We experience hope as the Spirit leads and encourages us. We experience hope in the Spirit's intercession for us. We have hope because Christ has given us His Spirit in our lives.

QUESTION 20

Match the following Scripture references with the corresponding ministry of the Holy Spirit.\

Scripture	*Ministry of the Holy Spirit*
Ephesians 4:30	The Spirit gives hope.
1 Corinthians 2:9-13	The Spirit enlightens our understanding.
Romans 8:14	We are sealed by the Spirit.
Acts 9:31	We are encouraged in the Spirit.
Romans 8:26-27	We are led by the Spirit.
Romans 15:13	The Spirit intercedes for us.

QUESTION 21

The filling of the Spirit happens only once, at the moment of salvation. *True or False?*

The article "The Holy Spirit in Me" talked about several ways in which the Holy Spirit works in and ministers to individual Christians. Because the Holy Spirit is God, His work is not limited to a simple list. You have probably recognized His work in your own life not only in some of the ways mentioned in the article, but in other ways as well. Take some time to consider the work of the Holy Spirit in your life as an individual Christian.

QUESTION 22

Open your Life Notebook and write a personal response to the article "The Holy Spirit in Me." Which of these ways that the Holy Spirit works in the life of the Christian is most meaningful to you? Why? Are there other ways that the Holy Spirit is at work in the life of the believer that were not included in the article?

Topic 6: Conclusion

As we examine the Scriptures provided in this lesson, we should come to understand and appreciate how the Holy Spirit's ministry in our life deepens. The Holy Spirit's work is an essential part of our relationship with Christ, and the extent of that work is much broader than we may have realized. We need to understand that the Holy Spirit indwells us, residing in our lives. The Spirit should be recognized as a helper, a source of power, and a giver of gifts. We should recognize the fruit that the Spirit desires to produce in our lives as well as the varied ways in which the Spirit helps us, bringing understanding, encouragement, and hope. We should marvel at the reality of the Spirit interceding for us when we don't know how to pray. We may find ourselves quietly praying, *Lord, You overwhelm me. Thank You for Your presence and the gift of Your Spirit; thank You for the difference He makes in my life.*

QUESTION 23

Choose at least one of the following Scriptures from this lesson to memorize. Write a paragraph in your Life Notebook explaining why you chose that particular Scripture.

- Romans 8:14-15
- Romans 8:26-27
- Romans 15:13
- 1 Corinthians 2:9-10

Lesson 3 Self Check: Christian Life

QUESTION 1

What is the meaning of the word Jesus used for the Holy Spirit when He promised His disciples that the Spirit would come?

A. Someone to be worshipped
B. A companion
C. Someone called alongside to help
D. A devoted one

QUESTION 2

Jesus said that the Holy Spirit would be with the disciples only when they wanted Him. *True or False?*

QUESTION 3

What grieves the Holy Spirit?

A. Sinful acts but not sinful words or sinful thoughts
B. Sinful thoughts but not sinful acts
C. Because the Holy Spirit is God, He cannot be grieved
D. All sin, whether acts, words, or thoughts, grieves the Holy Spirit

QUESTION 4

The lists of spiritual gifts in Romans, 1 Corinthians, and Ephesians, if taken together, form a complete list of all of the possible spiritual gifts. *True or False?*

QUESTION 5

Why does God give Christians spiritual gifts?

A. For the edification of the individual receiving the gift
B. For the good of all believers
C. As a reward for faithful service
D. To answer the prayer of someone who has prayed for a particular gift

QUESTION 6

Which fruit of the Spirit is essential to the effective use of spiritual gifts?

A. Love
B. Joy
C. Peace
D. Faithfulness
E. Self-control

QUESTION 7

Which of the following is not listed as part of the fruit of the Spirit?

A. Patience
B. Gentleness
C. Goodness
D. Prayer

QUESTION 8

In order for our lives to show the fruit of the Spirit, we must live in submission to the Lord. *True or False?*

QUESTION 9

When does the Holy Spirit come to indwell believers?

A. Once, at the moment of salvation
B. After salvation when we ask for the Holy Spirit
C. At multiple times when we need Him
D. When we go to heaven

QUESTION 10

What is always true of the Holy Spirit's intercession for believers?

A. God does not hear; He is waiting for the believer's prayer.
B. The Holy Spirit only echoes the believer's prayer.
C. The Spirit always intercedes according to God's will.
D. None of the above are always true.

Unit 1 Exam: The Christian Life

QUESTION 1

What was God's intention when he created man?

A. He wanted to replace fallen angels.

B. He wanted to enjoy a relationship with His creation.

C. He wanted minimal contact with man.

D. He wanted someone for Satan to tempt.

QUESTION 2

At its heart the Christian life is a relationship with Jesus Christ. *True or False?*

QUESTION 3

To whom was Jesus speaking when he used the image of the new birth?

A. Nicodemus

B. Peter

C. A Samaritan

D. Zacchaeus

QUESTION 4

Why did people despise Zacchaeus?

A. He hosted parties and did not invite them.

B. He was a tax collector who cheated people.

C. He was short and ugly.

D. They envied him.

QUESTION 5

Which of the following did Jesus not say was a mark of discipleship?

A. Loving one another

B. Bearing fruit

C. Following His teaching

D. Attending church

QUESTION 6

When Jesus used the image of the vine and branches, what did the vine represent?

A. Disciples

B. The gospel

C. Jesus

D. Unbelievers

E. The Jews

QUESTION 7

Which statement correctly describes the Christian's relationship with Christ?

A. It will begin in heaven.

B. It began at birth, ended at Calvary, and will resume in heaven.

C. It begins at salvation and ends with physical death.

D. It begins at salvation and lasts for eternity.

QUESTION 8

When Jesus began to call His disciples, he called them to be with him. *True or False?*

QUESTION 9

What did Jesus tell Zacchaeus that he came to do?

A. Build his church

B. Deliver oppressed Jews

C. Seek and save lost people

D. Find and heal sick people

QUESTION 10

What is spiritual death?

A. Separation from God

B. Crucifixion

C. The same as the grave

D. Not praying for an extended time

QUESTION 11

When Jesus used the image of the Shepherd and the sheep, who or what was represented by the door?

A. Disciples

B. Old Testament believers

C. Holy Spirit

D. The gospel

E. Jesus

QUESTION 12

In the story Jesus told about the good neighbor, who was the good neighbor?

A. A priest

B. An expert in religious law

C. An innkeeper

D. A Samaritan

QUESTION 13

The old things that should pass away when a person becomes a Christian include both values and behaviors. *True or False?*

QUESTION 14

Why did Paul consider his Jewish credentials to be worthless dung?

A. Because people persecuted him

B. Because knowing Christ was infinitely more valuable

C. Because unbelievers valued them

D. Because people thought he was a Pharisee

QUESTION 15

What word picture of the Christian life is the focus of Psalm 23?

A. Shepherd and sheep

B. Vine and branches

C. Good neighbor

D. Wise manager

QUESTION 16

The account of the rich young man who wanted to follow Jesus illustrates that people who are materially rich cannot become spiritually rich. *True or False?*

QUESTION 17

Which statement best describes the Christian's hope?

A. It is not significantly different from the non-Christian's hope.

B. It is focused on practical solutions to immediate problems.

C. It is anchored in the person and work of Jesus Christ.

D. It has little impact on day-to-day life.

QUESTION 18

How did Jesus repeatedly refer to the Holy Spirit?

A. Spirit of power

B. Spirit of comfort

C. Spirit of peace

D. Spirit of hope

E. Spirit of truth

QUESTION 19

Which statement best describes the indwelling of the Holy Spirit?

A. The Holy Spirit indwells the believer permanently from the moment of salvation.

B. The Holy Spirit comes to indwell the believer at some point after salvation and may leave.

C. The indwelling of the Spirit is no different from the filling of the Spirit.

D. The indwelling begins when a person recognizes his spiritual gifts.

QUESTION 20

Spiritual gifts are given as rewards for faithful and effective service. *True or False?*

QUESTION 21

Spiritual fruit is a better indication than spiritual gifts that a person is living by the Spirit. *True or False?*

QUESTION 22

Who is supposed to benefit from a spiritual gift?

A. The person receiving the gift should get the primary benefit.
B. The pastor or leader of the local church should get the primary benefit.
C. The body of believers should get the primary benefit.
D. Unbelievers should get the primary benefit.

QUESTION 23

What quality must be present in order for spiritual gifts to be effectively used?

A. Faithfulness
B. Love
C. Self-control
D. Gentleness

QUESTION 24

Spiritual discernment is not possible apart from the Holy Spirit. *True or False?*

QUESTION 25

One of the ways the Holy Spirit works in the Christian is to give hope. *True or False?*

Lesson 3 Answers to Questions

QUESTION 1: *Your answer*

QUESTION 2

C. Spirit of truth

QUESTION 3

Scripture	*Truth about the Holy Spirit*
Romans 8:9	Every Christian is indwelt by the Holy Spirit.
John 15:26	The Holy Spirit testifies about Jesus.
John 14:16	The Holy Spirit indwells believers permanently.
Acts 1:8	The Holy Spirit empowers believers for witness.
John 14:26	The Holy Spirit brings to mind what Jesus said.
John 16:8	The Holy Spirit convicts of sin.

QUESTION 4

B. Sexual immorality

QUESTION 5: *Your answer*

QUESTION 6

A. Grieve him

QUESTION 7: True

QUESTION 8

A. Indulging evil
B. Neglecting prayer
C. Ingratitude
D. Disrespect for spiritual leaders
E. Devaluing God's prophetic word

QUESTION 9: *Your answer*

QUESTION 10: *Your answer*

QUESTION 11: False

QUESTION 12

B. Listening to spiritually minded Christians who know me

QUESTION 13

A. Love

QUESTION 14: *Your answer*

QUESTION 15

A. Sexual immorality
B. Murder
C. Jealousy
E. Drunkenness
F. Sorcery

QUESTION 16: False

QUESTION 17: *Your answer should be similar to the following:*

Love, joy, peace, patience, kindness, goodness, faithfulness, gentleness, self-control

QUESTION 18: *Your answer*

QUESTION 19: *Your answer*

QUESTION 20

Scripture	*Ministry of the Holy Spirit*
Ephesians 4:30	We are sealed by the Spirit.
1 Corinthians 2:9-13	The Spirit enlightens our understanding.
Romans 8:14	We are led by the Spirit.
Acts 9:31	We are encouraged in the Spirit.
Romans 8:26-27	The Spirit intercedes for us.
Romans 15:13	The Spirit gives hope.

QUESTION 21: False [Incorrect. (For clarification, re-read the article, "The Holy Spirit in Me" in Lesson 3)]

QUESTION 22: *Your answer*

QUESTION 23: *Your answer*

Lesson 3 Self Check Answers

QUESTION 1

C. Someone called alongside to help

QUESTION 2: False

QUESTION 3

D. All sin, whether acts, words, or thoughts, grieves the Holy Spirit

QUESTION 4: False

QUESTION 5

B. For the good of all believers

QUESTION 6

A. Love

QUESTION 7

D. Prayer

QUESTION 8: True

QUESTION 9

A. Once, at the moment of salvation

QUESTION 10

C. The Spirit always intercedes according to God's will.

Unit 1 Exam Answers

QUESTION 1

B. He wanted to enjoy a relationship with His creation.

QUESTION 2: True

QUESTION 3

A. Nicodemus

QUESTION 4

B. He was a tax collector who cheated people.

QUESTION 5

D. Attending church

QUESTION 6

C. Jesus

QUESTION 7

D. It begins at salvation and lasts for eternity.

QUESTION 8: True

QUESTION 9

C. Seek and save lost people

QUESTION 10

A. Separation from God

QUESTION 11

E. Jesus

QUESTION 12

D. A Samaritan

QUESTION 13: True

QUESTION 14

B. Because knowing Christ was infinitely more valuable

QUESTION 15

A. Shepherd and sheep

QUESTION 16: False

QUESTION 17

C. It is anchored in the person and work of Jesus Christ.

QUESTION 18

E. Spirit of truth

QUESTION 19

A. The Holy Spirit indwells the believer permanently from the moment of salvation.

QUESTION 20: False

QUESTION 21: True

QUESTION 22

C. The body of believers should get the primary benefit.

QUESTION 23

B. Love

QUESTION 24: True

QUESTION 25: True

Unit 2: Intimacy— A Growing Relationship with God

Introduction

When you became a Christian, you began a relationship with Jesus Christ. Some relationships between people do not grow very much if there is little opportunity for intimate communication. But when those involved in a relationship are able to share their deepest thoughts and feelings with one another, their knowledge of each other deepens and intimacy grows. That pattern should be true of a Christian's relationship with the Lord.

In this unit we will focus on that growing intimacy. Lesson 4 examines the role of worship in our relationship with the Lord. Lesson 5 looks at how our interaction with God's Word enhances the relationship. Lesson 6 focuses on prayer as the way we communicate with the Lord. Each of these is a necessary ingredient of a healthy, growing, intimate relationship with Jesus Christ.

Unit Outline

Lesson 4: Building Intimacy through Worship—Responding to God

Lesson 5: Building Intimacy through the Word—Listening to God

Lesson 6: Building Intimacy through Prayer—Communing to God

Lesson 4: Building Intimacy through Worship—Responding to God

Introduction

The Christian life is a relationship, and relationships involve discovering what the other person in the relationship is like. No matter how well a bride thinks she knows her bridegroom, inevitably she will know him better after a few months or years of married life as they discover more and more about each other. When you became a Christian, you knew some things about the Lord; as you have grown in your relationship with Him, your understanding of who He is and what He does has grown as well. Ideally you have moved from knowing about the Lord to knowing Him in a personal and ever-deepening way. As you come to know Him more deeply, the appropriate response is to worship Him.

God's intention is for worship be a joyful and integral part of every Christian's life. However, some Christians find it difficult to worship in a meaningful way. As you move through this lesson, you will have the opportunity to deepen both your understanding and experience of worship.

This lesson focuses on worship in the life of the Christian. In the first three topics you will explore the nature of worship, both what it is and how it is a response to who God is and what He does. The next two topics focus on biblical examples of worship in the Old and New Testaments. Topic six will help you to apply what you know about worship to your own life as an individual Christian and to your church fellowship.

Lesson Outline

- Topic 1: What Worship Is
- Topic 2: Responding to Who God Is
  - Discovering God's Character
  - Connecting Worship to God's Character
- Topic 3: Responding to What God Does
  - Remembering What God Has Done
  - Works You Have Witnessed
  - Connecting Worship to God's Works
- Topic 4: Old Testament Examples of Worship
  - Lessons from the Temple
  - Musical Worship
- Topic 5: Worship in the New Testament
  - Integrated Worship
  - Individual Worship
  - Unending Worship
- Topic 6: Worship Here and Now
- Topic 7: Conclusion

Topic 1: What Worship Is

Sometimes when non-Christians attend a worship service they will find it boring, and they may conclude that all Christian worship must be boring and should therefore be avoided. And there are times when some Christians may find worship to be boring. Suppose for a moment that you had the opportunity to participate in worship in many different church settings and many different cultures. Probably no two worship experiences would be exactly alike, and probably there would be a wide spectrum of experience. What is it that makes worship what it is?

QUESTION 1

As you begin this lesson, open your Life Notebook and write a description of what worship is, as you understand it. What are the possible elements of worship? Which of these are essential? What must be present in order for worship to take place?

Keep your response to Question 1 in mind as you read the following article, "What Worship Is. When you have finished the article, answer the questions that are found below it.

What Worship Is

For many people worship equates to a block of time in the rhythm of their lives. They go to a place of worship one day each week and worship is what happens while they are there. While it might be true that worship happens during these regularly scheduled slots in their lives, to define worship in that way is to limit it to something far more shallow than what God intended. Possibly what they experience during these scheduled worship times is not worship at all.

When Jesus engaged in conversation with a Samaritan woman at a well, her concept of worship was geographically focused. Should worship take place in Samaria or in Jerusalem (Jn 4:19-20)? The answer Jesus gave exploded her geographical presuppositions. He pointed out first that worship required a relationship with the one being worshipped. "You people," He said, "worship what you do not *know*" (Jn 4:21-22, emphasis added). By contrast, He said that the Jews worship what they do know. Those who worshipped false gods and idols went through the motions of trying to please or appease their gods; there would and could be no attempt to try to know those gods or to enter a relationship with them. What they called worship was really nothing more than the fulfillment of a perceived religious obligation.

Jesus did not have in mind an unknown god as the object of worship; He referred to God the Father. Years later Paul encountered in Athens an altar dedicated to an unknown god (Acts 17:22-31). One cannot experience a relationship with a god who is unknown, and so for Christians the concept of worshipping an unknown god is an oxymoron. True worship should be the natural response to a relationship with the true God. Paul responded to the altar to the unknown god by attempting to introduce the Athenians to the God whom they did not know.

Worship without relationship is likely to be nothing more than meaningless ritual. Christians are called to worship because they have been called into a relationship with the Lord. The more a Christian knows the Lord, the more that Christian will be able to worship the Lord. Worship is the response of a heart that is discovering who God is.

Sometimes Christians think and speak of worship as a set of activities such as singing, reading Scripture, praying, or even some body movements. However, it is possible for Christians to engage in those activities without worship ever taking place. Worship does not begin as actions; it begins as an attitude. What worship looks like at a particular time and place is secondary; whatever the form, worship will both express and respond to the Lord's worth. A believer who has begun a relationship with Christ has at least started to develop an understanding of Christ's worth. Understanding who the Lord is should lead one to an attitude of reverence and a desire to honor Him. As that attitude finds its expression, worship happens.

Jesus told the Samaritan woman that true worshippers would worship the Father in spirit and truth (Jn 4:23-24). True worship, therefore, must involve Jesus, who would later tell His disciples, "I am the truth" (Jn 14:6). Through Christ we are brought into relationship with God; apart from Him true worship cannot happen. And true worship involves the realm of the Spirit. Apart from Him we are ill-equipped to worship God. Worship is not focused on a particular place or a particular activity; it is focused on the reality of the triune God who is worthy.

When John recorded his vision of heaven in Revelation 4–5, he described a scene in which worshippers repeatedly declared that God is worthy. Whether addressing the One on the throne or the Lamb, they affirmed that He is worthy of glory and honor. Their response was not commanded, prompted, or manufactured by others; it was simply a response to the presence of the wonderful One with whom they enjoyed a relationship. Adoration is like that. Worship cannot be commanded or prompted by others; it is the proper response of one who has been brought into a relationship and experienced the unlimited love and grace of God.

QUESTION 2

Worship should be viewed as a religious obligation. *True or False?*

QUESTION 3

In Revelation 5, who is the object of worship?

A. Only God the Father on the throne
B. Only God the Son as the Lamb
C. Only the Holy Spirit
D. Both God the Father on the throne and the Lamb
E. Both the Lamb and the Holy Spirit, but not the Father

QUESTION 4

Which of the following describe true worship? *(Select all that apply.)*

A. It requires a relationship with the one being worshipped.
B. It involves God the Father, but not Jesus or the Holy Spirit.
C. It is not restricted to a particular place.
D. It is a response to who God is.

Topic 2: Responding to Who God Is

When Christians worship God, they are responding to who God is, to His character and the characteristics that express His nature. In the Old Testament we see over and over that when men find themselves in the presence of God, their natural and automatic response is fear and worship. They fall to the ground, take off their shoes, bow and worship as they respond to our HOLY God. We recognize that HIS presence is worthy of a special, worshipful and holy response.

Worship is recognizing the wonder of God who is so much greater than us and at the same time beholding the truth that He loves each one of us as if we were His only child. It is an expression of ultimate gratitude to Him who breathed life into us and who sustains us every day. Worship is a way to magnify the attributes of God for the world to see and celebrate each attribute as Holy and Good; for Holy and Good are *defined* by *who* God is. You will learn more as you read the articles throughout this lesson.

Discovering God's Character

Understanding something of who God is makes worship possible. The more one comes to understand the character of God, the more readily one will be drawn to worship Him. Conversely, misunderstanding the character of God can become an almost insurmountable obstacle to worship.

Read the following article, "What's in a Name," and then answer the questions found after the article.

What's in a Name?

Shakespeare, the English playwright, had his character, Juliet, ask the question, "What's in a name?" She was trying to reconcile her love of Romeo with the fact that their families were sworn enemies. Romeo's family name—Montague—carried with it a stigma for Juliet's family, and she pondered the relationship between a person's character and his name. A name should reflect the character of the one bearing it, but that is not always true for humans. Because the bestowal of a name precedes the formation of character, sometimes there is a disconnect between the two. For a child growing up, a name can sometimes reflect a goal of the kind of person he or she will hopefully become. But for God, whose character has always been an eternal constant, His names and titles can serve as reliable reminders of the unchanging reality of who He is and what He is like. Consider a few of these names, titles, and descriptions of God and how they might inspire worship.

When Jesus' disciples asked Him to teach them to pray, He gave them a model prayer that referred to God as Father (Lk 11:1-4). Not only was it a name with which the disciples were familiar, it was also a term that spoke of relationship. The eternal, almighty God desires to relate to His people as a father to his children. Sometimes a father does not have a loving relationship with his child, but God's relationship to His children is always one of love. God's intent is for it to be a very close relationship. When a person is brought into God's family at salvation, the Holy Spirit enables a close and intimate relationship. Romans 8:15 says that the Spirit enables us to cry "Abba, Father." *Abba* is an Aramaic term for father that connotes an especially close relationship. (Aramaic was the common language among Israelites when Jesus was with them.) When you are very close to someone, you can easily express in a variety of ways how much that person means to you.

In the same prayer Jesus taught the disciples that the Father is holy. When Isaiah was in the presence of God, he was overwhelmed as he heard the angels declaring God's character: *holy,*

holy, holy! Because of his sin, Isaiah feared death as the consequence of being in the presence of a holy God. Yet Jesus invited His disciples to pray to this same holy God, who is now described as a holy Father. This Father is utterly unique; there is no one like Him. When two people are in love, they recognize and affirm the uniqueness of the one they love. It is unthinkable that they could exchange the one they love for someone else as easily as one changes clothes. Yet, according to Romans 1:18-23, that is what ungodly people have done; they have exchanged the true God for created things that they worship. They have failed to recognize God as unique and holy.

Both aspects of God's character—the closeness of Abba and God's holiness—are important to recognize, and both should prompt worship.

Several Scripture passages refer to God as sovereign or Most High. Using that term, Psalm 47:2 describes God as the awe-inspiring ruler and Psalm 57:2 as the sovereign judge who vindicates. Interestingly even those possessed by demons acknowledge Him as the Most High, but without enjoying a relationship with Him or Abba. Mark 5:7 and Acts 16:17 are examples of such demonic recognition of God's sovereignty. Christians have a Father who is absolutely sovereign.

Closely related to His sovereignty is the fact that He is the Almighty God, reflected in His name El Shaddai. God is not only sovereign, He is able, and He is enough. God does not need outside help to accomplish His purposes; He is all-sufficient. To worship a God who is all-sufficient requires people to move beyond a reliance on their own resources and abilities. Sooner or later everyone faces circumstances that are beyond his ability to manage. No matter how difficult a set of circumstances may be, they are never beyond God's ability. So no matter what the circumstances are, believers can worship the God who is able.

Abraham dramatically experienced God's sufficiency on Mount Moriah when He instructed him to offer his son Isaac as a sacrifice. Since Isaac was the son through whom God had already said Abraham would produce a great nation (Gen 21:12), obeying God would require a major step of faith. Abraham chose to obey because he was convinced that God would provide. When questioned by his son about the absence of a sacrificial lamb for the offering, he shared his conviction that God would provide (Gen 22:8). God, the sufficient provider, did provide the ram. In response Abraham attached the name and character of God—*The Lord Provides*—to the place that centuries later became the location of the temple (2 Chron 3:1). The place that would become the geographical focal point for worship for the Jews had already been christened with the character of God.

In a similar way Gideon united the name and character of God with a specific place as a reminder of what God had done. The Lord had appeared to Gideon and blessed him with peace; in response Gideon built an altar and named it "The Lord is peace," thereby linking a place of worship to the character of God (Judg 6:23-24). Gideon was in the midst of a distinctly unpeaceful situation, but he responded to the peaceful character of God. The New Testament identifies the God of peace as the One who not only gives peace but who also equips Christians to do His will (2 Thess 3:16; Heb 13:20). One might not think of a God who is an absolutely sovereign and almighty Father as peaceful, but peace is part of His character which is even evident in His judgment of sin. At the end of his letter to the Romans, in the context of crushing Satan, Paul called Him the God of peace (Rom 16:20). Believers are blessed to be able to respond to a God who not only *gives* peace, but who *is* peace.

Allowing the names, titles, or descriptions of God to prompt worship can work equally well for the Son and the Spirit as it does for the Father. The name Jesus, meaning "the Lord saves," identifies Him as Savior. Many songs and hymns have been written expressing worship in response to this name and what it communicates of the Lord's character. In Philippians 2 Paul quoted what was probably an ancient Christian hymn proclaiming that one day everyone in heaven, on earth, or below will bow at the name of Jesus and confess that He is Lord to the glory of the Father (Phil 2:5-11). That declaration of Jesus as Lord is at the heart of worship. It is a reflection of the wonder of the Trinity—that worshipping the Son glorifies the Father.

Jesus, the one who is Lord, described Himself in a number of different ways at different times, and all of these descriptions point to some aspect of His character. He is both the Shepherd and the Lamb. He is the Light of the world. He is the Bread of life. He is the Resurrection and the Life. He is the true Vine. He is the way, the truth, and the life. Each of these descriptions illuminates some aspect of who Jesus is, and each of them can easily stimulate praise from Christians, those who recognize who Jesus is.

One cannot be neutral or apathetic about the names, titles, and descriptions of Jesus. The expected response from those who love Him is adoration and worship. The response of those who reject the reality of His divine identity is markedly different. John 8:58 records a dialog between Jesus and the leaders of the Jewish establishment. Toward the end of that discussion Jesus declared His eternal nature: "before Abraham came into existence, I am." This bold *I am* declaration, reminiscent of God's identification of Himself to Moses at the burning bush in Exodus 3, was a clear claim to deity. That is what Jesus meant, and that is what the Jews understood. They interpreted His claim to deity as blasphemy and picked up stones to stone Him, the appropriate punishment for such blasphemy (Jn 8:58-59). When one honestly confronts the character of God, neutrality is not possible. For Christians the appropriate response will be worship that affirms and exalts the character of God.

We have discussed only a few of the names, titles, and descriptions of God, but it should be clear that they reflect His character. Because they do, each of the names, titles, and descriptions of God calls forth a response from Christians. We come to know Him better and desire to exalt Him as we reflect on who He is. What's in a name? In the case of the Lord, the answer is His character, and His character is worthy of praise.

QUESTION 5

Why are the names, titles, and descriptions of God significant for Christians? *(Select all that apply.)*

A. They reflect the character of God.

B. Christians are expected to memorize them.

C. They stimulate worship.

D. They help us understand who God is.

QUESTION 6

What does the term *Abba* indicate?

A. That God is holy

B. A father with whom one enjoys a close relationship

C. A follower of Jesus

D. That God is sovereign

Connecting Worship to God's Character

To know something of God's character is a wonderful thing, but that knowledge by itself is fruitless. As we saw in the article "What's in a Name?" to meaningfully come to grips with the character of God calls for some kind of response. For unbelievers that response might be to confirm or deepen their rejection of Christ, or like the Jewish leaders in John 8, to become increasingly hostile to Christ and His followers. For the believer who trusts in Christ, the response will likely be one of worship. As we understand more of God's character, we want to express His worth.

Worship arises from a relationship in which you are able to recognize and respond to God's worth. We live in a busy world, and sometimes it is hard to take the time to contemplate and respond to what God is like. But if we do not take the time to do that, then we cheat both ourselves and God out of the experience of worship. Expressing God's worth is what worship is about. The next question asks you to make a response of worship prompted by the character of God as it is reflected in His names or titles. Be sure to allow yourself adequate time to enjoy expressing your worship to God.

QUESTION 7

There are many more names and titles for God in the Bible than those included in the article you read, "What's in a Name?" Open your Life Notebook and list as many names or titles for God as you can. Try to list at least twenty. Choose eight of them that are especially meaningful to you. Write a letter to God or a prayer or a song expressing what these eight names or titles mean to you. Take your time with this exercise and make it a meaningful time of discovery and worship of God.

Topic 3: Responding to What God Does

There is an old proverb that says what you do speaks so loudly that nobody can hear what you say. Most people draw conclusions about a person's character on the basis of what he does. Character and actions should be consistent, and this has an important application to worship. God's character and actions are always consistent, and since worship is a response to God's character, then God's actions, which reflect His character, can be an important stimulus to worship. In this topic we will take a look at how that works.

Remembering What God Has Done

If you were to make a list of the things God has done in your life, how long would the list be? Most people's lives are focused in the present, and remembering the past is not a high priority. For God's people, however, remembering what God has done in the past serves to remind them of who He is and what He is like. These reminders can serve not only as personal encouragements at difficult times but also as significant stimuli to praise and worship, regardless of the current circumstances.

Read Psalm 77.

At the beginning of the psalm the psalmist is discouraged and depressed as he contemplates his current distress. But in a dramatic shift, the psalm turns to a recitation of the character and mighty acts of God. As the psalmist begins to focus on what God has done, he is encouraged and expresses praise to God. What makes the difference? The turning point is the decision to focus on what God has done, His "mighty deeds."

QUESTION 8

Psalm 77 expresses the psalmist's discouragement, focus on God's works, and praise of God. List two phrases from Psalm 77:1, 9, 12-14 for each type of expression.

Psalm 78 expresses a commitment to tell the next generation what God has done. It was important that the coming generation know what God had done because remembering His deeds would not only encourage obedience but would also stimulate a relationship with God. The bulk of the psalm then focuses on God's actions hundreds of years previously in the Exodus and how easily God's people forgot His actions. This is one of several psalms that recount part of Israel's history and God's work among them.

QUESTION 9

Read Psalm 102:18. Why was it important for the Israelites to create a written record of God's actions among them?

Read Psalm 103 and notice how God's character and actions are woven together in the psalm.

QUESTION 10

Open your Life Notebook and create a chart for Psalm 103 with two columns. The first column should be labeled "God's Actions" and the second column "God's Character." In the first column, list the actions of God that are recorded in the psalm. Next to each action, in the second column write down what aspect of God's character that action shows. Example: In the first column you might write "forgives all our sins" and next to it in the second column "God is merciful."

God's actions are always consistent with His character, and so recalling what God has done reminds us of who He is and can lead us to worship our God who is worthy of praise.

QUESTION 11

Get together with at least one other Christian and spend at least ten minutes brainstorming as many things that God has done as you can think of. Do not limit yourselves to your own experience of God's actions; begin with creation and move forward from there. Then declare God's character by telling each other and God what aspects of God's character are evident in these actions. Write a paragraph in your Life Notebook reflecting on this experience.

Works You Have Witnessed

Knowing what God has done stimulates us to worship, but that stimulus becomes much stronger when we have personally witnessed God at work. Every Christian has his own story of God's marvelous works in his life and in the lives of others around him. When you experience or witness God at work, that becomes a powerful prompt to praise.

On the evening of Resurrection Sunday as the disciples were huddled together, Jesus miraculously appeared before them. They saw the crucified and risen Christ with their own eyes. Thomas, however, was absent, and when the others told him, he refused to believe because he had not seen Christ himself. A week later when Thomas was there, Jesus again appeared, singling out Thomas and inviting him to feel for himself the Savior's crucifixion wounds. It was that first-person experience that prompted Thomas's words of worship: "My Lord and my God."

Read the following article, "The Waiting Room"—one man's first-person account of witnessing the work of God.

The Waiting Room

I was shaking. My wife had been hit by a truck, and now she lay unconscious and bleeding on the other side of the double doors. As I sat there in the hospital waiting room, stunned and praying for a miracle, I began to remember other times when I had actually sensed God at work either in my circumstances or in those of people close to me. My mind drifted back to the time a few years earlier when my father had seemed to be losing his sight. None of the treatments had had a lasting effect on his vision. Medication had failed to make a difference, and now it seemed that his recent surgery would prove to be unsuccessful. I had been invited to be present as two of my parent's pastor-friends visited and prayed with my father.

Why not? I had thought. *He's tried everything else; I guess a little prayer couldn't hurt.* But I did not really expect it to make any difference. I wondered if my parents really expected anything other than the comfort of a pastoral visit. *If God was going to make that eye work the way it's supposed to, he could have done it by now,* I thought. It seemed to me to be a waste of time with the risk of artificially raising expectations and then experiencing disappointment. But they were my parents, and they had asked me to come, and so I did.

There had been nothing spectacular about that afternoon. The visit had been warm, the conversation generally light and familiar, and the atmosphere relaxed. They had prayed, inviting God to heal while acknowledging His sovereignty. There had been no dramatic evidence that God had worked or even heard: no lights, no sensation of power, no clap of thunder, and when Dad opened his eyes, no improvement in his vision. *Well, that's about what I expected,* I thought to myself. *No harm done, I guess, except for wasting an afternoon.*

In light of that apparent failure the phone call from my mother the next day totally surprised me. "We just left the eye doctor's office," she said excitedly. "Your father's vision is markedly better!"

I mumbled a response that that was good news. Could it be that God had actually intervened and touched my father's eye? I wasn't sure. "What did the doctor say?" I asked.

"He had no explanation. Medically there was no reason for the sudden improvement. He said that sometimes the body works in unpredictable ways. I told him it was God, but he didn't say anything."

I hadn't said anything either.

A year later Dad died, and my mother handled the grief of that loss with a serenity that she attributed to the Lord. Of course, she grieved. But in the midst of her grief there was a quiet confidence that God was at work in her circumstances, even in the loss of my father.

Now my wife was on the other side of those double doors with doctors and nurses who were trying to stop the bleeding. *Lord,* I prayed quietly, *You are an awesome God. I have seen what You can do in situations that seem to have no human answer. You are the God who gave my father sight. You are the God who gave my mother peace. Now please, Lord, protect and restore my wife's life.*

I looked up as the double doors opened and the doctor came out to talk to me.

God was not obligated to heal this man's father or his wife. But because he had experienced God's intervention in the past, he was encouraged to acknowledge what God had done and trust God in the current crisis.

QUESTION 12

How do you think this man will respond if the news he hears from the doctor is not good? Answer in your Life Notebook and give reasons for your answer.

QUESTION 13

How have you personally experienced or witnessed God at work? Open your Life Notebook and record some of these ways that you have seen God work. How have these actions of God helped you to understand His character?

Connecting Worship to God's Works

Knowing, witnessing, and experiencing what God has done enables us to see His character more clearly. As God's people properly perceive His character, worship can happen more readily.

One good example of this connection between the acts of God and worship can be seen in the solemn assembly held at the conclusion of the Feast of Booths in the book of Nehemiah. Read Nehemiah 9 giving careful attention to the prayer in verses 5-37. The prayer in Nehemiah 9 beautifully weaves three themes together: confession of the people's unfaithfulness, recounting of God's acts throughout Israel's history, and acknowledgment and praise of God's character.

QUESTION 14

Key phrases in Nehemiah 9:29-32 can be placed into three categories: confessing sin, God's works, and God's character. Match each phrase with the appropriate category.

Category	*Key Phrase*
Confessing sin	"You are a merciful and compassionate God."
God's works	"You solemnly admonished them."
God's character	"They sinned against your ordinances."

All three of these components are appropriate elements of worship as you consider what God has done and respond to Him.

QUESTION 15

Keeping in mind the pattern of the prayer in Nehemiah 9, spend some time creating a personal prayer that weaves together confession of sin, acknowledgment of God's work in your life, and praise of His character.

Topic 4: Old Testament Examples of Worship

Just as God's works help us see His character, worship in Scripture helps us visualize the possibilities for worship in our own lives and settings. In this topic and the next we will explore several examples of worship in the Bible. Some characteristics of worship in the Bible are timeless; others are appropriate for the particular time and place in which they existed. As we look at these examples, try to discern what is timeless and transferrable and what is not.

Lessons from the Temple

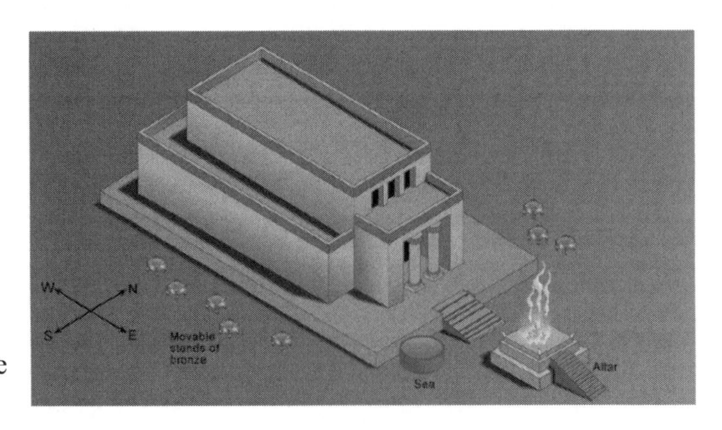

For God's people in the Old Testament, the temple, and its predecessor the tabernacle, was the focal point for worship for much of their history. We have already seen that for Christians, worship does not need to have such a geographical focus. Nevertheless, we can find some helpful principles to apply to our own practice of worship by observing the Jewish worship practices.

The following article, "Worship Hints from the Temple," focuses on some of the principles underlying worship practices in the Old Testament. Read this article and then answer the following question.

Worship Hints from the Temple

If a Christian were able to go back in time and worship with the Jews during the days of the temple or the tabernacle, he would find it a shockingly different experience from that of contemporary worship. Much of the specific activity that happened at the temple would not be welcomed in most Christian congregations. Yet underlying those worship practices we might consider alien are timeless principles that should be present in our own worship. Let us consider just a few of these temple practices.

Cleansing: Both the tabernacle and temple provided a basin between the altar of sacrifice and the holy place. Before entering, the priests would wash their hands and feet. The issue in this ritualistic cleansing was not the literal dust that they might carry with them; the washing was symbolic of the removing of sin. When Christians come to worship, it is not only appropriate but also necessary that they come cleansed of their sin through Christ. In worship, we come into God's presence to exalt Him and affirm His worth. Since God is holy, those who worship Him must come cleansed from sin. Though it may be painful to seek forgiveness, it is of benefit that our approach to a holy God illuminates the sin in our lives that might otherwise go unnoticed or ignored.

To atone for sin the Israelites sacrificed a spotless animal, its blood shed in a foreshadowing of what Christ would accomplish at Calvary. Today Christians do not rely on the blood of an animal sacrifice for their salvation, but on the blood of Christ. Christians who worship today do not need to foreshadow what has already taken place, though we do remember Christ's sacrifice every time we celebrate communion. A conscious awareness of Christ's sacrifice certainly ought to call forth worship from us. The bread and the cup of communion are visible and tangible reminders of Christ's perfect and sufficient sacrifice, and they are reminders that prompt a response of worship.

A second principle may be noted. The animals brought for sacrifice had to be the best. Offering anything less to God was unacceptable. It might seem wasteful or impractical to offer a perfect animal if there was one that was lame or diseased that should be destroyed anyway. Worship by its very nature may seem impractical, but God expects and deserves the very best. David plainly expressed the principle behind this apparent impracticality when he was securing land to build an altar for sacrifice, the land on which the temple would eventually be built. David was offered all he needed for the sacrifice as a gift, but he insisted on paying for it, declaring, "I will not offer to the LORD my God offerings that haven't cost me anything" (2 Sam 24:24). Real worship should be costly. To make worship a cheap priority, to limit it to the merely convenient, is the contemporary equivalent of offering a diseased animal. Our worship should reflect the depth of our love.

Restricted access and the presence of God: The holy of holies where the Ark of the Covenant rested was off limits to virtually all the Israelites. It was here that the visible representation of God's presence resided. Because of God's holiness His presence could be experienced only from afar. When Christ was crucified, the curtain that kept the holy of holies separate was miraculously torn from top to bottom, representing the access to God that Christ's sacrifice made available. Worship, of course, requires access to the Almighty, and Christians are invited to come into the presence of God as they worship. They need no priestly mediator other than Christ Himself. That access, however, in no way diminishes God's holiness. Our awareness of both God's holiness and our need for cleansing should be as clear as it was for Isaiah when he found himself a sinful man in the presence of the holy God (Isa 6:1-7).

Sensory cues: For the Israelites, worship was often a very sensory experience. They could smell the aroma of incense, see and almost taste the smoke of a sacrifice, feel the heat of the fire, hear the words of worship, lift their voices, play their instruments. All these helped them take their places in the drama of worship played out against the backdrop of the beauty of the temple itself. Among Christians there exists wide variety in the value placed on sensory prompts when it comes to worship. One of the lessons of the Old Testament is that worship does not need to be an exercise in sensory deprivation. The careful use of a variety of kinds of sensory cues can enhance the experience of worship and help the worshiper focus on the Lord, the object of our worship. The key is that these cues need to point to the Lord and not get in the way or distract from worship.

Corporate worship: The temple was a place where the Israelites *as a group* could come before God. While it is possible and appropriate for an individual to worship God alone, Scripture repeatedly portrays God's people assembled together both for teaching and for worship. There seems to be a synergistic value to corporate worship where together God's people can exalt Him in ways that they cannot do alone. New Testament passages such as Hebrews 10:22-25 reinforce this value with the reminder to not abandon meeting together. These verses reflect among New Testament Christians an Old Testament practice of corporate worship that was intended to be normative.

True, times and people change, but we can learn much from the examples of Old Testament worshippers. While the setting and methodology of worship may change, God does not change. He is still worthy of praise, and we still have the same privilege, responsibility, and invitation that these Old Testament saints had—an invitation to worship the Lord, who is worthy.

QUESTION 16

Which of the following should Christians learn by observing the worship practices of the Old Testament Israelites? *(Select all that apply.)*

A. We should sacrifice an animal.

B. Worship should be costly.

C. Sensory stimulation distracts us and should be avoided in worship.

D. Confession is an appropriate prelude to worship.

E. Aromas, music, and drama can all enhance worship.

F. Worshipping with other Christians is unnecessary if one worships alone.

Musical Worship

While it may be possible to worship without music, for most Christians the topics of worship and music are inseparably linked. There is a good reason for that link. Worship and music are closely related in the Bible as well. Psalms is a book of songs, many of which were written to express worship, but there are many other songs of praise in Scripture as well. We have already looked at several songs from the book of Psalms; now let's look at one of these Old Testament songs that is outside the book of Psalms.

When God miraculously parted the Red Sea for the Israelites and drowned the Egyptian army in those same waters, the response of God's people was to sing. Exodus 15 records the song, which was sung antiphonally—in alternating parts—and accompanied by drums.

Read this psalm in Exodus 15:1-21.

While the psalm was prompted by God's mighty act—delivering the Israelites from the Egyptians and destroying the Egyptian army—notice how the words of the song exalt various aspects of God's character.

QUESTION 17

What characteristics of God are included in the song of praise in Exodus 15? *(Select all that apply.)*

A. His power

B. His reign as King

C. His injustice

D. His uniqueness

E. His love

F. His relationship to His people

The psalms combined a poetic arrangement of the words themselves with singing, musical instruments, and sometimes dancing in an artistic expression of worship. Read the last two psalms (Ps 149–150) and notice the encouragements to musical worship.

QUESTION 18

What worship activities are encouraged in Psalms 149–150? *(Select all that apply.)*

A. Expressing joy

B. Using instruments such as flutes and horns

C. Dancing

D. Silently waiting

E. Using instruments such as drums or cymbals

F. Singing with other believers

Topic 5: Worship in the New Testament

Biblical examples of worship do not end with the Old Testament. New Testament Scriptures also provide frequent pictures of God's people worshipping Him. At a time in history when Christians were under the authority of the pagan Roman government and persecuted by the Jewish religious establishment, worship was clearly an important characteristic of their individual and corporate lives. Some of these pictures of worship are fresh expressions of the corporate worship practiced by God's people in the Old Testament.

Others illustrate individual acts of worship or ways in which worship affects every aspect of the lives of believers.

Integrated Worship

From the earliest descriptions of the church in the book of Acts, one can see that worship was an integral part of the lives of believers. The picture of these Christians that is painted in Acts 2:42-47 dramatically captures the vitality of their shared life in Christ and their relationship to the Lord. They are described as devoted to the apostles' teaching, to fellowship, to the breaking of bread (a likely reference to communion) and to prayer. The focus of the apostles' teaching was Jesus. The basis of their fellowship was their commitment to Christ. His sacrifice was the reality illustrated by the communion elements. He was the One they addressed in their prayers. The Lord was central, and in all that they did He was the focus.

This early description records no specific worship liturgy or hymns and seems to reflect few of the components of worship that some modern Christians consider essential. However, praising God was an inescapable characteristic of their lives and part of what identified them as Christians. Not that the trappings of worship were excluded from their lives; worship was so integrated into all that they did that it could not be confined to a Sunday morning liturgy.

Paul, in 1 Corinthians 10:31, indicates that everything that a Christian does should be done for the glory of God. Worship is not restricted to a particular time or place or to a limited set of activities. Ideally every act of a believer is an act of worship intended to honor and exalt the Lord.

QUESTION 19

Read Acts 2:42-47. What activities of the early Christians could have been done as acts of worship? *(Select all that apply.)*

A. Devoting themselves to the apostles' teaching

B. Praising God

C. Giving to meet the needs of others

D. Meeting together

E. Prayer

God's intention is that the lives of believers should be to the praise of His glory. We who have been brought into a relationship with the Lord can honor Him in all that we do.

Individual Worship

Because our entire lives can and should be to the praise of God's glory, our worship need not be restricted to times when we are with other believers for a commonly agreed time of worship. Such times are important, and Scripture encourages Christians to participate faithfully in shared corporate worship with other believers. However, because we are in relationship with the Lord, worship should permeate every part of our lives.

The Gospel writers record an instance when in the context of a dinner attended by Jesus, a woman carried out a private and individual act of worship that was misunderstood by many of those present. Read about this incident in Mark 14:1-9, and then read the article below, "The Broken Jar," that relates this incident as it might have been experienced by the worshipping woman.

The Broken Jar

Jesus was there, and I had to do something to show how important He was and what He meant to me. What could I do? Maybe I should have helped with the dinner party, but I am a terrible cook. While I was pondering what I could do, my eyes fell on the jar. It was my most valuable possession, and I knew that it was my answer.

It was a personal treasure. It wasn't a big jar, but with its long neck it was beautiful in its own way. And of course, there was no secret about what it contained: enough of that marvelous Eastern perfume for a single anointing, now sealed in this alabaster jar. I had often dreamed about the time when I might break it open and let its fragrance permeate the room. It would have to be a very special occasion to break open such a valuable gift.

And now Jesus was there, and the time was right. This would be the day; He would be the one to receive the contents of this jar. *Forgiven.* That is what He had said to me, and when He spoke the word, it made all the difference in the world. Now this jar represented something to honor Him.

Not everyone heard the crack as I broke the neck of the jar and poured the perfume on His head, but there could be no hiding the fragrance. Soon everyone there knew what had happened, and their attention focused on me instead of on Jesus. That was not what I wanted, and I never expected that people would be angry with me. It was a time to honor Jesus, and that was what I had tried to do. They called it a waste and said I should have sold it to feed the poor. But after all, it was my perfume to waste if I wanted. I suppose it was extravagant, but I could never call it a waste to give it to Jesus. He had changed my life forever. Nothing was too good for Him; nobody could be more worthy of the contents of that jar.

Then He spoke, telling the angry people to leave me alone. Their voices quieted down, but I could still see the disapproval on their faces. He said what I had done was something beautiful, and I relaxed, knowing that He understood. There is nothing wrong with feeding poor people, but that jar of perfume had nothing to do with the poor and everything to do with Jesus.

I had wanted to find a way to exalt Him and express my devotion, and He received my gift exactly as I intended it. It was worship, not a waste, and if I had another jar, I would do it again.

QUESTION 20

What did Jesus say about this woman's act of devotion? *(Select all that apply.)*

A. She did what she could.

B. She should have sold the perfume.

C. She anointed His body for burial.

D. Her act was wasteful.

E. People would remember and tell others what she had done.

QUESTION 21

Why can we call what this woman did an act of worship?

A. Because she sang as she broke the jar

B. Because the perfume was very expensive

C. Because other followers of Jesus were present

D. Because she exalted Jesus

E. Because she was a believer

The fact that many of those present disapproved, at least initially, of this woman's act of devotion in no way lessened its significance. She found a way to express her worship of Jesus that demonstrated His worth and her devotion. Any act that reflects God's worth and one's devotion to Him is an act of worship. These individual and personal acts of worship are not substitutes for corporate worship. They are consistent with and extensions of that worship, and they allow us continual opportunities to express and respond to God's worth.

Unending Worship

Because worship is an integral part of our relationship with Christ, it is not limited to our life on earth. Worship is a major activity in heaven even more so than it is here on earth. The images in the book of Revelation give us some idea of how pervasive worship will be when we are in the presence of the Lord unhindered by sin. Read the following passages in Revelation:

- Revelation 4:1-11
- Revelation 5:6-14
- Revelation 7:9-12
- Revelation 11:15-18
- Revelation 15:1-4
- Revelation 19:1-8

QUESTION 22

What worshipers are included in these six passages in Revelation? *(Select all that apply.)*

A. Four living creatures

B. Twenty-four elders

C. Angels

D. Large multicultural crowd of people

E. The beast

Though the mix of worshippers may change, there is one constant in these passages: The Lord is the one consistently recognized as worthy of worship. Without sin obstructing an awareness of God's worth, praise repeatedly flows to Him. It is not that heaven is one long, programmed, unending worship service; it is rather that a clear awareness of the Lord constantly prompts a response of worship. Like a person in love, we will have no difficulty expressing in a variety of ways our love for the Lord.

Topic 6: Worship Here and Now

A time is coming when worshipping the Lord will be the commonly shared experience of every believer. Philippians 2:9-11 and Revelation 5:13 describe every creature united in worshipping Christ. God has redeemed people from an almost immeasurable variety of cultures and languages, and in this life those cultures and languages will help define the ways in which we worship. What worship looks like may differ significantly from one group of believers to another. Language, culture, and musical forms may differ, and those differences will be reflected in the group's worship practices. Before concluding our study of worship, let's take some time to think about worship in your context. As you answer the following question, focus on the place, the language, and the culture that forms the environment in which you usually worship.

QUESTION 23

In this lesson we have touched on many different expressions of worship. Consider how each of the following might be used by the people in your local church to express worship and record your response in your Life Notebook. What differences do you see between your answer to this question and your response to Question 1?

- Prayers of praise
- Prayers of thanksgiving
- Scripture
- Acts of devotion and service
- Singing
- Various kinds of musical instruments
- Dancing
- Sensory cues
- Communion
- Physically acting out a reminder of what God has done
- Planning
- Spontaneity

QUESTION 24

Using your answer to the last question as a guide, plan a time of worship for the people in your local church that will help them exalt Christ.

Topic 7: Conclusion

There are many different styles and expressions of worship, and these may vary widely in different countries and cultures. Although the outward appearances of worship can be very diverse, the inward aspects of worship involve responding to who God is and what He does.

A believer's relationship with God should be one that grows and matures over time, just like relationships in a good marriage. As we walk with the Lord, we will get to know Him better, and our relationship with Him will deepen and our worship of Him will become more meaningful.

QUESTION 25

Take some time to tell God why worship is important to you. Record your thoughts in your Life Notebook.

Lesson 4 Self Check: Christian Life

QUESTION 1

Worship is the response of a heart that is discovering who God is. *True or False?*

QUESTION 2

How did Jesus describe the worship of true worshippers?

A. Worship in Jerusalem

B. Worship in spirit and truth

C. Worship is love and peace

D. Worshipping what is not known

E. Worshipping with music

QUESTION 3

True worship requires a relationship with the one who is being worshipped. *True or False?*

QUESTION 4

Because God is infinite, His names and titles are not a reliable reflection of His character. *True or False?*

QUESTION 5

With whom do you associate the name, "The Lord is Peace"?

A. Abraham

B. Isaac

C. Gideon

D. A Samaritan woman

QUESTION 6

Which of the following statements is true of God's actions?

A. God's actions are always consistent with His character and therefore prompt worship.

B. We do not need to focus on God's past acts since they do not always reflect His character.

C. God's acts in the past discourage us because we do not see Him acting now.

D. We should focus only on God's acts in the present.

QUESTION 7

Which of the following is not an important component of the worship prayer in Nehemiah 9?

A. Confessing acts of unfaithfulness

B. Asking deliverance from the Persian oppressors

C. Recalling God's acts in the Israelites' history

D. Recognizing and praising God's character

QUESTION 8

Worship has little to do with music. *True or False?*

QUESTION 9

What statement *best* describes the role of worship in the life of a Christian?

A. A good Christian will worship regularly on Sundays.

B. Christians should regularly pray prayers of thanksgiving.

C. We should embrace the music of psalms to worship well.

D. A Christian's entire life should be to the praise of God's glory.

QUESTION 10

When a woman anointed Jesus with an expensive jar of perfume, what did Jesus say about her act of worship?

A. She did what she could.

B. Others should do the same thing.

C. The perfume should have been sold and the money used for ministry.

D. The act was not significant and would soon be forgotten

Lesson 4 Answers to Questions

QUESTION 1: *Your answer*
QUESTION 2: False
QUESTION 3

D. Both God the Father on the throne and the Lamb

QUESTION 4

A. It requires a relationship with the one being worshipped.
C. It is not restricted to a particular place.
D. It is a response to who God is.

QUESTION 5

A. They reflect the character of God.
C. They stimulate worship.
D. They help us understand who God is.

QUESTION 6

B. A father with whom one enjoys a close relationship

QUESTION 7: *Your answer*
QUESTION 8: *Your answer should be similar to the following:*
Discouragement: "I will cry out to God and he will pay attention to me" and "Has God forgotten to be merciful?" Focus on God's works: "I will reflect upon your deeds" and "I will think about all you have done." Praise: "You are the God who does amazing things" and "O God, your deeds are extraordinary."
QUESTION 9: *Your answer should be similar to the following:*
So that future generations will worship the Lord.
QUESTION 10: *Your answer*
QUESTION 11: *Your answer*
QUESTION 12: *Your answer*
QUESTION 13: *Your answer*
QUESTION 14

Category	*Key Phrase*
Confessing sin	"They sinned against your ordinances."
God's works	"You solemnly admonished them."
God's character	"You are a merciful and compassionate God."

QUESTION 15: *Your answer*
QUESTION 16

B. Worship should be costly.
D. Confession is an appropriate prelude to worship.
E. Aromas, music, and drama can all enhance worship.

QUESTION 17

A. His power
B. His reign as King
D. His uniqueness
E. His love
F. His relationship to His people

QUESTION 18

A. Expressing joy
B. Using instruments such as flutes and horns
C. Dancing
E. Using instruments such as drums or cymbals
F. Singing with other believers

QUESTION 19

A. Devoting themselves to the apostles' teaching
B. Praising God
C. Giving to meet the needs of others
D. Meeting together
E. Prayer

QUESTION 20

A. She did what she could.
C. She anointed His body for burial.
E. People would remember and tell others what she had done.

QUESTION 21

D. Because she exalted Jesus

QUESTION 22

A. Four living creatures
B. Twenty-four elders
C. Angels
D. Large multicultural crowd of people

QUESTION 23: *Your answer*
QUESTION 24: *Your answer*
QUESTION 25: *Your answer*

Lesson 4 Self Check Answers

QUESTION 1: True

QUESTION 2

B. Worship in spirit and truth

QUESTION 3: True

QUESTION 4: False

QUESTION 5

C. Gideon

QUESTION 6

A. God's actions are always consistent with His character and therefore prompt worship.

QUESTION 7

B. Asking deliverance from the Persian oppressors

QUESTION 8: False

QUESTION 9

D. A Christian's entire life should be to the praise of God's glory.

QUESTION 10

A. She did what she could.

Lesson 5: Building Intimacy through the Word—Listening to God

Lesson Introduction

In order to thrive, relationships need communication. Imagine for a moment what the relationships of your own life would be like without any communication. The relationship may be with a child, a parent, a spouse, a coworker, or a friend. If communication ceases, the relationship will wither. Since the Christian life is a relationship, communication with the Lord is essential. This lesson and the next one focus on the importance of communication in the Christian's relationship with the Lord.

How is it possible to have a meaningful relationship with a God we can't see or hear? While we can't see or hear God in the same way we see and hear each other, there are many different ways of 'hearing' somebody. For example, people today frequently communicate via text messages and emails. We also communicate with phone calls which allows us to hear voices. But just as we can read words that are communicated electronically and hear voices on the phone, we can read God's Word in the Bible. Even though I can't see God, or hear His voice audibly, He still communicates. It would be a pretty poor relationship if He didn't!

This lesson focuses on listening to what God has said in His Word. We will start in the first two topics by looking at why God's Word is important and some of the ways in which we can hear that Word. Then in topic three we will look in more detail at making the devotional method a part of one's life. Topic four will deal with the disciplines of meditating on and memorizing the Word. Then we will look at the practical issues of applying God's Word and developing a consistent habit of spending time in God's Word.

Lesson Outline

- Topic 1: Why the Bible Is Important
  - Understanding What It Is
  - Understanding Its Value
- Topic 2: Ways of Listening to God
  - Hearing Others
  - Personal Study
- Topic 3: The Devotional Method
- Topic 4: Making God's Word Accessible
  - Meditating on the Word
  - Memorizing the Word
- Topic 5: Applying God's Word
- Topic 6: Developing a Habit
- Topic 7: Conclusion

Topic 1: Why the Bible Is Important

Communication is no less necessary to a relationship with Jesus Christ than it is to relationships between human beings. Without communication, any relationship will suffer, including the relationship that is the Christian life. But at least on the surface, it seems that communication with a God we do not physically see or hear would be a difficult challenge. Fortunately, God can handle this challenge. He has not left us merely to guess about what He wants to communicate.

Understanding What It Is

While a study of the doctrine of revelation and the place of Scripture is valuable, such a detailed doctrinal study is beyond the scope of this course. Our purpose is to understand the role that Scripture plays in the Christian life. Let's start by considering what the Bible says about itself in two passages. First, read 2 Timothy 3:16-17.

QUESTION 1

According to 2 Timothy 3:16-17, for which of the following is Scripture useful? *(Select all that apply.)*

A. Teaching
B. Reproof
C. Correction
D. Training
E. Equipping

In this letter to Timothy, Paul declared two important truths about the Bible. First, he said that it is inspired by God, or God-breathed. By describing it as inspired, he was saying that Scripture originates with God rather than with the human authors God used to write it. While the personalities of the human authors certainly can be seen in the Bible, the writing of Scripture was superintended by God. That means that what the Bible says is exactly what God wants it to say; it is His communication to us.

The second truth that Paul declared in these verses is that all of Scripture is useful, particularly to God's people. Not that Scripture is useless to people who have not yet begun a relationship with the Lord; on the contrary Scripture exposes such people to the truth about who Jesus is and the good news of salvation. But for people who have already begun that journey, Scripture is a crucially important means of staying in touch with and listening to the Lord with whom they have begun a relationship. Scripture teaches us what God intends for our lives. Because it is useful for reproof, it shows us when we begin to depart from God's best plans. As correction it points us back to what God intended; it is a vital resource for training and equipping us for the life and ministry that God intends for us.

QUESTION 2

Open your Life Notebook and describe a time when God used Scripture in your life in one of the ways mentioned in 2 Timothy 3:16-17. What Scripture passage did God use, and what effect did it have on you?

Scripture not only communicates teaching from God; it also reveals the heart and character of God. This dimension is important. It has never been God's intent that His people become theoretical experts in biblical doctrine while failing to really know Him. Rather, what we know of Bible doctrine should flow out of a deepening relationship with the Lord. Let's look at a second Scripture. Consider what Jesus said to the religious experts of His day. Read John 5:39-40.

These religious leaders were experts in the Old Testament Law, and they believed that knowing and obeying that Law was the path to life. Jesus pointed out that they had approached Scripture without faith and had failed to recognize that Scripture—and particularly the Old Testament Scriptures that these religious leaders possessed and should have known—revealed Christ. While they knew much of the content of Scripture, tragically they were missing the very heart of what God intended.

People today are not immune from approaching the Bible with the same lack of faith that these religious leaders displayed. Even believers can fall into that trap. Read the article below "Losing My Hunger" for the testimony of a young Christian who temporarily lost his hunger for hearing the heart of the Lord even while continuing to read and study the Bible.

Losing My Hunger

I became a Christian several years ago when I was attending university. Those early days as a follower of Christ were simply wonderful. I wanted to know everything I possibly could about the Bible because I wanted to know more of Christ. Though my study schedule was busy, somehow I found the time to dig into the Bible. Sometimes I would get up early in the morning and spend those quiet times reading the Bible and praying. A couple of times I lost track of the time and was late getting to my first class of the day. Other times I would stay up late at night. It seemed I could not get enough of God's Word.

My new relationship with Christ was an adventure, and I was eager not to miss any part of that adventure. In some ways I was like a newlywed, thoroughly in love and not wanting to be separated from the one I loved, even for a moment. Church and Bible study were added to my busy schedule, but I did not resent that time at all. I was getting to know the Lord better day-by-day.

I'm not sure just when—or why—that passion to know Christ began to wane. I continued to spend time reading and studying the Bible, but it began to be more of a chore than a delight. I kept going to church, but the teaching there did not connect with me the way it had done earlier. I wondered if something was wrong with the church or the pastor. In my personal study of the Word, I continued to learn more of the facts about God, but that's what they were: just facts. They were divorced from the daily reality of my life.

I was surprised one day when a friend asked me what was the matter with me. "With ME?" I wondered. I did not think there was anything wrong with me. I was still a Christian. I still attended church. I read my Bible. I knew more than I used to, and I thought I was becoming something of an expert on the Bible. There was not anything wrong with me!

But my friend patiently pointed out some of the things he had noticed. As he described me, he described a person who had ceased to grow spiritually even while his knowledge of Scripture continued to increase. When he asked me if I was still excited about my times with the Lord in His Word, I had to admit that I was not. I had become a theoretical expert on the Bible while drifting away from a close relationship with the Lord. He asked me what I had recently read in the Word, and I had no difficulty in answering him. But when he asked how I had applied that Scripture to my own life, I had much more difficulty in responding. The sad fact was that I had drifted into a habit of considering the Bible irrelevant to my own life. As a result, I had started to tolerate sin that I once thought had been conquered.

I had lost my hunger for the Lord, but my friend was stirring up my appetite again. He reminded me of the passion I had when I accepted Christ, and he told me that Christ had never lost His passion for me. I began to regain my hunger, not just for the Bible, but also for the Lord Himself. As I once again made my study of Scripture personal and willingly applied it to my own life, I began to discover just how much I missed that close relationship with the Lord.

The relationship was restored, but I had made an important discovery. My relationship with the Lord is not something I can simply take for granted. It needs to be guarded and nurtured. I recognize now that if I do not nurture that relationship, then I risk drifting into the same condition of having lost my hunger for the Lord. I have experienced what that is like, and I would rather stay hungry!

QUESTION 3

Which of the following was true of the young man in the article? *(Select all that apply.)*

A. His knowledge of the Bible continued to grow.

B. His fellowship with God grew steadily stronger.

C. His interest in the Bible diminished.

D. He continued to apply Scripture to his own life.

E. He was not hearing the voice of God.

It is helpful to keep in mind that central to the Christian life is a relationship with Christ, who is revealed in Scripture. Disconnecting Scripture from the Lord whom it reveals will only harm that relationship. Because God has chosen to reveal Himself in Scripture, the Bible is the place where we meet Him and where the relationship grows. Without Scripture, a growing relationship with Christ is difficult. For Christians the Bible is vitally important precisely because through it, God communicates Himself to us.

Understanding Its Value

We have already seen in 2 Timothy 3:16-17 some of the benefits and value of God's Word. Perhaps one of the most extensive declarations of the value of God's Word is found in Psalm 119. This psalm, the longest in Scripture, differs from most psalms in that it focuses not so much on the mighty acts of God as on the Word of God. The psalm is intricately constructed as an acrostic in 22 stanzas, one for each letter of the Hebrew alphabet. Its very construction reflects the care with which God's Word should be handled.

Take time to read through Psalm 119 carefully and thoughtfully before answering the next question.

QUESTION 4

Open your Life Notebook and list at least ten benefits of the Word of God that you see in Psalm 119. Note the verse(s) that speaks of each benefit.

The psalmist considered God's Word to be of enormous value and in this psalm, he wrote of its practical benefits in the life of the believer. These benefits are equally available today to the Christian who is willing to invest time in God's Word, listening to what He has to say.

Topic 2: Ways of Listening to God

Christians come into contact with God's Word in a variety of ways. Probably the most obvious is when a Christian opens the Bible, reads what is there, and takes time to assimilate and apply it to his own life. But for many, their introduction to hearing God's Word in Scripture comes through other people.

Hearing Others

Before we dig into the subject of personal study, let's look at some of the ways in which we hear God's Word through others.

Sometimes there is real benefit in hearing from someone else, especially a person who has been a Christian a long time. Pastors, elders, and other experienced believers, who may have been Christians much longer than we have, are often good at explaining something, so it is easier for us to understand.

Wise people recognize that others can provide valuable help when it comes to understanding what the Bible is saying. This does not mean the Bible is difficult to understand. Most of the time we can figure out what the words of Scripture mean without too much difficulty. Sometimes, though, in spite of recognizing clearly what a passage of Scripture is saying, we have difficulty fitting that Scripture into what we already understand of God and His Word. This is not so much a case of our saying, "I do not know what this means," as it is a case of our saying, "I know what this means, but I do not understand how it can be applied." At times like this we can benefit from the wisdom and insights of others. They may be more experienced or more mature than we are, or it may be that they can approach the passage in question without the same mental blocks that we may bring to it.

We hear God through other people in a variety of ways. Perhaps the most obvious example is hearing God through the preaching and teaching that we encounter in church. Because this is a common experience for many Christians, some people mistakenly conclude that they can hear God only through experts or Bible scholars. Such a conclusion, of course, is incorrect. First, not all pastors and teachers are experts, even if they hold a position that might make us think that they are. Second, teaching must always be evaluated by the Word itself. Acts 17:11 commends the Jewish believers in Berea for examining the Scriptures to see if what Paul and Silas were teaching was true. Third, most of us have more interaction with ordinary Christians than with supposed experts. In our relationships with family and friends, we have abundant opportunities to hear from the Lord.

For some people the availability of communication technology makes it possible for them to hear God through others without ever having face-to-face contact with those people. The potential advantages of print and electronic media are great, but such communication methods also heighten the need for careful evaluation. No matter what the source, we have the same responsibility as those Bereans of old to evaluate that input carefully, and in the absence of face-to-face fellowship, such evaluation is even more crucially important.

QUESTION 5

Most problems in understanding the Bible are because we do not understand the meaning of the words. *True or False?*

QUESTION 6

Through which of the following people might a Christian hear God speak? *(Select all that apply.)*

A. A pastor

B. A spouse

C. A Bible study leader

D. A friend

E. A son

F. A daughter

Personal Study

Because the Christian life is a relationship with the Lord, Christians can hear what He has to say without always needing to rely on others. As indicated above, God has communicated to us in the Bible. While other people can be helpful to us in explaining Scripture, there is no substitute for personal time in God's Word, where we listen to Him as we seek to grow in our relationship with the Lord.

But what does it mean to spend personal time in God's Word? As we begin to explore the area of personal Bible study, read the article below "A Multitude of Methods" and then answer the questions that follow.

A Multitude of Methods

Studying the Bible is an adventure, but it is an adventure that is different from studying other books. The Bible is unique in that it is God-breathed. In spite of the fact that God used many different human writers over many centuries, what the Bible says is exactly what God wanted it to say. Though different parts of the Bible had different audiences in differing cultures and at different times, all of the Bible contains God's truth for each generation.

Recognizing that it is God's Word, Christians have developed many different methods of studying the Bible. Some of these are described briefly below. It is not our purpose here to explain exhaustively each of these methods; rather the purpose is to recognize the breadth of methods available and provide a common vocabulary for talking about Bible study. There is no single method that is right or best or perfect for every person, every setting, or every portion of Scripture. You will need to decide which method or methods are appropriate for you, keeping in mind that the real goal is not merely knowing the Bible, but knowing God.

Chapter study: Some Christians enjoy studying the Bible one chapter at a time. In doing a chapter study, they focus on a single chapter, for example Romans 12. They bring to that chapter questions that seek to analyze, interpret, and apply it.

Book study: Sometimes rather than tackling a single chapter, a person might want to study an entire book, for example Romans, looking for what the entire book has to teach. While chapter studies are usually analytical in nature, book studies are more likely to involve synthesis rather than analysis, bringing together the various parts of the book into a cohesive whole.

Topical study: Rather than focusing on a particular passage of Scripture such as a chapter or a book, topical studies focus on a particular topic such as persecution. A person doing a topical study might compile a list of many Scripture references that relate to the topic. Those Scriptures then become the biblical base for the study.

Character study: A character study is really a specialized form of topical study, but here the topic is a person in the Bible such as David, Moses, or Mark. The Bible, particularly the Old Testament, is a rich source of information about hundreds of different people, and their lives have much to teach us. A character study will focus on the verses that relate to the person being studied.

Comparative study: In a comparative study a person seeks to compare two or more similar things. Such a study might focus, for example, on comparing the gospel of Matthew with the gospel of Mark. Or it might compare the reign of King Rehoboam with the reign of King Jeroboam. It might compare the actions or words of a person in the Bible at two different times in the person's life. A comparative method can be applied to many of the other Bible study methods.

Word study: A word study focuses on understanding a particular word as it is used in Scripture. A person might wonder, for example, exactly what is meant by the term "disciple" or by the word "repentance." Doing a word study involves not only the immediate context in which you found the word, but other places where that word is used as well. An exhaustive concordance and a Bible dictionary can be helpful in doing a successful word study.

Devotional study: In a devotional study, the emphasis is on personal application. Application is always an important goal of Bible study, no matter what the method. But in a devotional study, application is central. The key question is, How can I apply this passage to my life? The devotional method can be combined with almost any other method so long as the central purpose remains application to one's life.

While these different methods may take different approaches to studying the Bible, they share a few common characteristics.

First, all of them are intentional. Bible study is not a matter of simply opening the Bible and reading whatever catches your eye. While it is possible to hear from God in a random approach like that, such a lack of intentionality misses the point. To say that the Bible is inspired is to affirm that God was intentional in what was recorded. If we are truly interested in a relationship in which God speaks to us, we will also be intentional in listening to what He has said in His Word.

Second, Bible studies involve asking questions about the passage being studied regardless of which passage of Scripture it is or what kind of study method is being used. You can read the Bible without engaging your mind, letting the words simply wash over you, but that kind of reading is not study. The questions you bring to the biblical text will depend on the kind of study you are doing. The article on devotional Bible study will suggest several questions that you might want to answer as you study God's Word.

Third, no matter what study method you are using, it will be helpful to write down the answers you find and the insights you gain. Keeping some kind of written record of your study will help in at least two ways. First, it can save you time. By writing down things like cross-references and answers to the questions you have asked, you save yourself the trouble of finding them again. Second, the very act of writing will help you remember what you have written. Recording your insights can enhance the value of your study.

Fourth, personal application is important whenever you study the Bible. It is possible to become an expert in the content of Scripture without ever applying it to one's own life. But to do so is a serious mistake. Christians who devote time to Bible study and ignore application risk becoming like the Pharisees of Jesus' day who knew the Old Testament but did not really know the Lord.

The Christian life is a relationship with the Lord, and the Bible is God's Word. Those facts make Bible study important. You may use any number of methods to study the Bible, but the ultimate goal is always knowing and hearing from our loving, sovereign God who has called us into a relationship with Himself.

QUESTION 7

The real goal of Bible study is to know the Bible. *True or False?*

QUESTION 8

Match each of the following Bible studies with the method you would most likely use for it.

Bible Studies	*Method*
The life and ministry of Simon Peter	Book study
Philippians 2	Comparative study
Appearances of angels	Topical study
Differences between John's gospel and Mark's gospel	Character study
The prophecy of Amos	Chapter study

QUESTION 9

Which of the following methods would be most effective in a study of the book of Jonah? *(Select all that apply.)*

A. Chapter study
B. Word study
C. Book study
D. Character study
E. Topical study

The plea for God to break His silence is found in many psalms. It is not difficult to understand that desire. We who have been called into a relationship with God need to hear Him. The good news is that He is not silent; we can hear Him as we open His Word and read and study what it says. We have briefly looked at several ways of hearing and studying His Word. In the next topic we will look in more detail at the devotional method of reading and studying the Bible.

Topic 3: The Devotional Method

In devotional study, one is not trying to fully and rigorously explain a particular passage of Scripture; one is simply trying to hear what God is saying to him. While academic and factual knowledge of the content is important; hearing from God and applying His Word, letting it shape one's life, is the primary focus. This focus on application does not lessen the need to understand the truth of Scripture, nor does it allow one the liberty of imposing a meaning on the text that is not there. There may, however, be unanswered questions about the text that can be answered later and that do not get in the way of applying the truth of the Scripture to one's life.

What it is

The goal of devotional Bible study is the application of Biblical truth to one's personal life. In a sense it is Bible study in its most basic form. As we have already seen, application should be a part of every Bible study method; it is not unique to the devotional method.

The devotional method, while quite simple, is more than simply reading the Bible. Christians can easily fall into the trap of reading the Bible without making any personal application, and in doing so, to think that they have somehow fulfilled a spiritual obligation. The devotional method is simple enough to be made a regular, perhaps daily, part of the Christian's life. Ideally we will do so not merely out of a sense of obligation, but from a desire for a deepening relationship in which we want to hear from God and apply what He says.

Taking the time each day to read God's Word with a desire to apply it to one's life is a discipline that will help build a healthy, growing relationship with the Lord.

QUESTION 10

The goal of devotional Bible study is personal application. *True or False?*

How to do it

A new Christian may be overwhelmed by being handed a Bible and told that he needs to read it and apply it to his life. Where should he start? How much should he read? How can he tell exactly what God wants to say to him? The answers to questions like these will be shaped by his contacts with other Christians and the ways in which they interact with God's Word. Sometimes a person is just left to stumble toward some method of studying and applying God's Word without much guidance at all. In the previous article, "Losing My Hunger," you read the testimony of a young man who drifted into a habit of not applying Scripture to his own life. It took the questions of a friend to nudge him back into regularly applying to his own life what he was reading.

Now, read "Discovering Devotions" below for the testimony of another Christian who had difficulty discovering what it meant to spend devotional time in God's Word.

Discovering Devotions

One of my friends introduced me to Jesus shortly before I began training to be a nurse. It was a wonderful discovery! Knowing that God loved me and wanted a relationship with me was great and realizing that He had paid the penalty for my sin staggered my mind. I wanted to learn all that I could about Jesus, but I was not quite sure how to go about it.

"Sarah," my friend told me, "you need to start having devotions." Unfortunately, she did not tell me what having devotions meant. When I asked, she said that I should start having a "quiet time with the Lord." That comment was not very helpful to me either, but not wanting to look stupid, I did not ask her what she meant. The idea of simply being quiet held some appeal for me since I live a pretty busy life. However, I could not understand how doing that by itself could be of much help. I tried it, and sure enough, it was not much help.

I tried opening the Bible and reading it. I did not know where to start, so I started at the beginning. The first couple of chapters of Genesis were interesting, but I could not see how it related to me. The fact that God created everything provided some fascinating mental images, but I was sure that what I was experiencing was not what my friend meant by "having devotions."

It was a day or two before I was going to leave for my training program, and I was frustrated. I was missing something, but I did not know what. Finally, my frustration overcame my pride. I asked my friend what "having devotions" meant, and I did not care how stupid I sounded.

As it turned out, she did not think I was stupid at all. In fact, she apologized for not explaining it to me more clearly. She encouraged me to have a regular time of Bible reading and prayer each day. She also showed me how to read and ask the kinds of questions that would help me to make the truth I was reading a practical part of my own life. The simple method she showed me made good sense and helped me to get into God's Word in a way that helped me grow closer to the Lord and made a practical difference in my life.

In retrospect, having devotions should not have been that difficult a discovery. I am really glad that my friend introduced me to a practical way of spending time with the Lord.

Perhaps, like Sarah, you have had a variety of experiences in trying to develop a devotional practice of spending time with the Lord.

QUESTION 11

Before reading the next article on the devotional method, open your Life Notebook and briefly describe your current devotional practice, if any.

What was it that Sarah's friend told her that made a difference in her devotional life? Read "Devotional Bible Study" (refer to the Articles section at the end of this lesson), and then answer the following questions.

QUESTION 12

Which of the following characteristics need to be present for effective devotional Bible study? *(Select all that apply.)*

A. Directed

B. Simple

C. Complex

D. Practical

E. Regular

QUESTION 13

Put the following questions in the order in which you would normally answer them in a devotional Bible study.

Order	*Question*
First	What does it say?
Second	What should I study?
Third	How could this passage be applied?
Fourth	What application shall I make to my life?
Fifth	What does it mean?

QUESTION 14

Study Colossians, chapter 1 using the method discussed in the following "Devotional Bible Study." Open your Life Notebook and record your personal application. Then write a paragraph reflecting on the experience of using this method.

Devotional Bible Study

Most Christians are aware that devotional Bible study is an important part of the Christian life. They may have heard someone they respect, such as a pastor, tell them that it is important. They may have experienced for themselves its value in building and maintaining a healthy relationship with the Lord. They may have seen its importance demonstrated in the lives of other Christians. Yet in spite of knowing that it is important, some Christians struggle with the practice of devotional Bible study.

Three characteristics need to be present for a successful devotional Bible study. It needs to be *simple*, *practical*, and *regular*. Frequently the struggles a Christian has with devotional Bible study involve one or more of these areas. A devotional study that is lacking in one of these characteristics will likely soon fade out of a Christian's life, leaving behind a nagging sense that something important is missing. Before looking at some simple suggestions for devotional Bible study, let us briefly consider each of these three requirements.

Devotional Bible study needs to be *simple*. A study that is too complex will become discouraging, particularly to a new believer. If the instructions are long and involved, a Christian, even one who wants to know the Lord better, may ask himself, "Why bother?" The passage that is chosen for the devotional study needs to be short enough to manage in a reasonable amount of time. A chapter at a time will be easier to manage than lengthy passages. Keep it simple, both in length and methodology, is the first guideline for successful devotional study.

The heart of a devotional Bible study is application. The study needs to be *practical*. Whatever the passage is, the goal is that you apply that Scripture in practical ways to your own life. If this element is missing, then one will inevitably begin to wonder, "What's the point; why bother?" The goal of devotional study is neither the accumulation of knowledge nor the ability to critique somebody else's spiritual life; it is devotion. Unless the study has been practical enough to include personal application, it is not devotional study.

Remember that healthy relationships need communication like a plant needs water. Without ongoing communication, relationships soon begin to dry up and die. The Christian life is a relationship that needs to be nurtured with regular communication, and God speaks to us in His

Word. We need to listen *regularly* by making devotional Bible study a habit. If it is a practice that occurs only occasionally in our lives, then we demonstrate the low value we place on our relationship with Christ. It is then likely that devotional Bible study will cease to be a part of our lives.

How then does one have a devotional Bible study that is simple, practical, and regular? The suggestions that follow include a short list of questions that, successfully answered, will help you meet that goal. The first question you need to answer is, *What shall I study?* There are many good ways to answer that question. The key is to have a plan and then follow it. You might choose to study the gospel of John or the book of Romans as the focus for a devotional study stretching over some period of time. Remember that you do not need to study the entire Bible in the next two or three months. The goal is to hear from God and apply what He says. Aim for a passage of manageable length. Some people have developed the practice of reading until they sense God speaking to them through His Word, and then stopping there. In a sense, it is not important where in the Bible you begin since God is able and faithful to speak through all of His Word. However, it is important that you begin somewhere and develop the habit of listening to God.

After you have selected the passage to study, read it. You want to be able to answer the question, *What does it say?* Sometimes this question will be very easy to answer. A good way to check on whether you know what a particular passage of Scripture says is to try to put the passage into your own words.

Once you know what the passage says, ask yourself, *What does it mean?* Here you are digging a little deeper than the general "What does it say?" You might consider what the passage has to say about God, about man, about God's creation, about the church, about sin. You want to have some sense of the meaning and significance of what you are reading. It may be that there are questions about this passage for which you would like to find the answer. In a devotional study it is not essential that you answer all those questions immediately, but it can be helpful to jot down the questions for future study.

As you continue to meditate on the passage, you will want to consider the question, *How can this passage be applied?* Is there an example to be followed, or a sin to be avoided? Perhaps there is a command to be obeyed. You might see some reasons to praise God or some truth to internalize. Is there a promise to claim, and if so, does it apply to you and are there conditions that need to be met?

In your prayerful meditation on the passage, God's Spirit may move you to focus on some specific application. At this point your study becomes extremely practical as you answer the question, *What shall I do to apply this passage to my own life?* If you are having difficulty answering that question, ask God to help you. Writing out your answer to this question will help you clarify the application as well as remember it. This also gives you an easy way to check up on yourself to see if you have actually followed through with the application. A later article will cover some specific application questions.

Be sure that your application is personal, that is, that it applies specifically to you. Use first-person words, such as I, me, my, rather than general words, such as they, people, Christians, when you write your application. Making it practical means that it will be something that applies to you and that you can achieve. Sometimes your application will call you to a specific and difficult action that you have been resisting. Other times your application may be as simple as personally praying a passage back to the Lord. Whatever it is, talking to God in prayer about your response will help you carry through with the application. You will find it to be an exciting and rewarding process as you hear God speaking through His Word to the specifics of your own life.

We've looked briefly at five questions:

1. What shall I study?
2. What does it say?
3. What does it mean?
4. How can it be applied?
5. What shall I do to apply this passage to my own life?

Answering these five questions is one way of carrying out a successful devotional Bible study. This is not the only way, and these questions may generate others in your mind. As you spend time studying God's Word in a simple, practical, and regular way, you will nurture a growing relationship with the Lord who loves you enough to communicate with you.

Devotional Bible study is a simple way of listening to God and then applying what He says to one's own life. Making it a regular part of one's life helps to maintain a healthy and growing relationship with the Lord.

Topic 4: Making God's Word Accessible

Simply having a copy of the Bible available does not guarantee that a person will actually listen to God. Some people who have a Bible either do not read it or they read it without really trying to hear what God is saying to them. Others who want to listen to God have limited access to a copy of the Bible and do not have one handy when they want and need to hear from the Lord. Let's take a look at two practical ways of making God's Word accessible.

Meditating on the Word

When they see the word "meditate," some people think it means a mindless recitation of some phrases or emptying our mind and repeating something over and over again.

To Christians, meditation isn't mindless at all. Instead it involves significant mental work. When we read a passage in the Bible, we should take time to ponder what it actually says, to think through the passage and to try to hear what God might be saying to us. For example, we should ask ourselves questions about the passage that help us to understand it more completely. Sometimes we may sense a need to talk to God about the passage or to ask Him to help us understand it or apply it. When we meditate on a passage in the Bible, we think about it; we let our mind dwell on it. It is a helpful process in understanding God's Word. Meditation isn't exclusively religious; it is possible to meditate on anything.

Sometimes non-Christians have the mistaken idea that Christianity is somehow anti-intellectual and that becoming a Christian forces a person to turn off his mind. Nothing could be further from the truth. The Bible says much about the mind and the ways in which Christians should use it. Focusing the mind on God and His Word is a repeated theme in Scripture. Consider Psalm 1, for example, which compares the godly man with the wicked one; the godly man who is blessed is described as meditating day and night on God's Word. This pictures a person who invests significant time focusing his mind on what God has said.

Earlier in this lesson you read Psalm 119, a long and intricately written song focused on God's Word. This psalm includes many encouragements to meditate on God's Word. Reread Psalm 119, taking particular notice of the variety of circumstances in which the psalmist meditated.

QUESTION 15

Match the following verses with the appropriate descriptions of meditation.

Verses	*Descriptions of Meditation*
Psalm 119:47-48	Anticipating meditation at night
Psalm 119:23	Meditating to gain insight
Psalm 119:148	Meditating in the context of worship
Psalm 119:97-99	Meditating while experiencing opposition

There is nothing mystical or even complex about meditating on Scripture. This is simply a process of allowing one's mind to dwell on a particular passage, taking whatever time is needed to digest it. This might involve asking questions about the passage. Or it might involve putting yourself into the passage or imagining what it would have been like to live a particular scene in Scripture. Meditation is not an emptying of your mind; it is a focusing of your mind.

Toward the end of his letter to the church at Philippi, Paul gave the believers there some immensely practical advice. Read Philippians 4:8. When Paul told these Christians to "think about these things," he was in effect telling them to meditate on those things.

QUESTION 16

Which of the following should be subjects of meditation for Christians according to Philippians 4:8? *(Select all that apply.)*

A. Things that are true

B. Things that have been read recently

C. Things that are worthy of praise

D. Things that are just

E. Things that are pure

Interestingly, each of the descriptive phrases in Philippians 4:8 can be accurately applied to God's Word. In other words, when we meditate on Scripture, we are obeying the instructions of this verse.

In Mark 12:28-34, Jesus was asked by an expert in Jewish law which command was the greatest. He responded by referring to a passage in Deuteronomy. "Love the Lord your God with all your heart, with all your soul, with all your mind, and with all your strength." Loving God does not involve just the emotional part of man; it involves the intellect as well. We are to love God with our minds as well as our hearts. The Jews of the Old Testament made no artificial distinction between the "mind" and the "heart" as the center of one's being. They recognized the mind as an integral part of one's personhood. Using our minds to meditate on God's Word is one of the ways in which we can obey the command to love God with our minds.

Memorizing the Word

The incident in Mark 12:28-34 referred to in the previous section where Jesus responded to the scribe's question is one of many times when Jesus quoted or paraphrased Scripture that He had memorized. (It appears that Deuteronomy was a particular favorite of Jesus to memorize since He quoted from it often.) Clearly Jesus considered memorizing Scripture to be a worthwhile use of His time and effort. Each time He referred to Old Testament Scripture from memory in the presence of His disciples, He provided a living example for them to follow.

Before the Israelites entered the Promised Land, God gave them some practical instructions regarding His Word. Read Deuteronomy 6:6-9 and Deuteronomy 11:18-21.

QUESTION 17

What were the Israelites supposed to do with God's Word? *(Select all that apply.)*

A. Carry it as a reminder.

B. Teach it to their children.

C. Depend on the Levites to tell them what it said.

D. Talk about it.

E. Fix it in their minds.

While some of these instructions in Deuteronomy related to physical copies of the written Word, others focused on what the Israelites would actually do with it. The Israelites were expected to know what God had said. To talk about it at home and away from home, and to teach it to their children, required that they had internalized God's Word—fixed it into their minds. Most Christians today do not physically attach portions of God's Word to their bodies or write it on their doors or gates. However, their need to fix it in their minds is no less than that of the Israelites.

Memorizing Scripture is a discipline of great value. When you memorize Scripture, you are making God's Word available for Him to use in your life at any time, whether or not a written copy is available. For some people, memorizing Scripture requires little effort; for others, it is a difficult discipline. Regardless of how much effort it requires, it is a practice that can strengthen one's relationship with the Lord because it increases the time spent listening to Him.

Read the article below "Why I Memorize Scripture" and then answer the questions that follow.

Why I Memorize Scripture

Shortly after I became a Christian, a friend gave me a Bible. I valued that gift highly and enjoyed reading and exploring God's Word. I was surprised at first when my friend suggested I memorize verses of Scripture. After all, I had a copy of the written Word that I could use at my leisure; why go to the trouble of memorizing parts of it as well? My friend assured me that I would find it valuable, and so I gave it a try, even though my expectations were rather low.

It did not take long for me to discover that my friend was right. Memorizing Scripture was indeed valuable in ways that I would not have guessed, though I might have discovered some of them eventually. I realized that simply having a physical copy of the Bible was not enough. God's Word needed to become a part of me, and memorizing would help to make that happen. Let me give you a few of the reasons why I memorize Scripture.

Spiritual battles: It usually does not take too long for a person to discover that the Christian life is not free of trouble and spiritual conflict. The Bible describes Satan as the enemy of our souls, a roaring lion who seeks to devour us. When Jesus encountered Satan and was tempted by him, His consistent response was to quote Scripture. Read Matthew 4:1-11 and notice how Jesus repeatedly says, "It is written…." Even when Satan misused Scripture in trying to tempt Jesus, Jesus responded with appropriate Scripture that He had memorized. Jesus did not carry Old Testament scrolls with Him into the wilderness when Satan tempted Him. He already knew the Scripture and was able to quote it from memory.

Paul reminded the Ephesian Christians that they were engaged in a spiritual battle, and he encouraged them to use the armor of God in the battle (Eph 6:10-17). The pieces of the armor are defensive in nature, with the exception of the sword of the Spirit, the Word of God. That is the weapon Jesus used in His spiritual battle with Satan, and it is a weapon that we can use with effectiveness as well.

The problem is that we frequently encounter the battle at times when a physical copy of the Bible is not available. If we have not memorized Scripture, then we find ourselves caught in the battle without an effective weapon. We are trying to fight without a sword. Memorizing Scripture equips us for the spiritual battles of life.

Avoiding sin: Sometimes it is not so much the actions of Satan as the habits of the old sinful life that trip us up. As a Christian, I want to live a life that pleases God, and that means avoiding sin. In Psalm 119:9-11, the psalmist deals with the question of how to maintain a pure life. His answer is to store God's Word in the heart. As with the attacks of Satan, temptation does not limit itself to times when we have an open Bible in front of us; if it did, life might be easier! We live in a world that surrounds us with temptations to sin. If we have memorized Scripture, we can counter those temptations with God's Word no matter where we are or what we are doing. When I recognize an area in which I am vulnerable to temptation, I have found it helpful to memorize Scripture that specifically addresses that temptation. It turns out that the psalmist was right; storing God's Word in one's heart does help one to avoid sin.

Guidance and correction: I would be the first person to admit that I have not yet mastered the Christian life. I am still learning, and God is still shaping me into the person that He wants me to be. Sometimes in spite of having memorized Scripture, I find myself yielding to temptation or feeling like I am losing the spiritual battle. Paul told Timothy that Scripture is useful for exposing and correcting our errors (2 Tim 3:16-17). Unfortunately, it is during the times of temptation that I am least likely to pick up my Bible and start reading. I have found that God's Spirit can take Scripture that I have memorized and call it to my attention as a way of helping me see where I have gotten away from what He intended and how to get back on track.

God brings memorized Scripture to mind not only to correct me but also to keep me on the right track. Paul called it "training in righteousness" (2 Tim 3:17). The psalmist also understood that God uses His Word to guide His people. In Psalm 119:105 he likens God's Word to a lamp that sheds light on a person's path. God has used His Word to help shape the direction of my life. I have found it helpful to memorize verses that He has used in that way. Recalling those verses helps me to continue following the path God has set for me.

Encouraging other people: Countless times in my life a brother or sister in Christ has encouraged me with words from Scripture. I want to be that kind of encourager to others as well, but I have noticed that those opportunities do not necessarily come when I have a Bible in hand. Just a few days ago I had an unplanned encounter with a friend who shared with me a significant problem he was having. God brought to my mind a couple of verses of Scripture that I had memorized, and I was able to share them as an encouragement.

Sharing the gospel: Those opportunities to encourage others with Scripture do not just happen with fellow Christians. I have been able to share the gospel with unbelievers because I have memorized verses that explain the basics of the gospel. Verses that speak of God's love and holiness, man's sin, and Christ's sacrifice and invitation equip me to share my faith with others. They also remind me of how great a gift God has given me in salvation. In 1 Peter 3:15 believers are encouraged to be ready always to give an answer to anyone who asks about their hope. Sometimes those questions come at unexpected moments. I think that the times when I have been most effective in sharing my faith are the unplanned times, usually when there has been no Bible readily available.

Fellowship with God: I have discovered that the Christian life is an adventure. Listening to Him is important to me, and it remains important even if there is no open Bible in front of me. When I review verses that I have memorized, I can hear in a fresh way God speaking to me from His Word. Even though I have already heard those specific words, I need to hear them again and again. One of the blessings of my childhood was hearing my mother frequently tell me that she loved me. I never got tired of hearing those words. I do not tire of hearing God's words either. Because I have a relationship with the Lord, I value what He has said. Remembering memorized Scripture helps me to focus on Him.

For me, memorizing Scripture has not been particularly easy, but it has been worth it for the reasons I have given and more. When you memorize Scripture, you will likely discover other reasons. Admittedly, this is a discipline that takes time and effort, and once those verses are memorized, you need to review them in order to retain them. I am blessed to have available a written copy of God's Word. I am even more blessed to be able to treasure that Word in my heart.

QUESTION 18

Match the Scripture reference with the reason it supports for memorizing Scripture.

Scripture Reference	*Reason to Memorize Scripture*
1 Peter 3:15	Spiritual battles
2 Timothy 3:16-17	Avoiding sin
Matthew 4:1-11	Guidance and correction
Psalm 119:9-11	Sharing the gospel

QUESTION 19

The author of "Why I Memorize Scripture" gave six reasons for memorizing. Four of them are listed in the previous question (share the gospel, guidance and correction, spiritual battles, avoiding sin). What are the other two reasons for memorizing Scripture given in the article but not mentioned in the answer to the previous question?

QUESTION 20

Choose two verses from the article "Why I Memorize Scripture," and memorize them. Record these verses in your Life Notebook.

Topic 5: Applying God's Word

Most Christians come to realize quite quickly that the real challenge of Bible study is application. Sometimes applying Scripture to our lives is difficult or even painful, and so to avoid the difficulty or the pain, we avoid the application. Sometimes we would rather apply Scripture to other people's lives. For pastors and teachers, those who have a specific responsibility to declare and clarify biblical truth, the temptation to avoid personal application must be avoided. If we attempt to apply truth only to others and not to ourselves, people will soon come to regard us as hypocrites and cease listening to what we say. It is no accident that God often gives us the opportunity to live out a passage of Scripture in our own lives before we preach or teach that truth to others.

Studying God's Word without applying it is like listening to a friend with your mind already made up that you will ignore what that friend says. Such an attitude devalues the relationship and needs to be avoided. One helpful habit is to pray every time you open God's Word, asking Him to show you how you can apply His Word to your life.

In this lesson you have already had the opportunity to begin thinking about and practicing applying Scripture to your own life. The following article entitled, "Application Questions" will give you a list of practical questions to keep in mind as you approach Scripture that will help you uncover ways of applying that Scriptures to your own life.

Read "Application Questions" before answering the questions that follow.

Application Questions

Applying God's Word should be intentional in the life of the Christian, not accidental. Sometimes Christians can fall into the bad habit of reading, studying, and even memorizing Scripture without ever applying that Scripture to their own lives. This can happen because when they begin to study the Bible, they have no plan to identify an application. Christians who apply God's Word to their lives can develop a greater intimacy with Christ because through application lives are transformed. This short article provides you with a set of questions you can use to make application an intentional part of your Bible study.

The seven questions that follow are not the only ones that will lead you to an application. They are, however, intended to help you to be intentional about applying God's Word to your life. You may not be able to answer all of these questions because not all of them will apply to every passage of Scripture that you study. But those that you can answer will lead you toward a personal application that you can make in your own life to grow in your relationship with Christ.

##What do I learn about God that makes a difference in my life? God's Word reveals who He is and what He values. If the Word reveals something about God that is new or exciting to you, do not ignore it. Take time to think about what this means to you and how it helps you grow in your relationship with Him. Based on your reflection, ask yourself how it makes a difference in your life. You might, for example, be reading Psalm 23 and realize that the fact that the Lord is your

Shepherd relieves you of the need to worry. You may find a promise to claim, but make sure it applies to you or an encouragement to take to heart.

##*What command is there in this Scripture for me to obey?* Sometimes the passage that you are studying will include a command that you recognize you need to obey. Applying that Scripture will involve being specific about how you will obey that command. If you were studying Romans 12, for example, you would find a number of commands that God's Spirit might impress on your heart for personal application.

##*What example in this passage do I need to follow or avoid?* In Scripture you will find an abundance of both kinds of examples—good examples to be followed and bad examples to be avoided. Some passages will include both kinds of examples. If you were reading the account of the man with two sons in Luke 15 for example, what examples would you see there to be followed or to be avoided?

##*What warning is there in this passage for me to heed?* You might encounter, for example, in the teachings of Jesus a warning to avoid pharisaical hypocrisy. This may connect with your circumstances or perhaps with a personal attitude you need to adjust. Biblical warnings are there for our benefit. As you apply God's Word you have an opportunity to take personally the warnings of Scripture.

##*What sin in this Scripture do I need to confess and/or avoid?* Sometimes as you read Scripture, the Holy Spirit will bring conviction of some sin that needs to be confessed and forsaken. You can be thankful for this practical ministry of the Spirit in your life as He uses Scripture to shed light on sin you need to leave behind. Identifying these areas of sin in prayer and confessing them before God is one way of applying Scripture. Not every sin you encounter in Scripture will lead you to confession. Sometimes you will encounter a sin in the passage you are reading that does not personally affect you at the moment, but it is an area to avoid in the future, and so vigilance is necessary.

##*What action does this Scripture prompt me to take?* The Scripture you are studying may direct you to some specific action that you need to take. Matthew 5:23-24 for example presents the need for reconciliation before presenting a gift at the altar. If in studying that passage you sense a need for reconciliation with another believer, then you need to take the necessary action to contact that person and seek reconciliation.

##*How does this Scripture prompt me to pray?* You may be reading a passage that you can simply pray back to God, perhaps as an expression of praise, a statement of confession, or an acknowledgement of a need. Using Scripture as you pray not only applies that Scripture; it will also enhance your communication with the Lord. It may be that rather than praying the specific Scripture, you find that the passage you are reading triggers a reminder to pray about some concern you have or to thank God for what He has done for you.

Each of these questions arises specifically from the Scripture that you are studying. It is important that your applications be legitimately drawn from the passage you are reading. Sometimes people read into a text an application that the text does not support. To do so is a dangerous misuse of Scripture since it puts one in the position of inferring that a passage says something that it in fact does not say. That is why a correct understanding of what the text says and what it means should precede wise application.

The nature of the text will usually determine the nature of the application. Do not expect to be able to answer every question about each Scripture passage you study; not all of the questions will apply. You should expect, however, to be able to use at least one of these questions to lead you to a practical and personal application of that Scripture that fits the circumstances of your life. God, after all, is a personal God who desires and intends a loving relationship with His people, and so what He says should enable you to make a specific personal application.

Making the application specific and personal is sometimes uncomfortable. As a result, Christians sometimes tend to express an application in general terms that either apply to a group of people or call for a response that cannot be measured. "I should pray more" and "My church could support a missions outreach in Nigeria" are not personal and specific. "I will begin to pray with my spouse every day" and "I will memorize Philippians 1:9-11" are better examples of applications that are personal and specific.

As you approach His Word, you can expect God to use it to speak to you. His Word is truth, and the challenge of application is to translate that truth into specific action. Applying Scripture personally to your life is part of the joyful adventure of a relationship with the Lord. It is a joy you do not want to miss.

QUESTION 21

According to the article, why is application important to Bible study?

A. Believers do not seek out application.

B. The truth of the passage is in question until you apply it to your life.

C. A believer's relationship with Christ will be more intimate.

D. It is a sin to not apply God's Word.

QUESTION 22

Which of the following is the best example of a specific personal application?

A. It is not good to gossip.

B. I will apologize this week to Mary for sharing a rumor about her.

C. I will not listen to gossip.

D. My church should address the issue of gossiping.

QUESTION 23

Using the application questions in the article, study a chapter of Scripture of your own choosing. Write your application in your Life Notebook.

QUESTION 24

Open your Life Notebook and indicate which of the application questions you think will be most useful to you, and why. Write down any other questions you can think of that could help you make a personal application of a passage of Scripture.

Applying the Scripture that you study will help you to grow in your relationship with the Lord. Writing down the application will help clarify and solidify the application in your life. Some Christians like to memorize verses of Scripture that express what they are seeking to apply to their lives. Memorizing those verses helps keep the application fresh as you continue to review those verses.

Topic 6: Developing a Habit

Communication needs to be current. If a couple got married but never spoke to each other after the words they shared in the marriage ceremony, they would quickly become dissatisfied with the relationship. In a healthy, growing relationship with the Lord, a Christian needs to be continually hearing what God says. That means that the Bible—God's Word—will always be an important part of the believer's life.

Maintaining a habit of regular, daily time in God's Word can be a challenge. Most Christians live busy lives, and it is easy to let that important time in the Word be crowded out by other activities that seem more pressing. The battle between the urgencies of life and the importance of time with the Lord is a constant battle for many Christians. Keeping a written record of one's time in the Word is a tool that many have found helpful in maintaining a regular time in God's Word. For some who enjoy journaling, maintaining a written record is not a difficult discipline. For others, it may require more effort. Take a look at the "Devotional Record" below. This brief form is a simple tool for keeping a written record of your devotional times for a week.

QUESTION 25

Use the "Devotional Record," or a similar format in your Life Notebook, to keep track of your time in God's Word for a week. Be prepared to share one of your applications with others.

Devotional Record

Date:____________________ Scripture I read today____________________________

What I sensed God saying to me: (*or*... What seemed especially significant to me in this passage?)

____

____

How I will apply this Scripture to my life: (*or*... What will I do about it?)

____

____

◈ ◈ ◈

Date:____________________ Scripture I read today____________________________

What I sensed God saying to me: (*or*... What seemed especially significant to me in this passage?)

____

____

How I will apply this Scripture to my life: (*or*... What will I do about it?)

____

____

◈ ◈ ◈

Date:____________________ Scripture I read today____________________________

What I sensed God saying to me: (*or*... What seemed especially significant to me in this passage?)

____

____

How I will apply this Scripture to my life: (*or*... What will I do about it?)

____

____

Topic 7: Conclusion

Everyone recognizes that the physical nourishment we get from food is essential to our health and well-being. Similarly, the spiritual nourishment we get from God's Word is essential to our spiritual well-being. The Bible is part of the communication between the Lord and us. Failure to spend time in God's Word will cause us to get spiritually hungry, and if we go too long without it, we'll get spiritually malnourished.

Lesson 5 Self Check: The Christian Life

QUESTION 1

Which of the following is NOT a use of Scripture in 2 Timothy 3:16-17?

A. Teaching
B. Confidence
C. Correction
D. Training

QUESTION 2

If a person knows the content of Scripture, he will understand the heart of what God intends. *True or False?*

QUESTION 3

What is the ultimate goal of Bible study?

A. Learning God's law
B. Becoming a church leader
C. Knowing the Bible
D. Knowing God

QUESTION 4

What is the purpose of a devotional Bible study?

A. Personal application
B. Accurate exegesis
C. Knowing Biblical content
D. Developing a teaching outline

QUESTION 5

What three characteristics are required for successful devotional Bible study?

A. Simple, challenging, directed
B. Occasional, practical, regular
C. Impersonal, challenging, long
D. Directed, regular, occasional
E. Simple, practical, regular

QUESTION 6

The devotional method is the same thing as simply reading the Bible. *True or False?*

QUESTION 7

Which of the following is NOT true about meditating on God's Word?

A. It might involve asking questions about the passage.
B. It is taking the time to digest a passage of Scripture.
C. It requires a focused mind.
D. It requires emptying the mind.

QUESTION 8

Jesus memorized Scripture. *True or False?*

QUESTION 9

What is the real challenge of Bible study?

A. Understanding the text
B. Memorizing the text
C. Meditating on the Word
D. Applying the Word
E. Declaring the Word

QUESTION 10

Which of the following is the best example of a specific personal application?

A. This passage makes me appreciate prayer more.
B. My church needs to start a ministry of intercessory prayer.
C. I will pray with my spouse each evening.
D. Christians should spend more time praying with one another

Lesson 5 Answers to Questions

QUESTION 1

A. Teaching
B. Reproof
C. Correction
D. Training
E. Equipping

QUESTION 2: *Your answer*

QUESTION 3

A. His knowledge of the Bible continued to grow.
C. His interest in the Bible diminished.
E. He was not hearing the voice of God.

QUESTION 4: *Your answer*

QUESTION 5: False

QUESTION 6

A. A pastor
B. A spouse
C. A Bible study leader
D. A friend
E. A son
F. A daughter

QUESTION 7: False

QUESTION 8

Bible Studies	*Method*
The life and ministry of Simon Peter	Character study
Philippians 2	Chapter study
Appearances of angels	Topical study
Differences between John's gospel and Mark's gospel	Comparative study
The prophecy of Amos	Book study

QUESTION 9

A. Chapter study
C. Book study
D. Character study

[A word study and a topical study might help shed light on Jonah, but because these methods also require considerable study of the word or topic outside of the book of Jonah, they would probably be less effective as a primary means of studying the book itself.]

QUESTION 10: True

QUESTION 11: *Your answer*

QUESTION 12

B. Simple
D. Practical
E. Regular

QUESTION 13

Order	*Question*
First	What should I study?
Second	What does it say?
Third	What does it mean?
Fourth	How could this passage be applied?
Fifth	What application shall I make to my life?

QUESTION 14: *Your answer*

QUESTION 15

Verses	*Descriptions of Meditation*
Psalm 119:47-48	Meditating in the context of worship
Psalm 119:23	Meditating while experiencing opposition
Psalm 119:148	Anticipating meditation at night
Psalm 119:97-99	Meditating to gain insight

QUESTION 16

A. Things that are true

C. Things that are worthy of praise

D. Things that are just

E. Things that are pure

QUESTION 17

A. Carry it as a reminder.

B. Teach it to their children.

D. Talk about it.

E. Fix it in their minds.

QUESTION 18

Scripture Reference	*Reason to Memorize Scripture*
1 Peter 3:15	Sharing the gospel
2 Timothy 3:16-17	Guidance and correction
Matthew 4:1-11	Spiritual battles
Psalm 119:9-11	Avoiding sin

QUESTION 19: *Your answer should be similar to the following:*
Encouraging other people; fellowship with God

QUESTION 20: *Your answer*

QUESTION 21

C. A believer's relationship with Christ will be more intimate.

QUESTION 22

B. I will apologize this week to Mary for sharing a rumor about her.

QUESTION 23: *Your answer*

QUESTION 24: *Your answer*

QUESTION 25: *Your answer*

Lesson 5 Self Check Answers

QUESTION 1

B. Confidence

QUESTION 2: False

QUESTION 3

D. Knowing God

QUESTION 4

A. Personal application

QUESTION 5

E. Simple, practical, regular

QUESTION 6: False

QUESTION 7

D. It requires emptying the mind.

QUESTION 8: True

QUESTION 9

D. Applying the Word

QUESTION 10

C. I will pray with my spouse each evening.

Lesson 6: Building Intimacy through Prayer—Communing with God

Lesson Introduction

In the previous lesson we noted how essential communication is to any relationship. That truth is particularly important in the Christian's relationship with Christ. The focus in lesson five was on listening to what the Lord has said. However, communication does not flow in only one direction; listening is only part of what is needed. God has graciously chosen not only to speak to us but also to listen to us. Can you imagine a relationship in which the communication was all in one direction, a relationship in which you were expected to listen, but you never had the opportunity to speak or provide feedback? It is hard to imagine such a relationship lasting very long because relationships need two-way communication.

One of the fundamental truths about Christianity is that we can actually communicate with God. Unfortunately, some people erroneously think that God is not interested in hearing from them. They think that if God is really God, why He would bother listening to any human being? After all, haven't we really messed things up? Maybe, they think, God is unapproachable. Even if it is possible to communicate with God, what could humans say that He doesn't already know? How can you know what is important enough to talk about with the Almighty?

Looking at this from outside of Christianity, the idea of prayer might not seem to make sense. But we must remember that Christianity is not merely a religious system; it is a relationship. What kind of friendship would we have if we never talked to each other?

Conversation with the Lord is a vitally important part of our relationship with Him. It makes no sense to think of life as a Christian without prayer being an integral part of our daily living.

In this lesson we will focus on prayer, the other part of our communication with the Lord. We will begin in the first two topics by looking at the paradox of communication with God and the necessity of faith to healthy communication in a relationship with the Lord. In topic three, we will see how prayer is integrated in our relationship with God and look at the model prayer Jesus gave to His disciples. Topic four explores how prayer is involved in a Christian's relationships with other people. Then in topic five we will look at some practical ways of growing in prayer.

Lesson Outline

Topic 1: The Paradox of Prayer

- Facing a Holy God
- Overcoming the Separation of Sin

Topic 2: The Necessity of Faith

- The Characteristics of Faith
- The Demonstration of Faith

Topic 3: Learning from Jesus How to Pray

- His Example
- His Teaching

Topic 4: Praying for Others

The Privilege of Intercession

Prayer and Evangelism

The Encouragement of Prayer

Topic 5: Becoming a Person of Prayer

Praying Always

A Growing Experience

Topic 6: Conclusion

Topic 1: The Paradox of Prayer

Prayer is an astounding gift that God gives us. He earnestly desires to communicate with us by hearing what we have to say. Prayer is our intentional conversation with God. Through prayer we acknowledge our dependence on God and our need of Him to accomplish His purposes in our lives. The holy God of the Bible wants to be a central part of our lives. Often times this can be mind boggling. Who are we that the God of the universe wants to have a relationship with us? This intimacy is like nothing we could have ever hoped to have with Him.

Facing a Holy God

One of the difficulties that may be encountered in trying to understand prayer is the difference between God and man. Why would God choose to listen to human prayers? In fact, is it even possible for a sinful human being to come into the presence of a holy God long enough to say anything without being destroyed? In sensing that difficulty, we may experience some of the same tension with which God's people lived in Old Testament times. They believed that for a sinful human being—and we are all sinful—to come into the presence of God who is holy would mean death.

Let's consider a couple of examples from Scripture. Jacob encountered God on multiple occasions. His father Isaac sent him from Canaan to the land from which Abraham had come so that Jacob could find a bride. On his way, Jacob had a dream at a place he would call Beth-el in which God extended to Jacob the promise He had made to his father, Isaac, and his grandfather, Abraham. Read about his dream in Genesis 28:10-17.

QUESTION 1

What was Jacob's response to having seen the Lord in his dream at Bethel?

A. He ignored the dream.

B. He was filled with peace and joy.

C. He rejected God.

D. He was afraid.

E. He died.

Jacob did not return to Canaan for another twenty years. On his journey back to the Promised Land, he would have another unexpected encounter with the Lord during the night. This time it was in the form of a physical struggle with someone whom Jacob first assumed to be a man but later realized was the Lord. At this time the Lord gave Jacob the name *Israel*. Read Genesis 32:24-30, noticing again Jacob's response.

QUESTION 2

Jacob was surprised that he had seen God face to face and survived. *True or False?*

Jacob's expectation that death would be the result of being in the presence of a holy God was not unusual. His expectation flowed out of a correct understanding of the reality of God's holiness. For example, many years later when Moses was on Mount Sinai, he boldly asked to be shown God's glory. Part of God's answer was to tell Moses that no one could see Him and live. That was why the Lord had insisted that there be boundaries around the mountain (Ex 19) before Moses ever went up. In response to Moses' request, God graciously revealed His glory, but Moses was not permitted to see God face to face.

Another example can be seen many years later. When Isaiah found himself in the presence of the Lord (Isa 6), his response was that of someone who had experienced the worst possible thing rather than the best. Isaiah expected death, and the basis for that expectation was God's holiness and Isaiah's sin. Read about this encounter in Isaiah 6:1-8.

QUESTION 3

Why did Isaiah not die when he was in God's presence?

A. It was only a dream.

B. His sin was cleansed.

C. God had a job for him to do.

D. He was a prophet.

Sin separates people from God. There is no way human beings can overcome that separation on their own. On the surface it would seem that coming into God's presence through prayer is an unreasonable expectation. Prayer does indeed bring us into the presence of God, but if He is holy and we are sinful, then how can we pray? While man cannot solve this problem, God can.

Overcoming the Separation of Sin

In his vision in Isaiah 6, Isaiah recognized the dilemma created by being the sinful man in the presence of a holy God, and, acknowledging his sinfulness, he expected to be destroyed. Graciously, God's messenger, a seraph with a burning coal, brought him cleansing and forgiveness. Only then was Isaiah ready and able to engage in conversation with the Lord.

Later Isaiah challenged God's people, calling them to repentance and reminding them about the impact that sin had on their prayers and on their relationship with the Lord. Read Isaiah 59:2.

QUESTION 4

According to Isaiah 59:2, which of the following are consequences of sin in the lives of God's people? *(Select all that apply.)*

A. They will be alienated from God.

B. God will reject them.

C. They will not know how to pray.

D. God will not listen to their prayers.

This picture of a broken relationship stands in stark contrast to New Testament passages that speak of our freedom to come before the Lord. This does not mean God has somehow changed and overcome His own holiness. Instead, He has changed those who trust Him through the work of Christ. Read Hebrews 4:14-16.

Given the universal fear of coming into God's presence in the Old Testament, the invitation of these verses to come confidently before His throne is startling. God is the same in the New Testament as He is in the Old, and His holiness does not change. What enables that confidence is God's gracious provision. It is no accident that Scripture refers to His throne as a *throne of grace*. Jesus, as our high priest, has paid the price for our sin and satisfied the demands of God's holiness. Prayer requires a relationship, and our relationship with God depends on His grace. Because Christ died in our place, we are able to access this grace. Prayer is one of the key ways in which we abide in Him and thus maintain our faith.

In the following article, "Finding Grace," we see a young girl about to be on the receiving end of grace. With no expectation that her situation would improve and having done nothing to earn the intervention of someone who can fix her broken leg, she meets the one who can bring healing to her.

Finding Grace

Carmen and Michael had eagerly looked forwarded to the arrival of their new baby, but through a series of events over which she had no control, baby Grace would be an orphan. Her father had worked in the mines, and two months before Grace was born, he had tragically died, one of eight victims when a mine tunnel had collapsed. A month before the accident, her parents had decided that if the baby was a girl, her name would be Grace, and even in her grief Carmen determined that the child's name would be a reminder of God's goodness. In the midst of her labor pains, Carmen wondered how she would cope with both the birth and the prospect of raising the child alone. *I'll just have to trust that God will graciously provide*, she thought. What she did not know was that in a few short hours, she too would be dead, giving her life in childbirth.

It quickly became apparent that parents were not the only things missing in Grace's young life. She was born with congenital deformities to her face and one foot, and after several months in an orphanage, her caretakers discovered that her vision was impaired as well. Some of her contemporaries were adopted as toddlers and others as older children, but Grace was not considered adoptable. Many adults simply shunned her because of the disfiguring effects of her birth defects. Her vision problems sometimes enabled people to avoid her without Grace even noticing, and so in a sense, that deficiency saved her from some pain. Yet the child was aware that to most adults, her presence was unwelcome, and so she learned to avoid people. The child lived with the underlying inescapable awareness that for her, life was qualitatively different.

Though her interaction with adults was limited, her imagination was keen, and she used to imagine what it would be like to have parents. The mother and father she created in her mind were, of course, ideal. He would be strong and tender, telling her stories each evening. Her imaginary mother's dominant characteristic was a warm smile that reflected a deep inner kindness. As this imaginary family of three walked together, both parents slowed their pace without complaint to match Grace's awkward, stumbling gait. They were only imaginary, but they were all Grace had.

One fateful day when she was eight years old, Grace tripped near the bottom of the stairs, the weight of her body landing on her good leg. She heard the bone snap, not understanding what the sound meant. What she knew was that her pain was intense and trying to move made it worse.

The next couple of hours were a blur in Grace's mind. In pain, she was eventually carried out and taken to a local hospital. The pain dulled her awareness of everything else. She thought briefly about her imaginary parents, telling herself that they would never have let her fall, though she did not know how they could have prevented it.

She heard a voice breaking through the blur of noise and light that surrounded her. "You have a broken leg, Grace, but I think we can fix it."

She opened her eyes to gaze into the face of the doctor who had spoken, and she was startled. Her vision was not sharp, but the face reminded her of the father that she imagined. She pulled back, instinctively withdrawing, and squeezed her eyes shut again. The words did not penetrate Grace's preconceptions. In her eight short years, she had never seriously considered herself fixable; why should it be different now? With her eyes still closed, she mumbled, "No, you can't fix me."

"Grace, I *want* to fix you," the doctor declared. "Will you let me?" It seemed a strange question to ask of an eight-year-old, but the doctor was drawn to this young patient and sensed her need to find hope and trust.

Grace opened her eyes again and looked at the doctor wordlessly for a few moments. Then she spoke one word. "Why?"

The question stirred the doctor's heart. It was not a question he was used to. He thought for a moment before answering, and when he did, his words were gentle and deliberate. "Why do I want to fix your leg? Because I can," he said. "And because you can't." He looked into Grace's eyes and went on. "Grace, do you know what your name means?"

She shook her head.

"Grace is good that comes to you that you have done nothing to deserve. I want to give grace to Grace." He smiled. "Is that okay?"

She nodded, wondering if the father she had imagined had been incarnated before her eyes.

"Then let's go," he said, as he moved around to wheel her to surgery.

Grace is at the heart of the Christian life. Notice how Paul describes the Christian life in Romans 5:1-2. We stand in grace. It is because of what Christ has done that we have peace with God and are able to communicate with Him in prayer. Every time a Christian prays, he is demonstrating the grace that has made it possible to communicate in peace with a holy God.

Writing to the Ephesians, Paul says it is by grace that we are saved (Eph 2:4-9). Then he pictures them seated *with Christ* in the heavenly realms as a lasting future witness to the incomparable grace of God. It is God's grace that makes possible a relationship with Christ. Such grace, of course, is not cheap and should not be taken for granted. In a different context, Paul reminds the Corinthian Christians that the grace they freely experience came at a staggering cost (2 Cor 8:9).

QUESTION 5

Open your Life Notebook and reflect on the above article, "Finding Grace." How is this story like God's grace? In what ways is God's grace greater? Why do you think the little girl initially rejected the doctor's offer?

God's invitation to us to pray is an expression of His grace. Before moving on, take time to thank God for His work of grace in your life.

Topic 2: The Necessity of Faith

Faith is absolutely necessary for the Christian life. Without faith, we cannot properly grow in our relationship with Christ. Faith is essential to understanding prayer. In prayer we actively put our faith in God to hear us and respond to us. We also acknowledge His role in our lives and our dependence on Him.

The Characteristics of Faith

Sometimes people wonder whether God really exists, and even if He does exist, that maybe He has no interest in listening to us. They think they would feel foolish talking to a 'god' who isn't listening or isn't even there.

Perhaps it would help us to realize that it is much more foolish to ignore a God who *is* there and *is* listening. It comes down to an issue of faith. We don't 'see' Him the way we see each other when we're talking, but we know that He's there and He hears us when we pray.

Faith is absolutely essential to the Christian life. The need for faith permeates every aspect of our relationship with God. You have already seen that need in your study of this course, and you will continue to explore this life of faith as you continue the course. There is probably no part of the Christian life where the need for faith is more obvious than in prayer, so it is appropriate that we look at the nature of faith and how faith is expressed in our prayers.

The writer of Hebrews defines faith and gives examples of a host of people whose lives demonstrated their faith in God in various ways. Read Hebrews 11:1-6.

It is important to remember that the words, "believe," "faith," and "trust" all share the same root word in the original Greek language of the New Testament. They can be used interchangeably with respect to their meaning. They are only restricted by the rules of grammar. ("Believe" and "trust" are verbs. "Faith" is a noun.)

QUESTION 6

According to the writer of Hebrews, what is faith? *(Select all that apply.)*

A. Evidence of spiritual maturity

B. Being sure of what we hope for

C. Hoping only for what we know through reasoning

D. Being convinced of what we do not see

E. Not being convinced of what we see

QUESTION 7

It is impossible to please God without faith. *True or False?*

Sometimes people get the idea that faith only comes into play when we have major needs that seem to require miraculous intervention. But that is not what these verses and the rest of the chapter, and indeed the rest of Scripture, say. Since it is impossible to please God apart from faith, then living a life of faith is necessary whether we are facing great difficulty or not. God's desire and expectation is that we trust Him—all the time. A child walking next to her father and holding his hand does not trust him *only* if they face great danger; she is trusting him all the time. If they face great danger as they walk together, that danger simply makes it easier to see her faith. Whether we are currently facing a critical need, God's encouragement to us—because we are in a relationship with Him—is "trust Me."

The verses you read in Hebrews 11 included a couple of examples of Old Testament people whose lives demonstrated faith. The chapter then cites others—Noah, Abraham, Sarah, Isaac, Jacob, Joseph, and a host of others, even the prostitute Rahab. Though their lives differed in many ways, what they had in common was faith in God that was seen in their obedience to Him, whatever the circumstances. In chapter 12 we get the reason for all of these examples of faith. Read Hebrews 12:1-2. Faith enables us to run with endurance the race set before us, no matter what the particular course may be, with our eyes fixed on Jesus. The Christian life is all about Him, and it is by faith that we can remain focused and in contact with Him.

QUESTION 8

How is the fact that you trust God evident in your life? Open your Life Notebook and record one or two ways in which your life reflects faith in God.

The Demonstration of Faith

One does not have to look very far to find examples of living by faith in Scripture. The list of people in Hebrews 11 is just the beginning. There are countless examples in both Old and New Testaments of people who chose to trust God. Studying these examples can be both instructional and encouraging as we seek to become more consistent in our exercise of faith. One individual whose faith in God clearly intersected with his practice of prayer was Daniel. Read the following article "From the Palace to the Pit" along with all of the Scripture passages that are cited in the article, and then answer the question below.

From the Palace to The Pit—The Faith of Daniel

This was not the best time to be an Israelite. God had warned His people through the prophets that judgment was coming, and now that judgment had arrived in the form of the invading Babylonians led by their king, Nebuchadnezzar. Some of the Israelites were taken captive and exiled to Babylon. Additional waves of exiles would be taken by the Babylonians until Jerusalem and the temple were destroyed some twenty years after the initial invasion.

Among those taken in the first deportation was a bright young man with obvious potential named Daniel. He was one of a group of young men destined for three years of special training in preparation for entering the service of the Babylonian king. For Daniel, the Babylonian captivity led to a position of relative privilege and opportunity. Humanly speaking, it would not have been difficult for Daniel to abandon his faith in God and assimilate himself fully into Babylonian society, including the worship of Babylonian gods. Instead he chose to remain faithful to God and trust Him in the midst of his new circumstances. You can read in Daniel 1 about one of Daniel's early decisions to trust God and how God honored that commitment.

Daniel's faith and integrity led to unique opportunities to speak truth to Nebuchadnezzar for whom Daniel interpreted two dreams (Dan 2; 4). Later he interpreted the handwriting that Belshazzar saw on the wall declaring the end of his rule. Belshazzar rewarded Daniel by declaring him third in charge over the kingdom.

The incoming ruler was Darius the Mede, whose identity is unclear, but who was probably appointed to rule Babylon by Cyrus, the king of Persia. Interestingly he also recognized Daniel's spirit and "intended to appoint him over the entire kingdom" (Dan 6:3). This decision would have made Daniel third in charge after Cyrus and Darius. The other governors, jealous of Daniel's power and influence, began to seek some way of removing him from power. The plan they came up with was to appeal to the pride of Darius and to convince him to issue an unchangeable edict forbidding prayer to any person or god other than Darius for a month.

Because many Christians today consider prayer to be a personal and private matter, they might have little difficulty with such an edict. Since other people may not witness their praying, they could consider that they were safe from detection. But there was nothing private about Daniel's faith. His relationship with God was not compartmentalized; it affected every aspect of his life. People knew that he believed in God, trusted God, and talked to God. Nobody knew that better than his rival governors.

In many ways this was an ingenious plan. Darius valued Daniel, and there was virtually no chance that the ruler would look favorably on a request to diminish Daniel's influence. His competence and integrity were unquestioned. Rather than trying to find some area of failure in his duties, Daniel's critics focused on his faith. When they approached Darius, they never mentioned Daniel. Appealing to the ruler's pride, they succeeded in getting him to declare that only the king could be the object of prayer.

The trap was set, and the penalty had to be sufficiently severe that once caught in that trap, Daniel would not be able to escape. The penalty was indeed severe. Anyone guilty of praying to any person or god other than the king would be thrown to the lions. All that remained was to catch Daniel in the act, something that proved to be remarkably easy.

Daniel was not unaware of the edict. His response to this new command was to continue to do exactly what he had always done: regularly pray three times a day without trying to hide it. How could he maintain a relationship with the Lord while at the same time cutting off communication with Him? It was not a difficult decision for Daniel in spite of the possibility of a painful death. The one new element in Daniel's practice of prayer was to incorporate this edict as a topic of concern as he talked to the Lord. When Daniel's enemies found him, he was "praying and asking for help before his God" (Dan 6:11). Knowing that lions mauling him to death would likely be the consequence of his actions, Daniel continued to pray, trusting that God somehow could bring good out of what looked like impossible circumstances.

The only person surprised when Daniel was accused of illegally praying to God was Darius. The king found himself having to choose between two difficult options. If he protected Daniel, it would mean breaking his own law. If he carried out the law, it would mean losing a trusted and respected leader. He agonized before finally issuing his decision under pressure from the officials who had brought the accusation. Read about these events in Daniel 6.

Darius did not claim to be a believer in Daniel's God, but his only hope that Daniel would be alive the next morning was that somehow his God would do what Darius had not done and spare Daniel's life. Daniel was thrown to the lions, and the king spent a sleepless night worrying about Daniel's fate. The next morning Daniel was bought up out of the pit unharmed, giving witness both by his words and his presence that God had delivered him. Scripture is clear that Daniel was unharmed "because he had trusted in his God" (Dan 6:23).

Consider for a moment a couple of other scenarios. What if Daniel had been attacked by the lions? Sometimes people trust God, and things do not turn out the way they want them to. Such instances do not necessarily reflect a lack of faith. It is not uncommon to trust God without fully understanding what it is that God desires to accomplish in a particular set of circumstances. Faith does not require that I know how things will turn out; Daniel did not. A Christian's faith reflects his relationship with the Lord. Recognizing that He is Lord means that faith will not restrict God's ability to act as he wishes.

Or suppose that Daniel had not trusted God and, faced with the threat of death, stopped praying. The outcome would have been radically different. Daniel might have avoided the lion's den, but he would have compromised a consistent testimony developed over many years. Daniel was not the only one to benefit from his deliverance from the lions. The king, recognizing that it was God who had delivered Daniel, acknowledged Daniel's God as the living God who endures forever. He issued a new edict encouraging the worship of this living God. Daniel's accusers were themselves thrown to the lions and attacked before they reached the bottom of the pit. Daniel would be free to govern as an acknowledged believer in the Lord. As a result, countless other people who otherwise might not have done so would be able to consider the reality of who God is.

The effects of living by faith always extend beyond the immediate circumstances of that faith. Throughout the period of the Babylonian captivity and into the reign of the Persians, Daniel stood as an example of a man who chose to live by faith. Daniel's choice to trust God resulted in the Lord being lifted up in Persia. It resulted in favor being shown to Daniel. And it expressed and strengthened the reality of his relationship with the Lord.

QUESTION 9

What reasons does Scripture give for how Daniel was able to come out of the lion's den without any injury? *(Select all that apply.)*

A. God judged him innocent and sent an angel to protect him.

B. The pit was unsealed allowing Daniel to escape.

C. Daniel had obeyed the law of the king.

D. Daniel had trusted God.

E. Darius restrained the lions.

The account of Daniel's consistent faith provides a model for us to emulate. Daniel's circumstances were unique. We may never have the opportunity to serve in a Babylonian palace or as a counselor to kings. We may never be thrown in a den of lions. It may be difficult for us to point to examples of God's deliverance as dramatic as Daniel's. But in spite of those differences, our need to live by faith is no less than that of Daniel's. We have a relationship with the same God Daniel served, and we are invited and challenged to trust Him no matter what the circumstances of our lives may be.

QUESTION 10

Take some time to thank God for specific ways in which you have seen Him to be trustworthy in your life. Open your Life Notebook and record one or two ways in which the example of Daniel challenges you to trust God in the specific circumstances of your own life.

Topic 3: Learning from Jesus How to Pray

Jesus' life was full of prayer. While the Bible does not record every prayer Jesus prayed, we do know He prayed often and taught believers to do the same. This topic will look at what Jesus did and what He taught about prayer.

His Example

Some people think they would be intimidated by the idea of actually talking to God because they wouldn't know what to say. Others have no trouble talking with God. For them it is quite natural. The question is then: How do we learn to pray?

This question may remind you of a request that one of Jesus' disciples made. Read Luke 11:1-4. His disciples had many opportunities to witness the importance of prayer in the life of Jesus. Now, having seen Him pray again, one of the disciples asked Jesus to teach them to pray. There must have been something about Jesus praying that stirred a desire in the hearts of the disciples to want to pray as He did.

The verses that follow record some of the times the disciples could have witnessed Jesus praying. Read these verses:

- Matthew 14:23
- Mark 1:35-38
- Mark 15:34
- Luke 6:12-16
- Luke 9:29
- Luke 22:39-46

QUESTION 11

Match the following descriptions with the verse references.

Description	*Reference*
Jesus' appearance was changed as He prayed.	Mark 1:35-38
After praying, Jesus left crowds to minister elsewhere.	Luke 9:29
Jesus submitted to the Father's will as He anticipated His coming crucifixion.	Luke 22:39-46

QUESTION 12

If you had observed all these prayer incidents in the life of Jesus, what would you have learned about prayer? Open your Life Notebook and write a summary of what you would have learned by observing Jesus.

The longest recorded prayer of Jesus in the Bible is in John 17. In the previous four chapters Jesus had met with His disciples in the upper room for Passover. He had encouraged them, taught them, and challenged them as He prepared them for His crucifixion. The conversation continued as they left the room. Now, apparently still in the presence of the disciples, He prayed. Read this prayer in John 17:1-26 and consider about whom and what Jesus prayed.

QUESTION 13

For whom does Jesus pray in His prayer in John 17? *(Select all that apply.)*

A. Himself

B. The high priest and Jewish officials

C. His disciples

D. Roman officials

E. All believers

The incidents of Jesus praying that are recorded in the Bible give us a hint about the importance He placed on prayer. But these incidents are just a small fraction of what His followers witnessed. His disciples must have seen and heard Jesus pray many other times. Jesus did not hesitate to pray about anything, and the times He spent praying seemed to shape His actions. The disciples had seen in Jesus a devotion to prayer that they themselves did not have. What they witnessed in the life of Jesus created a hunger within them for the same kind of intimate communication that Jesus had with His Father. Inevitably sooner or later one of them would ask, "Lord, teach us to pray."

His Teaching

That request—*teach us to pray*—presented Jesus with an opportunity that He would not miss. Here were followers who wanted to learn to pray, and in Jesus they could have no better teacher. The model for prayer that He gave them was very similar to, though slightly shorter than, the brief prayer Jesus had used as a model in the Sermon on the Mount (Mt 6:5-14). Jesus clearly intended that prayer was to be an integral part of a meaningful relationship with the Lord and not an exercise to demonstrate religious merit. Pompous public prayer designed to garner the praise of men makes no more sense than parading one's spouse in public so that other people will notice how good-looking he or she is. The relationship is what is important. We strengthen that relationship when we spend time with the Lord in prayer.

The brief model prayer that Jesus gave His disciples in Luke 11 has much to teach them and us about communication with the loving Lord. Read the first two sections ("Teach us" and "Father") of "Teach Us to Pray" and then answer the question that follows.

Teach Us to Pray

Teach Us (section 1)

When Jesus called His disciples, He called them to be with Him. Spending time with Jesus would shape their lives as He impacted their values and behaviors. It must have been an intriguing adventure as they watched Jesus, conversed with Him, and learned from Him. Through His teaching and example, Jesus would affect many different areas of their lives, but there was one characteristic they saw in the life of Christ that prompted them to ask Him specifically for instruction. They had observed the prayer practices of Jesus. They had seen in His life the value He placed on communication with the Father. Now, having witnessed again something of the prayer life of Jesus, one of them asked Him, "Lord, teach us to pray."

Both the request itself and the response Jesus gave imply that effective praying is something that can be taught. The answer Jesus gave did not promote long prayers or flowery language. It was a short, simple, and focused prayer, so short, in fact, that many Christians have memorized it and recited it as part of their own prayer experience. More important than mechanically reciting the prayer is considering the meaning underlying those few words. The short model prayer Jesus gave His disciples in response to their request is known as "the Lord's Prayer." More accurately it would be called the disciples' prayer because it can be a helpful guide to followers of Christ in any age who desire to deepen their communion with the Lord in prayer. Consider, then, a few of the phrases Jesus used in this model prayer.

Father (section 2)

Effective praying begins with a relationship. The Christian who prays should not be talking to a stranger. When Jesus began this model prayer, He addressed His Father using a term that implies relationship. He did not have to. He could have addressed God the Father using a more formal term, but He did not. It is likely that one of the things the disciples had noticed about Jesus' praying was that there was nothing stilted or ritualistic about it. They already knew Jesus enjoyed a close relationship with the Father, and the communication of prayer was an important part of that relationship.

God's people were not in the habit of addressing Him as Father. Perhaps it was not all that strange that the one who claimed to be the Son of God should address God as His Father. But now as Jesus responded to the disciples' question, He invited them to affirm that same relationship by calling God their Father as well. It was a simple concept, but an awesome one, that Jesus set before His disciples. They too were to enjoy relating to God as a child does to its father. Addressing God as the ultimate authority or the ultimate power in the universe, is one thing, but quite another is to call Him Father while not diminishing His authority and power. The God of the universe, the Creator, the Holy One, welcomes His children the way a father welcomes a son, and that is good news when we pray.

When we converse with our Father, we are talking to someone who loves us, and the fact that He loves us affects the nature of the conversation. We can talk to God about anything that concerns us. Because He is our Father, what concerns us concerns Him. There is no need or burden so great—or so trivial—that He does not want to hear from us. He is our Father, and He listens with all of the love and attentiveness that a father could give. God always cares for us and loves us.

Because He is our Father, He loves us enough to discipline us. When we approach God as our Father, we are communicating with the one who knows when we need discipline and has the right to carry out that discipline. Proverbs 3:11-12 reminds us that discipline is a function of the Father's love. He disciplines those in whom He delights. There will be times for the Christian when that discipline and the circumstances that led to it will be an appropriate topic for conversation with the Father. Though discipline is usually not fun, the wise discipline of a loving father restores and deepens a relationship and makes communication sweeter and more meaningful.

We who are Christians do not pray to a stranger. We are not like the Athenian philosophers of Acts 17 who established an altar to worship an unknown god. God is our Father, and He welcomes conversation with His children.

Honored (section 3)

That God is our Father does not lessen at all the reality of His holiness. When we speak to God in prayer, we are talking to the one who is more worthy of honor than anybody else. So, in our conversation with the Lord, it should be important to us that we bring honor to the Lord who is worthy and express our worship to Him.

In this model prayer Jesus gave to the disciples, He spoke of honoring the Father's name. The Bible records many descriptive names for the Lord. Reflecting on the meaning of those names can lead one into specific practical worship. If, for example, He is Shepherd, then I can declare to Him my commitment to honor Him in that role in my life by following Him. Or I might honor Him as Shepherd by confessing times that I have gone astray. Since He is Jehovah Shalom—the God of Peace—I can honor Him in that role by expressing my choice to avoid unnecessary conflict or my commitment to be a peacemaker. When you pray, let the names of the Lord be more than a mere formality of address. Let those names prompt you to worship God.

Incorporating worship into prayer should not be difficult if we realize to whom we are speaking. Worship that is not expressed is difficult to imagine; how can one affirm the infinite worth of the Lord without doing or saying *something*? When Christians worship, they are communicating with God. Whether a person identifies that process as "prayer," clearly prayer is what it is. Because worship by its very nature involves expressing God's worth in some way, it is difficult to draw a sharp and definitive line between worship and prayer.

The ways in which you worship God can be incorporated into a time of prayer when you are communing with the Lord. If music is an important part of your worship, you can bring music into your prayer by singing or playing for Him either aloud or in the quiet of your heart. If you enjoy standing in awe before the Lord as you worship, you can do so in prayer. If, like Mary, you sometimes sit at the feet of the Lord to listen to Him and enjoy His presence, you can do that in prayer. To pray does not mean that you have to talk all the time.

Of course, it is good to talk *some* of the time and to take words with you when you go the Lord. Just as parents delight to hear their children's expressions of love, so does God. He who created you for a love relationship is no less delighted than a human parent when that love is expressed in the communication of the relationship.

In the busyness of life it is not hard to temporarily lose sight of the wonder of who God is and to focus on our own needs. Jesus gently reminded His disciples to take time to honor the one to whom they prayed.

King (section 4)

Most Christians have no difficulty acknowledging God as the ultimate Ruler. Also most believers realize that much in this present world resists coming under His authority and rule. He is a king whose kingdom seems to be not yet fully realized. The writer of Hebrews expresses this seeming paradox (see Heb 2:5-9). He acknowledged that the Father has put everything under Christ's control. Then in the next breath he wrote that we do not yet see everything put under His control. God may not be limited by time, but in this life we are, and so the paradox is easy to see. One does not have to look far to see aspects of this present world that are in rebellion to the Lord. A time will come when everything will be in submission to God and when everyone will acknowledge Him as the ultimate Ruler. But we do not yet live in such a time. Jesus encouraged His disciples in this model prayer to express to the Father their desire to see God's kingdom realized.

Imagine what the world you live in would look like if the Lord were the acknowledged Ruler. What would be different? How might the attitudes and actions of people be different than they are today? As you begin to recognize some of those differences, you are giving shape to the desire to see God's kingdom realized. To pray for God's kingdom to come is to pray that those parts of creation that are in rebellion against Him will instead acknowledge Him as the Sovereign King.

In order for someone to pray meaningfully for God's kingdom to come, one must first recognize that God is King. By providing this model to His disciples, Jesus encouraged them to acknowledge that God is the Sovereign King. His kingdom—His reign—is most easily seen in one's own life. To pray "may your kingdom come" while one is reluctant to let the Lord reign in his own life would be gross hypocrisy. When we pray, it is good to be reminded that the One to whom we pray is indeed the King who has the right to rule, both in our lives and beyond. Having acknowledged God's right to rule in us, we will find it easier to pray that the Lord's reign will be extended in the lives of others.

Provider (section 5)

Many people begin praying by focusing on their own perceived needs. Often those needs motivate a person to pray to God in the first place. Jesus invited His disciples to expose their needs to God in prayer, and to do so on a regular basis. This makes sense because the one who is the sovereign Ruler is also the source for meeting our needs.

Jesus also specifically encouraged His followers not to worry about the basic needs of life like food and drink and clothing (see Mt 6:25-34). Jesus reminded His followers that they are of immeasurable value to God and deeply loved. He told them that their heavenly Father already knows what they need. But if God loves us, and He already knows what we need, why would Jesus encourage us to ask the Lord to supply those needs of which He is already aware? It seems to be a paradox. Why tell God what He already knows? Why ask Him to meet a need that He already recognizes?

The paradox begins to resolve when we recall the nature of prayer and of our relationship with God. As Christians, we are involved in a growing relationship with the Lord and communication is an important aspect of that relationship. If we are experiencing a need, it is a natural and expected part of this relationship to talk about that need to God who loves us and is able to meet our needs.

The question is not, *Why tell God what He already knows?* The question is, *Why wouldn't I talk to God about what concerns me?*

When Jesus encouraged His disciples to pray about what they need, He focuses on a need that they will experience every day for as long as they live: bread. Implicit in this request is an admission of one's ongoing dependence on God. This is not a one-time request for God to provide the food we need for the rest of our lives. It is a request for daily provision that can be brought daily to the Lord. Today He supplies what we need for today. Tomorrow He will supply what we need for tomorrow. We continue to expose our present need to God, and He continues to meet that present need.

The pattern for this daily provision of need was not unfamiliar to the disciples. They knew enough of their history to recall how God had provided for the Israelites centuries earlier when they had left Egypt but had not yet arrived in the Promised Land (Ex 16). At that time God provided manna each morning, enough for the day, and each day the Israelites would gather what they needed. With the exception of the Sabbath, they were not able to successfully save any manna for future use. God's provision—and their dependence—was very much a daily issue.

Jesus intended the same kind of daily dependence for His disciples. He taught them to ask for *daily* bread, not weekly, monthly, or yearly. Talking about what they needed for each day was to be an integral part of their relationship with the Lord. Relying on Him each day for the provision of those needs would strengthen the relationship.

Forgiver (section 6)

Some people find it difficult to talk about their sin. Most people would prefer to talk about their successes rather than their failures. But when it comes to sin and our relationship with God, avoiding talking about sin is not a viable option. Jesus encouraged His disciples in the model prayer He provided to confess their sins and seek God's forgiveness. Confession, agreeing with God about one's sin, however distasteful it may be, is a necessary part of the process that leads to salvation. Having once opened ourselves to God by admitting our sin, we would be foolish then to ignore, hide, or sidestep the issue of sin in our lives. To do so would get in the way of the kind of growing relationship with the Lord that is central to the Christian life.

Unconfessed sin will obstruct communication with the Lord. God is undeniably and consistently gracious, and He will always be ready to forgive sin when it is humbly confessed and forsaken, just as He did when we first accepted Christ as Savior. Sometimes people are tempted to try to take advantage of that grace and assume that God will respond positively to their prayers even though they are harboring unconfessed sin in their hearts. The Bible, however, is clear on this matter. Sin is destructive to our relationship with the Lord. When we hang on to sin and refuse to confess, we are inviting Him not to listen to our prayers. The following verses are just three of many examples in the Bible that speak of the effect sin has on our prayers: The psalmist in Psalm 66:18 says that if he had harbored sin in his heart, the Lord would not listen. Isaiah reinforced this message in Isaiah 1:15 where God says that He will look the other way and not listen. The following verse (Isa 1:16) is a strong call to repentance. Isaiah 59:2 explains that sin alienates people from God and causes Him not to listen. How frustrating it is to talk to someone who will not listen!

To pray while being unwilling to confess known sin is utterly foolish. Anytime we recognize sin in our lives, we should be honest with the Lord about it and confess. To do otherwise will interrupt our communion with the Lord.

Experiencing God's forgiveness ought to motivate Christians to be ready to forgive other people. Sometimes, however, we are much less ready to offer to others the forgiveness we ourselves have been given. Jesus recognized the possibility of this reluctance and addressed it in the model prayer He gave His disciples. The request for God's forgiveness is linked to an affirmation of our readiness to forgive other people who sin against us.

Forgiveness is a transaction that must be given and received. In the case of God forgiving us, God is always ready to offer forgiveness. We simply need to confess and ask for His forgiveness in order to actuate it. Effecting forgiveness then, depends on our confession. But in the case of us forgiving others, there is no guarantee that forgiveness will be both offered and received. Someone who has wronged us may confess, even publicly, and yet we may refuse to forgive. Jesus addressed this possibility, and expanded on His answer to Peter's question about how often to forgive, with a powerful and visual story (Mt 18:21-35). The parable and the model prayer show that Jesus intended His followers to be ready to forgive other people. Forgiveness among people can be completed only when both parties are willing. The offended must be willing to forgive, and the offender must be willing to confess and be forgiven.

A healthy indication of the Spirit's convicting work in our lives is that God will bring to mind a personal wrong we have suffered. When we experience that, we need to be ready to offer forgiveness and not follow the example of the slave in the story Jesus told who was forgiven, but unwilling to offer forgiveness to someone else.

Protector (section 7)

At first glance, the request that God not lead us into temptation seems somewhat strange. After all, a God who loves us surely would not deliberately lead us into danger. However, this petition should not be taken as an expression of fear that God would maliciously lead us into the hands of the enemy. On the contrary, it recognizes the truth about both the world in which we live and the God who loves us.

We live in a fallen world that is a dangerous place. We are never far from the influence of sin and the temptation to turn from God. Even Jesus was subject to temptation. The Bible records three specific attempts by Satan to tempt Jesus (see Mt 4:1-11) and there may have been others that were not recorded. Each time He was tempted, Jesus responded by quoting God's Word. What Jesus experienced was not so much the Father leading Him into temptation, but the Father through His Word leading Him out of it.

As long as we live in a world that is marred by sin, we will experience temptation. Prayer needs to be an important ingredient in our response. The prayer Jesus taught His disciples recognizes that the Lord is our leader, and that His leadership is effective in our moving away from temptation rather than toward it. Sometimes you may find yourself taking a step toward temptation instead of away from it. While temptation is inescapable, yielding to temptation is not. It is in times of temptation that we face our most obvious need to follow God's leadership, and in so doing to find the way out that we need (1 Cor 10:13).

In a well-loved and familiar psalm, the psalmist recognized God as his leader (Ps 23). The Lord, he said, leads him down the right paths. Temptation confronts us with a moral fork in the road where we have a choice to make. The Lord's leadership is always to the right path, not the wrong one. We do not need to wait until we reach the fork in the road to follow the Lord's leading. Asking for that leadership and affirming our intention of following it at times when we are not experiencing temptation, helps prepare us for the next fork in the road where we will face a choice that has the potential to disrupt our fellowship with the Lord.

Conclusion

Each part of this model prayer Jesus gave to His disciples can teach us something about the Lord and motivate us to know Him more deeply. Each phrase has the potential to stimulate us to thanksgiving and praise as we see more clearly and specifically what God is like and what He has done. Each topic might move us toward confession as we become aware of ways in which we have fallen short of God's standard. Each statement can help us ask the Lord for what is in keeping with His will. As you reflect on this short model prayer that Jesus gave to His disciples, let Him teach you to pray as He taught them.

QUESTION 14

What important things about your relationship to God are reflected when you address Him as Father? *(Select all that apply.)*

A. You are God's child.

B. He is a distant God who is hard to know.

C. God loves you.

D. God will discipline you.

E. Since He is God, He is not concerned with the things that concern you.

God is our Father, and He desires to have a close relationship with us. Acknowledging that truth by drawing close to God in prayer is a great privilege for believers. The fact that God is Father does not in any way diminish the reality of His transcendent holiness. His character invites a response of worship and submission. This side of God's character is also incorporated into this short model prayer. Now, go back and read section three ("Honored") and section four ("King") of the above article, "Teach Us to Pray," and then answer the questions below.

QUESTION 15

What does it mean to pray "may your kingdom come"? *(Select all that apply.)*

A. Restore the kingdom of Israel.

B. I recognize You as the sovereign King of my life.

C. I need the help of Your angels.

D. May those who rebel against You come to acknowledge You as King.

QUESTION 16

Imagine some of the ways in which your life and your world would be different if the Lord were universally acknowledged as King. Open your Life Notebook and record some of these examples. Then spend some time praying for the advance of His kingdom.

The model prayer that Jesus gave to His disciples does not begin by focusing on the person doing the praying. The initial focus is on the Lord, and that focus is appropriate. But the personal concerns of the one praying are not forgotten. Jesus encourages His disciples in this model prayer to include those concerns in their conversations with the Lord. Refer back to the article, "Teach us Pray" once again and read the next two sections (section 5, "Provider" and section 6, "Forgiver"), and then answer the three questions below.

QUESTION 17

A Christian who is willing to confess his sin should expect God to ignore his prayers. *True or False?*

QUESTION 18

Why should Christians pray about needs of which God is already aware? Open your Life Notebook and write a short explanation.

Jesus raises a third area of personal concern in this model prayer that He gave His disciples. He recognizes—and invites the disciples to acknowledge—both God's leadership role as a King who is in contact with His people and the reality of evil in the fallen world in which we live. Relying on the Lord's leadership is an intensely practical issue for Christians, and Jesus incorporates it into this prayer. Return to the above article, "Teach Us to Pray" one last time and read the final two sections, (section 7, "Protector" and the "Article Conclusion" before answering the next questions.

QUESTION 19

Which of the following statements about temptation are true? *(Select all that apply.)*

A. Because He is God, Jesus cannot understand what it is like to experience real temptation.

B. Yielding to temptation disrupts the Christian's fellowship with God.

C. Sometimes there is no way to escape giving in to temptation.

D. Following God's leading helps us to move away from temptation.

As you think about this short prayer Jesus used to teach His disciples, and as you review "Teach Us to Pray," you may find that one or more phrases from this prayer have particularly impressed you. Before you proceed with this lesson, take some time to talk to the Lord in prayer, using this model that Jesus gave to prompt you. Take as much time as you need to focus on the phrases that seem particularly appropriate for you at the moment. As you do so, you will be learning from the Lord Himself how to pray, using His example as a guide.

Topic 4: Praying for Others

Not only do we have the opportunity to pray for our own needs, but we also can pray for others. When we pray for other people, we help them to carry their burdens. Prayer can also be one way we reach out to unbelievers. We can bring any request to God; whether it is for ourselves, a friend at church, or a person who needs to know Jesus, prayer is a privilege.

The Privilege of Intercession

Praying for other people is one of the great privileges of the Christian life. Intercession, or praying for others, is one of the ways believers can help bear the burdens of other people. The Christian is involved in a growing relationship with Jesus Christ, and it should be a natural part of the communication of that relationship to talk about the needs and concerns of other people. Read the article below entitled, "Intercession" and then answer the following three questions.

Intercession

Intercession—praying for other people—is one of the greatest privileges and responsibilities of the Christian life. The Christian life is about a relationship with Christ, but that does not mean that all other relationships no longer matter. Every person is part of a web of relationships. Many of the people who are a part of that web have obvious burdens and needs. Some of those people talk to God in prayer about those needs, and others do not. But whether they themselves pray about their needs or not, Christians who know them have the opportunity to pray for them. As you explore some of the biblical examples of intercession in this article, consider how those examples might shape your own prayer practices.

When Christians pray for other people, they are following the example of the Lord Himself. John 17 records a prayer of Jesus shortly before His arrest and crucifixion. Much of this prayer is intercessory in nature, that is, Jesus is praying for other people. Some of those for whom He prayed were aware of His intercession; others were not. He prayed, for example, for the disciples' safety (Jn 17:11, 15), and the prayer must have been heard since John recorded it. What Jesus had in mind was more than mere physical safety, for He prayed that they would be kept safe from the evil one. Probably the disciples had much less awareness than Jesus had of their need for spiritual safety. This need was not one about which they themselves would have prayed. But Jesus saw the need and brought it to the Father in prayer.

Jesus then prayed for those who would become believers through the ministry of the disciples (Jn 17:20). In praying for these future believers Jesus interceded for people who would have no awareness at all that He was praying for them. Intercession does not require that the person for whom the prayer is offered be aware of the intercession. In this prayer of Jesus, some of those for whom He prayed were aware and others were not. Prayer, including intercession, is an expression of the relationship between the Lord and the one who is praying.

Sometimes when a Christian becomes aware of another person's need, the Christian responds by doing something other than interceding. He might offer constructive advice, practical help, or negative criticism. The first two are well intentioned, but they might not be well received, depending on the attitude and awareness of the person with the need. Negative criticism, of course, is almost never well received. Intercessory prayer, on the other hand, can always be a response to awareness of need. Some examples of intercession in Scripture are set in circumstances where, humanly speaking, some other response might have been more expected.

Consider, for example, the prayer of Moses for the Israelites in Numbers 14. Between Egypt and the Promised Land, the Israelites sent out a committee of representatives to investigate the land into which God was leading them. The committee had returned with a mixed report. In spite of the fact that the land was productive, most of the committee were scared of the inhabitants and did not believe that Israel could successfully conquer the land. As a result, the Israelites rebelled against the leadership of Moses, and they were prepared to choose a new leader to take them back to Egypt. Faced with that kind of rebellion and rejection, a lesser leader might have been tempted to curse the people rather than pray for them. God declared His readiness to judge the Israelites by disinheriting them and making Moses the father of the new nation, but Moses prayed, asking God on behalf of the people for a different outcome (Num 14:13-19). God's answer to that prayer would result in Moses spending the next four decades with the Israelites in the wilderness, waiting for an entire generation to die. It would have been far easier to invoke God's judgment rather than to ask for His mercy on the people.

Praying for the people one leads is not optional; it is required, even—perhaps especially—when those people do not want to follow their leader. Samuel makes clear this obligation to pray for the people one leads. The people of Israel, who had been led for many years by God-appointed judges, now insisted on a king. In fairness to them, they seemed to have some good reasons for doing so, and yet the path they were choosing was in effect both a repudiation of Samuel's leadership and a rejection of God as their king. But Samuel remained committed to praying for these people (1 Sam 12:23). He considered it sin to fail to pray for the people.

The apostle Paul is another example of an intercessor in the Bible. His letters include many prayers for those to whom he was writing. He expressed both prayers of thanksgiving and prayers of intercession. One example is Paul's prayer for the Ephesian believers that is recorded in Ephesians 3:14-21. Paul's prayer for them does not focus on a specific human material need, but rather on their spiritual need for a deeper understanding of God's love. Perhaps Paul recognized the danger to this church that would later be described in Revelation 2:4: "You have departed from your first love!" Years earlier than the description in Revelation, Paul interceded for the Ephesians, asking that they be rooted in love and understand more fully Christ's love for them.

Virtually every Christian will have the opportunity to lead others. That leadership may involve different sized groups of people. Some will be in a position to lead a church congregation or some other large group of people. Others may exercise leadership in their own families or other smaller groups. Sometimes a Christian will be given the privilege of leading just one other person. In every case Samuel's words are a solemn reminder. The call to lead is also a call to intercede.

The opportunity and responsibility to pray for others is not reserved just for leaders. Those who follow are challenged and encouraged to pray for their leaders as well. Paul made the matter of praying for those in authority a priority when he wrote to Timothy (1 Tim 2:1-4). Inevitably there will be times when you disagree with the actions of a particular leader, but whether you agree with the leader or not, interceding for that person is important. Even if the leader is ungodly, you can intercede, praying that God will work in that person's heart for his own good and the good of all the people he leads.

The beginning of Acts 12 records the persecution that came to the early church, ordered by Herod, including the execution of John's brother James. When Herod saw that that action was popular among the Jews, he ordered that Peter also be arrested at the time of Passover. The Christians in Jerusalem, fearing, and perhaps even expecting, that Peter would meet the same fate as James, prayed earnestly for his release. Read about this event in Acts 12:1-17.

Many of these Jerusalem believers may have sensed that they were praying for the impossible. Peter was heavily guarded, and Herod had already demonstrated his readiness to assassinate Christians. But they interceded anyway, even though they were unaware that God had miraculously answered their prayer. So when Peter, released by the Lord, showed up at the home of Mary in the middle of a prayer meeting, the initial reaction was that it could not be Peter; after all, he was in prison. After these Christians got over the shock of seeing Peter and began to realize that what they were seeing was in fact real, they may have been greatly encouraged. Peter had been miraculously delivered; their prayers, in spite of the low level of their faith, had been answered.

The value of intercessory prayer is not limited to the ones for whom the prayer is offered. The intercessor benefits as well. As a Christian is moved to pray for others and then is able to see God at work in harmony with those prayers, his faith is strengthened and his relationship with the Lord is deepened. God, being God, is able to do what He wants, when He wants, and how He wants in the lives of other people whether we pray or not. After all, He is God. Part of the mystery of God's great grace is that He allows and invites us to participate with Him in His work through intercessory prayer. But if we fail to intercede, then we miss the blessing of seeing Him at work and being partners with Him in that work. A believer's prayers for others are not only for their good; they are for his good as well.

An interesting case of divinely directed intercession is recorded at the end of the book of Job. Job, suffering deeply, had engaged in a lengthy conversation with some friends who came to comfort him but who ended up criticizing him. Toward the end of the book, God spoke to Job, revealing Himself, and Job was left with nothing to say. God also expressed His displeasure with Job's friends because they had misrepresented the Lord in their conversation with Job. They were told to prepare a burnt offering and that Job would intercede for them (Job 42:7-10). These three people had wounded Job with their words, and Job had described them as useless. Praying for them was probably not what he would have first chosen to do. But at God's direction he interceded for these friends.

After Job prayed for his friends God restored Job's fortunes. Clearly intercession was important to the Lord. We are left to wonder about a couple of questions: What might have happened if Job had not prayed? And what might have happened if his friends had interceded for Job instead of criticizing him?

When we intercede for others, we are, quite literally, doing what the Lord does. Read Romans 8:26-39. These few verses tell us that both the Holy Spirit and Jesus Christ intercede for us. There are times when we simply do not know how we should pray. But that is never true of the Lord. When we do not know how to pray, the Spirit intercedes for us, and God knows the mind of the Spirit. What a great thing it is to know that God the Holy Spirit is praying for us! Not only the Holy Spirit, but Jesus as well is our intercessor. He who died to redeem us and then conquered death in the resurrection now intercedes for us. When you ask God for forgiveness, it is not just you asking; it is Christ as well, the very one who has already paid the penalty for that sin.

Intercession is both the fruit and the fuel of a deepening relationship with the Lord. In intercessory prayer, Christians are able to join with the Lord Himself in bringing the needs of others before the Father. Effective intercession requires a close relationship with the Lord so that we can hear His heart and agree with Him in prayer. The practice of intercession will help that relationship grow as we come to understand more clearly the heart of the Lord.

QUESTION 20

What did Samuel conclude about praying for the Israelites?

A. Praying for them would be futile since they had decided to disobey God.

B. Not praying for them would be sin.

C. They did not deserve prayer because they had rejected Samuel's leadership.

D. The new king would pray for them, so Samuel did not need to pray.

QUESTION 21

Read the following passages and match them with the phrases that best describe the content of Paul's intercession.

Scriptures	*Description*
Ephesians 1:17-19	Spiritual strength and greater understanding of Christ's love
Ephesians 3:14-21	Increasing love and deciding what is best
Philippians 1:9-11	Knowing God's will and pleasing Him
Colossians 1:9-12	Encouragement and strength
2 Thessalonians 2:16-17	Spiritual wisdom and increasing knowledge of God

QUESTION 22

Open your Life Notebook and write an explanation of how intercessory prayer is of benefit to the person who prays.

Prayer and Evangelism

Sometimes when we ask God for something, we do not know with certainty that our request is compatible with God's will. But when we pray for another person's salvation, there can be no doubt that we are asking for something God wants as well. When Paul instructed Timothy that prayers be offered for all men, the reason he gave is that God wants everyone to be saved (1 Tim 2:1-4). Such evangelistic intercession includes not only the person for whose salvation you are praying, but also those in authority. The leaders who make decisions that affect other people's lives have the power to make evangelistic activity either easier and safer, or more difficult and dangerous. Whatever the circumstances are, God's will is for people's salvation. Praying for the salvation of others is one of the most important kinds of intercession we can offer.

Most people do not come to Christ in a relational vacuum; they are led to Christ by the words and actions of other people they have come to trust. Jesus not only recognized that reality; He intended it. He left with His disciples the responsibility and privilege of carrying the gospel to others and making disciples. Paul, writing to the Thessalonian Christians, described himself as one who was "entrusted with the gospel" (1 Thess 2:4). He understood and taught that Christians had been given the gospel as a trust, and like good stewards, they would be responsible to the Lord for how they handled it.

Since God has chosen to regularly use people in communicating the gospel, praying for the salvation of other people must include praying for those people who will be carrying the gospel to them. Jesus, talking to His disciples, used the metaphor of a field that was ready to be harvested. There was no shortage of the crop, but there was always the danger that there could be a shortage of harvesters. Jesus responded to this great evangelistic need by encouraging His disciples to pray (Mt 9:36-38).

To intercede in this way, asking the Lord to send workers into His harvest, is serious business. When Luke recorded Jesus using this same metaphor, Jesus made the disciples the answer to their own prayers by sending them (Lk 10:1-3). When we pray in this way, there is always the possibility that God will prompt us to action to help meet the need we have brought to Him in prayer.

QUESTION 23

Which of the following are appropriate ways to intercede for the salvation of other people? *(Select all that apply.)*

A. Pray directly for the person's salvation.

B. Pray that God will send someone to lead that person to Christ.

C. Pray for those in authority over the person.

D. Pray that God will use you to communicate the gospel to that person.

Read "Jean's Decision" and then answer the question that follows it.

Jean's Decision

I was born and raised in a small town on the outskirts of the city. Being the youngest child in a large family, I enjoyed being spoiled by my siblings as well as being teased by them. My parents, as well as my brothers and sisters, were devout Christians, but I had resisted accepting Jesus as my Savior. I usually went to church with my family—I did not really have much choice in the matter—but my reasons for being there had nothing to do with a commitment to Jesus Christ. For me it was simply a place to connect socially with other people.

As I grew into my teen years, social connections, particularly with members of the opposite sex, were the dominant force in my life. That fact, along with my resistance to Christ, concerned my parents, and they made no secret of their concern. My father tried to enforce reasonable and godly limits on me, but I became increasingly adept at breaking those limits, most of the time without getting caught. My mother most often expressed her concern by telling me that she was praying for me. Sometimes she would put her arm around me and pray aloud for me in my presence. I did not particularly like that, and it had little noticeable effect on me. I continued to live my young life in my own rebellious way and did my best to ignore my family's rules.

One day when I was fourteen I decided to visit a boy I liked. I knew my parents would not approve, and so I told my mother I was going to the store, hoping that she would not ask me to buy something. I suspected at the time that my mother knew I was lying, but she did not challenge me. All she said was, "Remember I'm praying for you, Jean." The words hardly penetrated my mind as I left the house. Little did I know that they would be the last words I would ever hear her speak.

When I returned home hours later, I knew immediately that something was wrong. Two of my sisters were talking quietly with tears on their cheeks. The conversation stopped when I came in. I asked what was wrong and discovered that Mother had collapsed and apparently suffered a stroke shortly after I left. I could not believe it, but Mother was lying unconscious on her bed. Within a few short hours, she died without ever regaining consciousness.

I was both stunned and crushed. Mother was dead. *How could it be?* I thought. And the last words I had spoken to her were a lie. It seemed to me that at the tender age of fourteen, my life was a wreck, and the tears began to flow. I wept as much for the mess I was making of my life as for the loss of my mother. My father and my brothers and sisters wept as well, but it seemed to me that there was no grief as deep as mine.

Somehow in the midst of my tears I remembered my mother's final words to me: *Remember I'm praying for you, Jean.* I knew that if my mother said she was praying, then she would indeed pray.

She had probably been talking to the Lord about me even as I closed the door behind me when I had left the house. Praying for me may well have been her last conscious act. I knew what the content of that prayer would have been; there could be no doubt. More than once I had heard my mother pray for my salvation.

Until that day I had managed to maintain a heart hard enough to resist God. *They can pray all they want*, I had thought, *I'll accept Christ when I'm good and ready, but not yet!* As I heard in my mind my mother's prayers for me, my resistance melted. That might seem a strange place for a spiritual decision, but there in the midst of my grief on the day my mother died, I confessed my sin to the Lord and asked Christ to come into my life as my Savior.

I have often wished that my mother could have lived to see the answer to her prayers. Somehow, though, I think she knows that the last hold-out in her family finally surrendered to the Lord. I suppose you could say that Mother prayed me into God's kingdom. I have sometimes wondered if I would ever have made that decision had it not been for her prayers for me. In a very real sense, my mother's prayers drove me to that decision to become a Christian on the very day she died.

QUESTION 24

Open your Life Notebook and compare your salvation story with Jean's. Who do you know was praying for your salvation? For whose salvation do you pray?

Before continuing with this lesson, take some time to thank God for the people who have prayed for you, and pray again for the salvation of those for whom God has given you a burden to intercede.

The Encouragement of Prayer

To have other believers interceding for you is an encouragement. Knowing that others care enough to pray brings comfort. The expression of faith that is implicit in the prayers of those who intercede will help strengthen your faith as well. Paul reminded us in Galatians 6:2 to carry one another's burdens. Praying for one another is one of the most effective ways of sharing the load of our burdens. This is also an expression of the kind of love Jesus said should be a mark of those who are His disciples (Jn 13:34-35). Some unbelievers may find it attractive that Christians pray for each other. Even unbelievers who deny the existence of God can delight in seeing people who carry one another's burdens.

In order for this encouragement of Christians to take place, believers need to be free to share with one another their current burdens and to allow others to pray for them. While the spiritual gift of discernment may prompt someone to sense another's burden, God has not given the gift of mind reading to His people. Taking the initiative to share a need with others who will join you in praying strengthens the fellowship of believers. Paul is a good example of a believer who did not hesitate to ask others to pray for him. His epistles are punctuated both by his prayers for those to whom he was writing and by invitations to them to pray for him.

QUESTION 25

Read the following Scripture passages in which Paul invited other people to pray for him. Which of these prayer requests focus on Paul's ministry of declaring the gospel? *(Select all that apply.)*

A. Romans 15:30-32

B. Ephesians 6:19-20

C. Colossians 4:2-4

D. 2 Thessalonians 3:1-2

E. Philemon 22

While the specific expression of Paul's burden was a bit different each time he shared it, there is a clear and repeated underlying theme that reflected Paul's ongoing concern to be a faithful and effective messenger of the gospel. He understood what his calling was, and he recognized that the prayers of other believers would be an important factor in his fulfillment of that calling.

Intercessory prayer may make a noticeable difference in the outcome of a particular situation. In some circumstances God may choose to delay action until His people pray. Paul, writing as a prisoner to Philemon, expressed the expectation that he would soon be able to visit him (Phm 22). Such a visit would require that Paul be released. He described that expectation as an answer to Philemon's prayer, implying that the prayers of Philemon and others would be effective in gaining his release.

Mark 9 records the interesting account of a failed attempt to heal a demon-possessed boy (Mk 9:14-29). The boy's father had asked some of Jesus' disciples for help, but they had not been able to cast out the evil spirit. After Jesus rebuked the evil spirit and restored the boy, the disciples asked Jesus why they were unable to cast out the spirit. Jesus responded that only by prayer would this kind of demon come out. Apparently the question that the disciples should have asked was, *Why did we not pray*?

James was equally direct. Writing about the role of spiritual leaders in praying for healing, he encouraged Christians to seek such prayer (Jas 5:13-16). He declared that the prayer of a righteous man is effective. That statement should remind intercessors that harboring sin in one's life will hinder prayer.

To say that intercessory prayer is effective does not mean that God is somehow reduced to a power to be controlled and manipulated by people. He is God, and He is sovereign. He will do what He will do. Sometimes the answer God chooses is not the one that we have in mind when we pray. That does not diminish either His love or His sovereignty. That God invites us to be part of the process of His action through intercessory prayer is an expression of His grace that should encourage both intercessors and those for whom they intercede.

QUESTION 26

Which of the following is true of the encouragement of intercessory prayer? *(Select all that apply.)*

A. Because prayer is private, intercessory prayer encourages only the one who prays.

B. Intercessory prayer is attractive to unbelievers who see Christians caring for one another.

C. Intercessory prayer is a way of bearing one another's burdens.

D. The opportunity to intercede for others is an expression of God's grace.

E. Intercessory prayer helps strengthen the faith of Christians for whom prayer is offered.

Topic 5: Becoming a Person of Prayer

Jesus' life was filled with prayer because of His close relationship with the Father. Our lives must also be filled with prayer as His followers if we are to maintain a close relationship with the Lord. A person of prayer is actively investing in his relationship with God and living the Christian life.

Praying Always

The Bible commands us to "constantly pray" (1 Thess 5:17), that is, to be in regular communication with God. Some people wonder what prayer is actually like. They wonder whether Christians must kneel down or pray in a special place or at specific times. Since we are commanded to pray constantly, it seems clear that prayer cannot, and should not, be limited to certain times and specific locations. Prayer is not supposed to be a religious ritual. Just as we all have conversations with our friends and family at all kinds of different times and in many different places, we should view communication with God in a similar manner. In other words, where we are located, and whether we are kneeling, sitting, or standing, isn't as nearly important as the fact that we pray.

Prayer is supposed to be an integral part of our lives just as Christ is an integral part of our lives. It is normal to experience growth in one's experience of prayer just as it is normal to grow in a relationship with the Lord. As the relationship deepens, prayer becomes an increasingly important factor in a Christian's life. Just as a baby's communication with its parents deepens as the child matures, prayer in the life of the believer deepens as that believer grows in Christ. Of course, at whatever level of maturity the child—or the Christian—is, a loving father delights to hear his children.

Since the Lord is always with believers—and He promised His disciples He would be—then conversation with Him is possible at any time and in all places. There is nothing about which the Christian cannot pray. At any time and in every circumstance talking, as well as listening, to the Lord is a normal part of the Christian's life. Whatever the level of his spiritual maturity, his prayers are welcomed by the Lord who delights to hear from His children.

To grow in prayer to the point that one's life is lived in the midst of a continual conversation with the Lord may take time. It might also require a shift in thinking about prayer. But such constant prayer should be the goal—and eventually the experience—of every believer.

QUESTION 27

Match each Scripture passage with what it says about prayer.

Scripture	*Message*
Matthew 6:5-6	Pray with others
Luke 11:5-10	Pray in every situation
Acts 12:12	Pray constantly
Philippians 4:6	Pray privately
1 Thessalonians 5:17	Pray persistently

A Growing Experience

While constantly praying may be the goal, most Christians recognize that prayer is one of the growing areas of their lives in which God continues to shape them. It is an area in which believers, particularly new Christians, struggle. Before leaving the important topic of prayer, we want to consider some practical strategies for encouraging growth in this important area of the Christian life. Read the following article entitled, "Prayer—A Better Conversation" before answering the question that follows.

Prayer—A Better Conversation

Carrying on a conversation with God in prayer is a central part of the Christian life. Most believers value the experience, yet many sense that their practice of prayer could somehow be better than their current experience. The sense that prayer could be better rests on the reality that prayer is part of a growing relationship with the Lord. As that relationship grows, one should expect that prayer, the communication we bring to the relationship, will also grow. Having said that, it is also true that there are specific strategies that a Christian can adopt with the potential to improve the prayer experience. The following are a few practical suggestions that might help to enhance or deepen one's prayer experience.

Before getting into these specific suggestions, a word of caution is in order. These are not commandments; they are suggestions and should be viewed as such. Some of them will work well for you; others may not. Incorporate those strategies that work for you but do so without becoming legalistic or mechanistic about it. Prayer is part of your relationship with God who loves you deeply. You should enjoy the time you can spend communing with Him.

Suggestions when you pray by yourself

Build a habit. True, prayer should be woven through every part of the Christian's life and every part of his day. However, deliberately set aside time that is reserved for talking with the Lord. Just as lovers delight in time that has been dedicated to time together, time dedicated to your conversation with the Lord will deepen your relationship with Him.

Give God your attention. Obviously, you should give your attention to the one with whom you are speaking, but this is easier to say than to do. Many distractions—visual, audible, and mental—can compete for our attention. So, choose a time and place where distractions will be minimized. Instead of yielding to a distraction, simply incorporate it into your praying; talk to God about it. You will not surprise Him.

Praise God. Focus on who God is. Meditate on His character and His attributes. Tell the Lord what you have noticed about Him. Think about what He has done and express your gratitude to Him. Tell God that you love Him.

Take time to listen. Prayer is a conversation, not a monologue. What does the Lord say to you? Have an open Bible handy, and let God impress His Word on your heart as He speaks to you. Silence is not a bad thing; simply being quiet before the Lord can help you hear Him.

Be honest about sin. To try to hide our sins from God is foolish. But because we are sometimes not honest with ourselves about our sin, we are not honest with God either. As His Spirit shows you your sin, confess it specifically and honestly to the Lord. Remember that unconfessed sin will make meaningful prayer impossible.

Incorporate Scripture into your prayers. Once again, using your Bible in prayer can be helpful. You can pray Scripture back to God, perhaps using prayers in the Bible that are appropriate to your particular circumstances.

Tell God specifically about your needs and burdens. Whether some need concerns you directly or somebody else, if it is on your heart, express it to the Lord in prayer. Express your concerns specifically enough that you will know when God answers. Do not worry if you have difficulty expressing a need; remember that the Spirit is interceding for you.

Exchange your anxiety for God's peace. Philippians 4:6-7 encourages us not to be anxious about anything but instead to pray about everything. The promise of Scripture is that when we do, God's peace will guard our hearts and minds.

Explore different postures and settings. Sometimes praying while you walk will help you sense God's presence. At other times kneeling might seem appropriate. For some people closing their eyes helps; others prefer praying with open eyes. Remember that the Lord is with you wherever you go.

Enjoy the Lord. You were created for fellowship with the Lord. Enjoy Him and let Him enjoy you.

Suggestions when you pray with other people

When you pray alone, it is just you and the Lord and the relationship you enjoy together. When you add other people, the dynamic become a bit more complicated. However, praying with one or more other people can help stimulate growth as you encourage and learn from one another. In addition to the suggestions above, the following suggestions can be helpful for those times when you are praying with others.

Brevity is good. In virtually any group, someone who monopolizes the conversation quickly becomes tiresome to other people. When you are praying with others, do not monopolize the conversation.

Let the Spirit lead. Resist the temptation to yield to what you think others might expect. Pray about what the Spirit prompts you to pray.

Listen—to others and to the Lord. You may have more opportunity in a group setting to listen, both when others are praying and when it is silent. Silence is still good.

Pray conversationally. In conversations people do not speak in a set order; they speak as they have something to say. Praying topically and allowing several to pray about a specific topic is more natural than a series of multi-topic monologues.

Expect variety. In any group there will be differences in the maturity level and the background of the participants. Expect that variety, and be thankful that God is at work in different ways in the lives of your fellow believers.

Take notes. As other people express needs and burdens in prayer, taking note of those needs will enable you to continue interceding for them.

Be as specific as possible. Remember that other people who are praying with you cannot read your mind. When you are specific in prayer, it will help others who may be prompted to pray for the same concern.

Enjoy the fellowship of prayer. The newly born church of Acts 2 is described as devoting themselves to teaching, fellowship, the breaking of bread, and prayer (Acts 2:42). The fellowship of prayer was one of their defining characteristics and part of what God intended for them. As you have opportunity to pray with others, enjoy it with thanksgiving.

Growing in prayer is a normal part of growing as a Christian. Consider the suggestions in this article, and implement those that will help you to grow in your conversation and relationship with the Lord.

QUESTION 28

Consider the lists of strategies for praying alone and for praying with others in the article "Prayer—A Better Conversation." Open your Life Notebook and indicate for both lists which strategies you want to implement in your life and how you plan to implement them. Explain why these strategies are important to you.

Topic 6: Conclusion

Studying prayer is a little like studying how to swim. Sooner or later, you have to get in the water. Christians will learn to pray by praying. Because prayer is such an intimate and integral part of the Christian's relationship with Christ, it needs to be developed within the context of that relationship.

QUESTION 29

Before you complete this lesson, set aside some time for prayer in which you practice some of what you have learned in this lesson. Then describe the experience in your Life Notebook.

Lesson 6 Self Check: Christian Life

QUESTION 1

What did Jacob expect would happen when he found himself in God's presence?

A. He expected to prevail in combat.

B. He expected to die.

C. He expected to be rewarded.

D. He expected to be strengthened.

QUESTION 2

How does God respond to a person who prays with unconfessed sin?

A. He does not listen to them.

B. He gives them what they ask for.

C. He immediately punishes them for their sin.

D. He overlooks their sin.

QUESTION 3

Faith in prayer is necessary only when facing a major need. *True or False?*

QUESTION 4

What did Daniel do when prayer to the Lord became illegal?

A. He stopped praying and obeyed the law.

B. He continued to pray, but privately so that no one would notice.

C. He asked the king to change the law.

D. He continued to pray openly.

QUESTION 5

Jesus intended that prayer be a religious exercise that would demonstrate spiritual merit. *True or False?*

QUESTION 6

How did Jesus teach His disciples to address God in prayer?

A. Holy One

B. God

C. Father

D. Lord

QUESTION 7

Asking God to meet the basic needs of my life is unnecessary and a waste of time since God already knows my needs. *True or False?*

QUESTION 8

Who benefits from intercessory prayer?

A. The one with the burden for whom prayer is offered
B. The one who prays
C. Both the one with the burden and the one who prays
D. No one benefits.

QUESTION 9

Sometimes prayer is necessary before God will work. *True or False?*

QUESTION 10

Constant prayer should be the goal of every believer. *True or False?*

Unit 2 Exam: Christian Life

QUESTION 1

Which of the following statements does NOT accurately describe true worship?

A. True worshippers worship in spirit and in truth.
B. True worship responds to God's character and his actions.
C. Worshipping with other Christians is unnecessary if one worships alone.
D. Worship is the response of a heart that is discovering who God is.

QUESTION 2

Worship requires that one have a relationship with the one who is being worshipped. *True or False?*

QUESTION 3

What did Jesus say in evaluating the act of the woman who anointed him with expensive perfume?

A. She did what she could.
B. Others should also have brought perfume.
C. It was a waste since it could have been sold to pay for ministry.
D. Her worship was more acceptable than that of others because of the perfume's value.

QUESTION 4

Worship should always be directed to the Father since Jesus and the Holy Spirit are subject to the Father. *True or False?*

QUESTION 5

Which of the following characteristics of Old Testament temple worship should NOT be present in contemporary Christian worship?

A. The need for cleansing
B. An awareness of the sacrifice for sin
C. Restricted access to God's presence
D. Sensory cues to enhance worship

QUESTION 6

Which of the following statements best describe the relationship between music and worship?

A. Music is essential to worship.
B. The Bible does not give us any good examples of musical worship.
C. Vocal music is acceptable in worship, but instrumental music without words is useless.
D. Music and worship are closely linked, and music can enhance worship.
E. The Bible has nothing to say about the relationship of music and worship.

QUESTION 7

Worship should be viewed as a religious obligation. *True or False?*

QUESTION 8

Which of the following statements best describe the role of worship in the life of a Christian?

A. Christians should worship God on Sunday.

B. The responsibility to worship should be left to those who are gifted in that area.

C. Everything a Christian does should be an act of worship.

D. Worship is for this life; once we are in heaven, we will no longer need to worship.

QUESTION 9

Communication is essential to human relationships but not to a Christian's relationship with Christ. *True or False?*

QUESTION 10

Which statement about biblical inspiration is NOT correct?

A. God used the personalities and styles of the human authors of Scripture.

B. Because God used sinful people to write Scripture, we need to be inspired to avoid its errors.

C. Since it is "God-breathed," what the Bible says is exactly what God intends.

D. Scripture originated with God rather than with the human authors.

QUESTION 11

Studying the Bible will ensure that a person has a growing relationship with Jesus Christ. *True or False?*

QUESTION 12

What is the ultimate goal of studying the Bible?

A. Gaining greater understanding of Bible doctrines

B. Knowing and hearing from God

C. Becoming a church leader or pastor

D. Increasing knowledge of biblical history

E. Being able to answer other people's questions

QUESTION 13

What is the most important characteristic of devotional Bible study?

A. Making personal application

B. Creating a teaching outline of the passage

C. Memorizing some or all of the passage

D. Reading the Gospels

E. Comparing the characters in the passage

QUESTION 14

The devotional Bible study method may be combined with almost any other method. *True or False?*

QUESTION 15

Which of the following is NOT a characteristic of a good devotional Bible study?

A. It is simple.

B. It is practical.

C. It is complex.

D. It is regular.

QUESTION 16

Which of the following is NOT true of meditating on God's Word?

A. Asking questions can be a helpful part of meditating.

B. Meditation requires emptying the mind.

C. Meditating takes time to digest a passage of Scripture.

D. Mental focus is important.

QUESTION 17

Through prayer Christians come into the presence of God. *True or False?*

QUESTION 18

What happens when a person prays without confessing known sin?

A. Nothing different; God is gracious and will answer.

B. God does not listen to the prayer.

C. The person is immediately punished for his sin.

D. God forgives, cleanses, and restores without the need for confession.

QUESTION 19

Why was Isaiah distressed when he found himself in the presence of God in Isaiah 6?

A. He expected to die because he had seen God.

B. He was scared of the angels.

C. He feared the tasks God might give him.

D. He heard God condemn him.

QUESTION 20

Why was Daniel thrown to the lions?

A. Darius wanted to replace him with a Persian governor.

B. He had been captured by other officials.

C. He was Jewish.

D. He had broken a law against praying to God.

QUESTION 21

Which one of the following statements best describes Daniel's faith?

A. He believed he could keep the lions from attacking him.

B. He believed that Darius would not punish him.

C. He believed his opponents could not destroy him.

D. He believed that somehow God could bring good out of impossible circumstances.

QUESTION 22

The model prayer that Jesus gave to his disciples implies that God will tempt them unless they ask him not to. *True or False?*

QUESTION 23

Which one of the following statements best describes the ministry of intercession?

A. Intercessory prayer is primarily the responsibility of leaders.

B. Intercessory prayer is primarily the responsibility of followers who pray for their leaders.

C. Intercessory prayer is a privilege that allows all Christians to bear the burdens of others.

D. Intercession is unnecessary for Christians because the Holy Spirit intercedes for us.

QUESTION 24

In public prayer meetings new believers should remain silent and let the mature believers be the ones who pray. *True or False?*

QUESTION 25

Maintaining a constant conversation with God is practical and should be every Christian's goal. *True or False?*

Lesson 6 Answers to Questions

QUESTION 1

D. He was afraid.

QUESTION 2: True

QUESTION 3

B. His sin was cleansed.

QUESTION 4

A. They will be alienated from God.
B. God will reject them.
D. God will not listen to their prayers.

QUESTION 5: *Your answer*

QUESTION 6

B. Being sure of what we hope for
D. Being convinced of what we do not see

QUESTION 7: True

QUESTION 8: *Your answer*

QUESTION 9

A. God judged him innocent and sent an angel to protect him.
D. Daniel had trusted God.

QUESTION 10: *Your answer*

QUESTION 11

Description	*Reference*
Jesus' appearance was changed as He prayed.	Luke 9:29
After praying, Jesus left crowds to minister elsewhere.	Mark 1:35-38
Jesus submitted to the Father's will as He anticipated His coming crucifixion.	Luke 22:39-46

QUESTION 12: *Your answer*

QUESTION 13

A. Himself
C. His disciples
E. All believers

QUESTION 14

A. You are God's child.
C. God loves you.
D. God will discipline you.

QUESTION 15

B. I recognize You as the sovereign King of my life.
D. May those who rebel against You come to acknowledge You as King.

QUESTION 16: *Your answer*

QUESTION 17: False

QUESTION 18: *Your answer*

QUESTION 19

B. Yielding to temptation disrupts the Christian's fellowship with God.
D. Following God's leading helps us to move away from temptation.

QUESTION 20

B. Not praying for them would be sin.

QUESTION 21

Scriptures	*Description*
Ephesians 1:17-19	Spiritual wisdom and increasing knowledge of God
Ephesians 3:14-21	Spiritual strength and greater understanding of Christ's love
Philippians 1:9-11	Increasing love and deciding what is best
Colossians 1:9-12	Knowing God's will and pleasing Him
2 Thessalonians 2:16-17	Encouragement and strength

QUESTION 22: *Your answer*

QUESTION 23

A. Pray directly for the person's salvation.

B. Pray that God will send someone to lead that person to Christ.

C. Pray for those in authority over the person.

D. Pray that God will use you to communicate the gospel to that person.

QUESTION 24: *Your answer*

QUESTION 25

A. Romans 15:30-32

B. Ephesians 6:19-20

C. Colossians 4:2-4

D. 2 Thessalonians 3:1-2

QUESTION 26

B. Intercessory prayer is attractive to unbelievers who see Christians caring for one another.

C. Intercessory prayer is a way of bearing one another's burdens.

D. The opportunity to intercede for others is an expression of God's grace.

E. Intercessory prayer helps strengthen the faith of Christians for whom prayer is offered.

QUESTION 27

Scripture	*Message*
Matthew 6:5-6	Pray privately
Luke 11:5-10	Pray persistently
Acts 12:12	Pray with others
Philippians 4:6	Pray in every situation
1 Thessalonians 5:17	Pray constantly

QUESTION 28: *Your answer*

QUESTION 29: *Your answer*

Lesson 6 Self Check Answers

QUESTION 1

B. He expected to die.

QUESTION 2

A. He does not listen to them.

QUESTION 3: False

QUESTION 4

D. He continued to pray openly.

QUESTION 5: False

QUESTION 6

C. Father

QUESTION 7: False

QUESTION 8

C. Both the one with the burden and the one who prays

QUESTION 9: True

QUESTION 10: True

Unit 2 Exam Answers

QUESTION 1

C. Worshipping with other Christians is unnecessary if one worships alone.

QUESTION 2: True

QUESTION 3

A. She did what she could.

QUESTION 4: False

QUESTION 5

C. Restricted access to God's presence

QUESTION 6

D. Music and worship are closely linked, and music can enhance worship.

QUESTION 7: False

QUESTION 8

C. Everything a Christian does should be an act of worship.

QUESTION 9: False

QUESTION 10

B. Because God used sinful people to write Scripture, we need to be inspired to avoid its errors.

QUESTION 11: False

QUESTION 12

B. Knowing and hearing from God

QUESTION 13

A. Making personal application

QUESTION 14: True

QUESTION 15

C. It is complex.

QUESTION 16

B. Meditation requires emptying the mind.

QUESTION 17: True

QUESTION 18

B. God does not listen to the prayer.

QUESTION 19

A. He expected to die because he had seen God.

QUESTION 20

D. He had broken a law against praying to God.

QUESTION 21

D. He believed that somehow God could bring good out of impossible circumstances.

QUESTION 22: False

QUESTION 23

C. Intercessory prayer is a privilege that allows all Christians to bear the burdens of others.

QUESTION 24: False

QUESTION 25: True

Unit 3: God's Family—Finding My Place as a Responsible Christian

Unit Introduction

Some people think that being involved in a church is not much different than belonging to a club or other organization that conducts social work and helps people out. These organizations may also provide fellowship and a sense of purpose for people. Some groups may even help their members advance in the world.

It's true that there are certain needs that are common to humanity. There is a need for friendship and a common purpose, as well as feeling like we're making a difference with our lives. But the church is fundamentally different than social organizations because it has a living connection with the living God. It is actually a living organism. Besides meeting the common human needs the other organizations do, it also serves the ultimate needs of humanity. But keep in mind that Christianity isn't just an organization; it's a relationship with the Lord, and that relationship lasts beyond this lifetime. The church focuses on eternal relationships. This means that what it does now continues into eternity. Jesus calls it losing our life to save it. That's not true with other organizations. While they accomplish a lot of good things, their focus is on our temporal life now—not with eternal issues.

The lessons in this unit will investigate this Christian life we now live, how it meets the common human need for fellowship, purpose, and meaning. Yet the Christian life does not stop at the end of this life, so we show how what we do now will continue into eternity. Lesson 7 explores how we relate to others in the living church and what our role is as a member of it. Lesson 8 looks at our calling to be stewards. It answers the question, "How do we live the life we're called to wisely?" Lesson 9 investigates the question, "How do we best find and then follow God's will?"

Unit Outline

Lesson 7: Called to Community and Service—My Relationships with Others and My Role in the Church

Lesson 8: Called to Be a Steward—Using Wisely All God Entrusts to Me

Lesson 9: Called to Follow—Making Wise Decisions

Lesson 7: Called to Community and Service—My Relationships with Others and My Role in the Church

God's intention is not that the Christian life be lived in isolation. He made us to be together, to have fellowship with each other on a regular basis. Just as we need to spend time investing in our relationship with God, we need to interact with other believers. We will take a look at both relationships in this lesson. We will see that all believers are interdependent and face the same challenge to serve God together as a witness to nonbelievers. This lesson examines God's call to make disciples and we will have an opportunity to assess how our lives fit into His call.

The focus of this lesson is on living out God's call on our lives within the context of a local church and fulfilling our responsibilities as a member of that body. We will start in the first topic by looking at the believer's call to worship God, examining what worship is and some biblical examples of it. In Topic 2, we will look at what needs are met by attending church with other believers, along with some dangers of not attending. Topic 3 continues by showing that the church is the equipping station for believers—a place where believers are equipped with the knowledge and tools needed to make disciples. Topic 4 addresses God's command to witness about Him to the world. In the final topic, we will look at the type of obedience we are called to and how our lives can best fit in with God's call.

Lesson Outline

Topic 1: A Worshipping Community

Topic 2: An Encouraging Fellowship

Topic 3: An Equipping Station

Topic 4: The Goal of God's Command

Topic 5: The Shape of My Obedience

Topic 1: A Worshipping Community

Have you ever wondered why God wants to be praised and worshipped? Perhaps you think this seems like He is egotistical.

In answering this important question, we need to realize that God's character is not changed by anything His creatures do or say. Worship is more for our benefit than for His. He is greater than us by nature and by what He's done for us. If we don't acknowledge that, it only hurts us. Besides, He is infinitely worthy, and it should be an honor and pleasure to worship Him. It's a way for us who belong to God to respond to Him.

Worship is about interacting with God. Worship directs the attention of the church body to God. God not only created us to have fellowship with Him but longs for us to be with Him. When humanity rebelled, God took the steps needed, at His own expense, to provide redemption for those who believe. Even before man fell, God was worthy of man's worship. For example, Job 38:7 describes when the earth was created "the morning stars sang in chorus, and all the sons of God shouted for joy." The heavenly beings in God's presence continually worship Him for His holiness (Rev 4:8). Those redeemed by God worship Him because He paid a high price to bring them back into fellowship with Him. Worship acknowledges that, in contrast to everything else, God is uncreated.

QUESTION 1

Please match the following reference with the aspects of worship they discuss.

Reference	*Aspect of Worship*
Genesis 24:26-27	God the Son is worshipped for Christ's redemptive work.
Exodus 34:8	God is worshipped for His holiness.
Job 38:4-7	Jesus accepted worship as the Son of Man.
Revelation 4:8	God must be worshipped in spirit and truth.
John 4:23-24	The Lord is worshipped for His faithful love for Abraham.
John 9:35-38	Moses worshipped by bowing down.
Rev 5:9-10	The angels sang for joy when the earth was created.

Please read "A Worshipping Community", which discusses important aspects of worship. Then answer the questions that follow the article.

A Worshipping Community

At its heart, worship means acknowledging the worth of someone or something. That is what we do when we worship God, we acknowledge His worth. God is infinite and infinitely worthy of praise. Because that is true, we can and will never run out of things to praise God for. We can expect that He will continue revealing new things to us about Himself, both His character and His works, in this life and throughout eternity. This will give us unending opportunities to sing His praise for everything new we learn about Him. Even the angels who are continually in His presence and have been for thousands of years, never tire of praising God for even His most simple attributes and actions. For example:

- In Psalm 46:6-7, often called a Song of Zion, the Israelites worshipped God for His omnipotence saying, "Nations make a commotion, kingdoms are upended. God gives a battle cry, the earth dissolves. The Lord, the invincible warrior is on our side! The God of Jacob is our protector! (Selah)."
- In Isaiah 6:3 the seraphs in Isaiah's vision of God in heaven called out to one another, "The Lord who leads armies has absolute sovereign authority. His majestic splendor fills the entire earth."
- In Revelation 4:8 the living creatures in heaven praise God for His holiness and His eternal presence. They never stopped to rest, saying, "Holy Holy Holy is the Lord God, the All-Powerful, who was and who is, and who is to come!" The twenty-four elders respond by praising God as the Creator, saying, "You are worthy, our Lord and God, to receive glory and honor and power, since you created all things, and because of your will they existed and were created!" (Rev 4:11)

The ultimate reason to praise God now is for His Son Jesus Christ (Col 1:15-20). The thorough but fruitless search throughout heaven and earth for someone else worthy to open the seals of judgment shows that He alone is worthy (Rev 5:9). God is worthy of praise because of who He is. He can also be worshipped for what He has done. Those who have been saved since Jesus' resurrection know His redemptive work in a special way. They acknowledge that they have been saved by this redemptive work by "singing a new song."

Note: singing a new song in Scripture often means that this is a unique experience limited to a special group of people who have experienced this in a personal way. See also the song of Moses and the song of the Lamb in Revelation 15:3 and the song of the 144,000 in Revelation 14:3.

Believers today know this work of God through Christ in a way that Old Covenant believers in God could not. Since He has finished for all time His redemptive work, "Through him then let us continually offer up a sacrifice of praise to God, that is, the fruit of our lips, acknowledging his name" (Heb 13:15).

In each of these references worship takes place in a group setting. While there is certainly value in worshipping God alone, Scripture repeatedly encourages God's people to worship Him together. There is a synergy to corporate worship in which Christians together help each other to praise the Lord who is worthy of worship.

Because Christians come from a variety of backgrounds, they may have some hurdles to overcome in corporate worship. Christians must understand that worship may be different in other cultures and churches. Some believers worship with hands raised while some do not. Some worship by singing hymns, while others sings choruses. Some worship with drums, some with guitars, and some with organs. King David even had a dispute with one of his wives about the way he worshipped the Lord. In spite of these differences in culture and practice, all appropriate worship needs to conform to God's guidelines in Scripture. Through the questions in this topic we will discover what some of those guidelines are.

Besides understanding what appropriate worship is, we need to know what it is not. God is uncreated, and believers ought not worship any created thing (Rom 1:21-23). This not only includes images, but people alive or dead and any other heavenly beings, including angels (Col 2:18). Twice in Revelation the apostle John was chastised for falling in worship at the feet of his angelic guide (Rev 19:10; 22:9).

One of the ways the early church worshipped was by testifying that God is the Creator. For example, after Peter and John were released from prison, the church worshipped, saying, "Master of all, you who made the heaven and the earth and the sea, and everything that is in them" (Acts 4:24). Christians today have the same opportunity to offer true worship to God by focusing on who He is and what He has done and together finding ways to declare His worth.

QUESTION 2

Which of the following is meant when the Scripture says a certain group of people could "sing a new song"? *(Select all that apply.)*

A. It was limited to a specific group of people.

B. It meant they knew the words of the psalm.

C. It meant they were a member of the temple choir.

D. It was something personally experienced by those people.

QUESTION 3

Identify one guideline for the church worship service in each of the following verses: 1 Corinthians 14:26, 31, 33, 40.

In the next question you will discover what happened when David worshipped the Lord in 2 Samuel 6:12-23.

QUESTION 4

Please read through 2 Samuel 6:12-23. Then open your Life Notebook and write out your answers to the following questions. When you answer them, note the verses from which your answer comes.

- What is David trying to do?
- What did David do each time those who carried the ark took six steps?
- What else was he doing before the Lord?
- What else were David and all Israel doing?
- Who saw David and how did she feel about his dancing?
- What did David do after he finished sacrificing?
- Besides a blessing, what else did David give to each member of Israel?
- What happened when David went to bless his own house?
- How did David reply to Michal?
- What happened to Michal because of her response?

Topic 2: An Encouraging Fellowship

In Topic 1 we saw that new believers will gain new friends as well as a spiritual family. What kind of relationships are these? Are they relationships only here on earth, or in heaven, or perhaps both?

When nonbelievers become believers, they often lose friendships and suffer some degree of loss in their family relationships. The same thing happened to Jesus when He began His ministry. The Scripture tells us His brothers did not believe in Him until after His resurrection (Jn 7:5). They even taunted Him saying:

Leave here and go to Judea so your disciples may see your miracles that you are performing. For no one who seeks to make a reputation for himself does anything in secret. If you are doing these things, show yourself to the world. (Jn 7:3-4)

Thankfully the Lord anticipated this problem. He comforts believers with the promise that "in this age" they would receive "homes, brothers, sisters, mothers, children, fields, all with persecutions—and in the age to come, eternal life" (Mk 10:30).

The Bible encourages Christians to enjoy fellowship with other believers. To learn more about fellowship read "An Encouraging Fellowship" below and answer the question that follows.

An Encouraging Fellowship

Believers are at a definite disadvantage in this fallen world. Satan rules it and believers are not welcome in it (Jn 12:31; 16:11). Immediately before Jesus left this world He promised that the world would hate us, as it hated Him (Jn 15:18; 1 Jn 3:13). The more a believer abides with Christ the more intensely the world will hate that person. This hatred will show itself in persecution.

So, when a person first believes in Christ, he severs his natural connection with this world and its ruler (Eph 2:1-7; 5:8). Though he still lives in this world, he is a citizen of God's kingdom, and his allegiance is to the Lord. Often, when his new faith becomes known to family and friends he is shunned or persecuted and isolated from them. In many parts of the world a new believer's life can even be in danger from his or her friends and natural family when they learn of his or her new faith. Some new believers therefore may seek to repair this severed connection by placing greater importance on the old relationships, returning to a love for this age. Demas is an example of a believer who deserted Paul "since he loved the present age" (2 Tim 4:10).

That is one of the reasons it is so important that new believers recognize the importance of their new spiritual family. Jesus pointed out in Mark 3:31-35 that His spiritual family, those that do God's will, are more important than His natural family. This new relationship is in the Lord and extends into eternity. This family relationship with other believers is extremely important in living an effective Christian life. Consider, for example, some of the things Scripture says about the value of the Christian's relationships with other believers:

- They are the ones who can encourage us with God's Word when we need it (1 Thess 4:18; 5:11).
- Our presence with them leads us to mutual comfort in one another's faith (Rom 1:12).
- Our lack of fellowship contributes to our lack of maturity in the faith (Heb 10:24-25).
- The presence of other believers can also restore us even when we have wandered from the faith and are in danger of chastisement from our Lord (Jas 5:19-20).

We are organically connected with one another from the moment we believe in Christ "for in one Spirit we were all baptized into one body" (1 Cor 12:13). Having come into a relationship with Jesus Christ, we are now also related to one another. It does not matter that we are from all different races and social classes for "we were all made to drink of the one Spirit" (1 Cor 12:13). But like all families, we can sometimes find it difficult to get along with our brothers and sisters, as the Corinthians did: "for you are still influenced by the flesh. For since there is still jealousy and dissension among you, are you not influenced by the flesh and behaving like unregenerate people?" (1 Cor 3:3).

However, as an antidote against quarreling, the Lord has commanded us "to love one another. Just as I have loved you, you also are to love one another" (Jn 13:34). When we keep this love fervent, our "love covers a multitude of sins" (1 Pet 4:8). This type of love is what we all desperately need. And it is qualitatively different than any natural love in the world (1 Jn 3:16). Love is the distinguishing mark of a disciple of Christ and a wonder and testimony to the world: "Everyone will know by this that you are my disciples—if you have love for one another" (Jn 13:35).

One of the great blessings of a growing relationship with Christ is discovering that He has brought us into a network of fellowship with other believers. We enjoy God's love, and we also find that He has made possible the encouragement that comes from loving one another.

QUESTION 5

Who does Paul say deserted him because he loved this present age (2 Tim 4:10)?

A. Demas

B. Epaphras

C. Mark

D. Timothy

Now read the story of James in the following article "Spirtual Family," which shows how Christians can be family for each other when their natural family members are not believers. Answer the question that follows the article.

Spiritual Family

When James became a Christian, he was scared to tell his family. His father and mother believed that having a Christian in the family would bring them disgrace. He knew that Christians worship the one true God, and he did not regret his decision to believe in Him. However, it would be difficult to participate in many family activities, like their weekly dinners together, now that he did not share his parents' faith. He knew that the Bible said he was a "new creation," but he wondered if his family could love this new James.

Lord, I need Your help to tell my family. I know You saved me, please show me how my family can be saved too. I trust You, Lord. Thank You for loving me so much that you redeemed me from my sins with Jesus' blood on the cross. Amen.

After praying this prayer, James went to the weekly dinner with his family and told them about his decision to believe in Christ. His parents were very upset and told him to leave their house and never come back. It hurt James to leave his family; he knew that he would miss the family interactions. More importantly, he wanted to share God's love but they were not interested in hearing anything about this God.

A short time after that dinner James met other Christians. Those new friends became like family to him. He missed his natural family and prayed for his parents and siblings because he wanted them to be part of his spiritual family. However, his spiritual family provided him the encouragement he needed to grow in his faith through prayer and Bible study. They were knit together by Jesus' work on the cross.

Spiritual families are not perfect; they are still subject to conflict. The Corinthians experienced this by "behaving like ordinary people" (1 Cor 3:3). The remedy to quarreling with brothers and sisters in Christ is to "love one another" as the Lord commanded in John 13:34. We all desperately need this type of forgiving love which is different from any worldly love. In fact, believers should be distinguished by their love for each other (Jn 13:35). James may have been rejected by his natural family, but his spiritual family loved him as their own brother.

QUESTION 6

Please match the following references with the corresponding teachings on our family relationship with other believers.

Reference	*Teaching*
Romans 1:12	The presence of other believers can also restore us even when we have wandered from the faith
1 Thessalonians 4:18; 5:11	Our presence with them leads us to mutual comfort in one another's faith.
Hebrews 10:24-25	Our lack of fellowship contributes to our lack of maturity in the faith.
James 5:19-20	They are the ones who can encourage us when we need it.

Topic 3: An Equipping Station

Perhaps you have heard some preachers say that God wants us all to be rich because it's easier for us to praise Him when we're rich. Some preachers have gone so far as to say that they have expensive jewelry, luxury cars, and fancy houses because God wanted them to be rich. They even have a magnificent church building made out of special materials.

The Bible says that the Corinthian church fell into the same trap almost two thousand years ago (1 Cor 4:6-13). Paul had to point out to them that they acted as if they had become kings, while he lived with hunger, thirst, and brutal treatment. The church doesn't exist to make people materially wealthy. The apostle Paul was a very successful evangelist, missionary, and church planter, yet he had few material possessions. He was dependent on the generosity of others to support his work for Christ. Paul even considered himself to be a slave for the sake Christ (1 Cor 9:17). He never focused on gaining material possessions. And Jesus said "Do not accumulate for yourselves treasures on earth, where moth and rust destroy and where thieves break in and steal. But accumulate for yourselves treasures in heaven, where moth and rust do not destroy, and thieves do not break in and steal. For where your treasure is, there your heart will be also." (Mt 6:19-21).

Even secular associations have purposes to accomplish, and they usually hold regular meetings to that purpose. Often the success of these associations depends on a gifted person or an abundance of earthly provisions.

The church likewise has regular meetings to help accomplish its goal or mission. Often the biggest churches have a gifted person and significant earthly provisions. But when you look at things from God's point of view, it may be that those churches are not the ones accomplishing the most in God's mission. In fact, the church that was praised the most in Revelation is the one at Philadelphia about whom Jesus said, "I know that you have little strength, but you have obeyed my word and have not denied my name" (Rev 3:8). This topic will look at what is vital in the Lord's eyes to accomplish the mission of the church.

Discipleship is often a great way to equip other believers. Believers invest in others' lives and encourage spiritual growth. Please read "Equipping to Serve," Because God had gifted Caleb and Sarah with an ability to help other Christians, David and Esther were able to discover some ways in which they, too, could be equipped to serve.

Equipping to Serve

David and Esther joined a local fellowship shortly after they married. They started by going to the weekly gatherings in the pastor's home. At first, they knew only Caleb and Sarah, who lived near them and had invited them to the fellowship. David and Esther had been Christians for many years but had never had a group of other Christians with whom to interact. Through this fellowship group they were able to meet more Christians and were encouraged to see that there are others who believe what they believe.

David and Esther wanted to know how they could help their brothers and sisters in Christ. They were unsure where to begin because they did not know what they should do. Caleb and Sarah were good at noticing needs that other people had and always tried their best to meet them. After one of the fellowship meetings David and Esther asked Caleb and Sarah about how they were helping others.

"When we pray for people, the Lord often brings neighbors, friends, and family to our minds. We try to do whatever we can," Sarah responded with a smile.

"Actually, a lot of what we are able to do is determined by how God made us. For example, Sarah is able to sympathize with people when they grieve. Sometimes people just need someone with whom to share their sorrow, and God made Sarah with the ability to do that," Caleb added.

"I can sew clothes; would that be something God wants me to do?" Esther asked.

"It can be, but more than that you can sew people together in relationships. I have seen how you connect people in relationship, Esther. I believe God made you to bring people together," Sarah said.

"Would you both like to come to our house this week so that we can talk more about the ways that God made you and what you can do to help others?" Caleb offered, while Sarah nodded her head.

"We would like that," David and Esther said together.

David and Esther began going over to Caleb and Sarah's home on a regular basis to talk about helping others and the gifts God had placed in them for this purpose. Over time the two couples became good friends and learned more about God together. They would often spend time in the Bible to see what God said about specific questions they had. They still continued to go to the local fellowship meetings and even started a small group together with other couples who wanted to learn more about God's plan for their lives. These men and women prayed, worshipped, and read together. During their time together they encouraged each other to discover and put into practice the gifts God had given them.

QUESTION 7

According to Ephesians 4:12-16, which of the following are supposed to result from the gifted men given to the church? *(Select all that apply.)*

A. Baptism in the Holy Spirit

B. Equipping the saints

C. Evangelism

D. Knowledge of the Son of God

E. Practicing the truth in love

F. Unity in the faith

QUESTION 8

According to Hebrews 10:25, believers who no longer meet together tend to lose the benefit of fellowship. *True or False?*

Topic 4: God's Command

If you were God, how would you accomplish the church's mission in the world? Some people have wondered why God didn't use angels because they are perceived as being more reliable than people.

The Bible says angels are valuable servants of God that minister to believers. But God has chosen to accomplish His purposes through ordinary people who trust Him. It might not seem to make much sense, but God accomplishes His work according to His wisdom, which often confounds human wisdom. For example, He saved the world by sending His own precious Son to die on a cruel cross for our sins. No human would have thought of accomplishing salvation that way! It doesn't seem to make any more sense than God working through people. But God actually enjoys accomplishing His goals through people even though we are weak in many ways.

God desires to restore His relationship with people that was broken by sin. To make that possible, He sent His Son to pay the price for people's sin. But in order for the relationship to be restored, a person needs to accept God's provision. In a similar way, this joining of God's sovereign action and provision with man's response is the pattern God often chooses to use to accomplish His purposes in the church. An example of this pattern can be seen in the work of many missionaries. God calls and equips them, but they depend on God's people to provide for their financial needs.

Though He chooses to work though people, God is not constrained by limited human resources. Jesus dramatically made this point when He fed the multitudes in Mark 6:35-44 and Mark 8:1-10.

The following matching question is based on the lesson Jesus was teaching the disciples in Mark 8:14-21. Please read the passage and then answer the questions below.

QUESTION 9

Please match the questions Jesus asked with the correct answers.

Question	*Answer*
How many loaves did the disciples have with them in the boat (Mk 8:14)?	Twelve
How many loaves were broken to feed the five thousand (Mk 8:19)?	One
How many baskets of bread pieces were left after feeding the five thousand (Mk 8:19)?	Seven
How many baskets were collected after the four thousand ate (Mk 8:20)?	Five

Please read "God's Command" and answer the questions that follow.

God's Command

The Great Commission is familiar to most Christians. Though it is stated similarly in several places in the New Testament, the most well-known version is Matthew 28:18-20:

> Then Jesus came up and said to them, "All authority in heaven and on earth has been given to me. Therefore, go and make disciples of all nations, baptizing them in the name of the Father and the Son and the Holy Spirit, teaching them to obey everything I have commanded you. And remember, I am with you always, to the end of the age."

Jesus' command is not limited to taking the gospel message to the world, bringing people to salvation, and then leaving them to continue their lives as before. Rather, it is to make them disciples by teaching them all about their Savior and how they should now live as ambassadors for God (2 Cor 5:20). The work of reconciliation, started by Christ, is continued by us (2 Cor 5:18-20). Though He finished His work of redemption, He has not finished His work of reconciliation. He has entrusted us with the message of reconciliation, which is why He gave us the great commission immediately before He left this earth to return to His Father's right hand in heaven (Acts 1:8-9).

God does not expect us to accomplish this mission without divine power. Remember how the disciples were gathered with other believers in the upper room (Acts 1:13)? They had not yet gone out to spread the Word because they had not yet received the power of the Holy Spirit (Acts 1:8). However, when they received Him, they went out and preached in the power of the Spirit to the Jewish crowd that had just crucified their Messiah (Acts 2:23, 36). Peter challenged them to completely change their mind about who Jesus is, and many of them responded to that challenge: Jesus was not a false prophet justly condemned; God had made this crucified Jesus both Lord and Christ (Acts 2:36). When He returned to the Father, as promised, Jesus did not abandon us as orphans, but gave us His Spirit, the Advocate, who would be with us forever (Jn 14:16-18).

There is another incident in the Gospels, besides the two miraculous feedings of thousands, which also shows our need to rely on God to accomplish the mission He has given to us. The disciples were sent out, with limited resources, and accomplished their mission (Mark 6:7-13).

Later they faced a new problem and they were expected to apply the lesson they learned from that previous mission to their new situation. Please read Mark 9:14-29 to discover why the disciples failed in this case.

QUESTION 10

The ultimate goal of the great commission is discipleship. *True or False?*

QUESTION 11

When Jesus left us to return to heaven, He expected us to carry the message of reconciliation. *True or False?*

QUESTION 12

When Jesus told the disciples in John 14:16-18 He would not leave them as orphans, what was He referring to?

A. His continuing intercession for them before the Father

B. His second advent

C. The coming of the Holy Spirit

D. The Father's omnipresence

QUESTION 13

Please briefly explain what the disciples' error was in Mark 9:14-29.

Topic 5: The Shape of My Obedience

Believers should be obedient to the Word of God above all other influences in their lives. If a believer is told to do something that contradicts the Word of God, he should not obey it. God wants us to be obedient to Him, even if they we do not understand why He directs us one way and not another. God's ways are not our ways, and we cannot accomplish His mission our way (Isa 55:8-9). Instead, we must be committed to living as His servants (Mk 10:45). This means that we do not seek to be served, but to serve others instead. We bless those who slander us and give up our self-serving lifestyle to gain a better life in eternity (Mk 8:34-38). We may not always feel like being obedient, but it is the appropriate response to the redemption offered to us by Christ. The only way we can live this out is through our total dependence on God. Read "Obedience." Then answer the questions that follow.

Obedience

How do we determine our role in God's mission? God does not usually outline His plan for our lives up front and in great detail. The Christian life is a relationship with the Lord that is lived out day by day. He reveals His plan step by step so that we are always living by faith. This living by faith is a requirement for the one who seeks to please God. Hebrews 11 discusses the role of faith in daily life.

As Paul stated the proper role of Christian leaders is to be “servants of Christ and stewards of the mysteries of God” (1 Cor 4:1). The main qualification for leaders is that they be faithful. Anyone can be faithful and that is all God asks of us. He does not ask us to do anything we are not capable of.

Even when we have done everything our Lord has commanded us to do, our response should be, “We are slaves undeserving of special praise; we have only done what was our duty” (Lk 17:10).

This level of obedience is supernaturally high. This is also what was expected of Jesus when He denied Himself and was obedient unto death. Christ humbled Himself not only when He served those He encountered, but most profoundly in His death on the cross. Our obedience to Him takes shape when we, by embracing Christ, count our lives as though we were dead and live to advance the kingdom of the One who has brought us into a relationship with Himself.

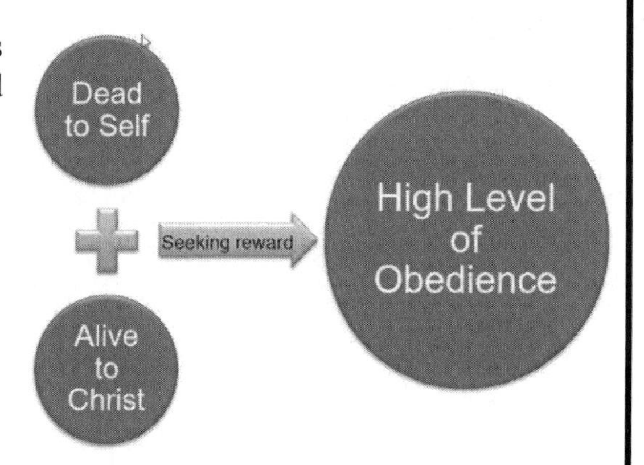

While this level of obedience may sound painfully difficult, it also has its rewards. When we leave everything and follow Him, as the disciples did (Mk 10:28), we are choosing the relationship that He has chosen, and we receive the reward “a hundred times as much” (Mk 10:30).

QUESTION 14

Please match the following references with the corresponding teachings about obedience.

Reference	*Teaching on Obedience*
Isaiah 55:8-9	We give our life to Christ to gain it in eternity.
Mark 8:34-38	Our obedience is an appropriate response to Christ’s redemption.
Mark 10:45	We bless even when we are reviled.
Romans 12:1-2	Rely on Christ for contentment no matter what you have or don’t have.
1 Corinthians 4:12	God’s ways are not our ways.
Philippians 4:12-13	We become total servants.

QUESTION 15

Please read Hebrews 11:13-16. When you are finished, write your own paraphrase of this passage.

QUESTION 16

According to 1 Corinthians 4:2, the requirement for a Christian steward is that he be found __________.

QUESTION 17

Please read Exodus 3–4. Then open your Life Notebook and note Moses' response to God's call in Exodus 3 and 4. Write out what the issues were. Then, for each issue, show how God and Moses resolved the issue. Also explain how Moses might have avoided these problems.

QUESTION 18

We will have reason to boast only after we have done everything that God has asked of us. *True or False?*

QUESTION 19

Rewards are promised to believers who sacrifice things in their earthly lives to serve God. *True or False?*

QUESTION 20

As a follow-up to Question 17, instead of listing Moses' issues, open your Life Notebook and list the issues you have with responding to God's call. Next write out your explanation of how you can resolve those issues.

Lesson 7 Self Check: The Christian Life

QUESTION 1

People singing a new song in Scripture implies these same people were personally involved in what they were singing about. *True or False?*

QUESTION 2

David humbly accepted Michal's criticism for dancing before the Lord in 2 Samuel 6:12-23. *True or False?*

QUESTION 3

Who deserted Paul because he loved this present age?

A. Silas

B. Mark

C. Luke

D. Demas

QUESTION 4

Hebrews 10:24-25 connects a believer's spiritual maturity with continuing to fellowship with other believers. *True or False?*

QUESTION 5

How many loaves did the disciples have with them in the boat in Mark 8:14?

A. None

B. One

C. Seven

D. Twelve

QUESTION 6

When Jesus left us to return to heaven He expected us to carry the message of reconciliation for Him. *True or False?*

QUESTION 7

Which of the following did Jesus say was the disciples' error when they failed to cast out the demon Mark 9:14-29?

A. A lack of authority

B. Jesus was not present with them

C. Not praying

D. Not abiding

QUESTION 8

Which of the following verses would be best to use to urge a fellow believer to give his or her life to God as a proper response to Christ's redemptive work on their behalf?

A. Isaiah 55:8-9

B. Romans 12:1-2

C. 1 Corinthians 4:12

D. Philippians 4:12-13

QUESTION 9

Which of the following paraphrases Hebrews 11:13-16?

A. You must hold firmly to faith and a good conscience.

B. Faith involves leaving your past life to follow God's promises.

C. These three remain: faith, hope, and love. But the greatest of these is love.

D. The righteousness of God is revealed in the gospel and the just shall live by faith.

QUESTION 10

Since believers have been rewarded by salvation, they need not look for any future reward for obedience. *True or False?*

Lesson 7 Answers to Questions

QUESTION 1

Reference	Aspect of Worship
Genesis 24:26-27	The Lord is worshipped for His faithful love for Abraham.
Exodus 34:8	Moses worshipped by bowing down.
Job 38:4-7	The angels sang for joy when the earth was created.
Revelation 4:8	God is worshipped for His holiness.
John 4:23-24	God must be worshipped in spirit and truth.
John 9:35-38	Jesus accepted worship as the Son of Man.
Rev 5:9-10	God the Son is worshipped for Christ's redemptive work.

QUESTION 2

A. It was limited to a specific group of people.

D. It was something personally experienced by those people.

QUESTION 3: *Your answer should be similar to the following:*

Let all things be done for the strengthening of the church. People speaking in the church should take turns so all can learn and be encouraged. God is not characterized by disorder but by peace. Do everything in a decent and orderly manner.

QUESTION 4: *Your answer should be similar to the following:*

- *What is David trying to do?* He wanted to bring the ark of the LORD into Jerusalem (2 Sam 6:12).
- *What did David do each time those who carried the ark took six steps?* He sacrificed an ox and a fattened calf (2 Sam 6:13).
- *What else was he doing before the LORD?* He was dancing with all his strength (2 Sam 6:14).
- *What else were David and all Israel doing?* They were shouting and blowing trumpets (2 Sam 6:15).
- *Who saw David and how did she feel about his dancing?* Michal saw him and despised him (2 Sam 6:16).
- *What did David do after he finished sacrificing?* He pronounced a blessing over the people in the name of the LORD of hosts (2 Sam 6:18).
- *Besides a blessing, what else did David give to each member of Israel?* A portion of bread, a date cake, and a raisin cake (2 Sam 6:19).
- *What happened when he went to bless his own house?* Michal told him that he showed himself as a vulgar fool (2 Sam 6:20).
- *How did David reply to her?* He said he was celebrating before the LORD! He also said he was willing to shame and humiliate himself more than this (2 Sam 6:21-22).
- *What happened to Michal because of her response?* She had no children to the day of her death (2 Sam 6:23).

QUESTION 5

A. Demas [There is a danger that new believers will seek to repair this severed connection with this present world. Demas deserted Paul "since he loved the present age" (2 Tim 4:10).]

QUESTION 6

Reference	*Teaching*
Romans 1:12	Our presence with them leads us to mutual comfort in one another's faith.
1 Thessalonians 4:18; 5:11	They are the ones who can encourage us when we need it.
Hebrews 10:24-25	Our lack of fellowship contributes to our lack of maturity in the faith.
James 5:19-20	The presence of other believers can also restore us even when we have wandered from the faith

QUESTION 7

B. Equipping the saints
D. Knowledge of the Son of God
E. Practicing the truth in love
F. Unity in the faith

[God made the church to be an equipping station for His saints. We were not meant to go it alone in the Christian life and be complete in ourselves.]

QUESTION 8: False

QUESTION 9

Question	*Answer*
How many loaves did the disciples have with them in the boat (Mk 8:14)?	One
How many loaves were broken to feed the five thousand (Mk 8:19)?	Five
How many baskets of bread pieces were left after feeding the five thousand (Mk 8:19)?	Twelve
How many baskets were collected after the four thousand ate (Mk 8:20)?	Seven

QUESTION 10: True

QUESTION 11: True [This work of reconciliation was started by Christ, but we are entrusted with carrying that message to the world (2 Cor 5:18). Though He finished His work of redemption, He has not finished His work of reconciliation.]

QUESTION 12

C. The coming of the Holy Spirit [Remember how the disciples were gathered with other believers in the upper room (Acts 1:13)? They had not yet gone out to spread the Word because they had not yet received the power of the Holy Spirit (Acts 1:8). When they received Him, they went out and preached in the power of the Spirit to the Jewish crowd that had just crucified their Messiah (Acts 2:23, 36).]

QUESTION 13: *Your answer should be similar to the following:*

Jesus told them, "This kind can come out only by prayer." He implied that the disciples had attempted to cast out the demon without prayer, relying on themselves and their experience rather than relying on God.

QUESTION 14

Reference	*Teaching on Obedience*
Isaiah 55:8-9	God's ways are not our ways.
Mark 8:34-38	We give our life to Christ to gain it in eternity.
Mark 10:45	We become total servants.
Romans 12:1-2	Our obedience is an appropriate response to Christ's redemption.
1 Corinthians 4:12	We bless even when we are reviled.
Philippians 4:12-13	Rely on Christ for contentment no matter what you have or don't have.

QUESTION 15: *Your answer should be similar to the following:*

The people who please God by faith left the lives they knew by sight and experience and turned instead to follow God's promises of future heavenly blessing.

QUESTION 16: Faithful [Anyone can be faithful and that is all God asks of us. He does not ask us to do anything we are not capable of.]
QUESTION 17: *Your answer*
QUESTION 18: False [Even when we have done everything our Lord has commanded us to do, our response should be, "We are slaves undeserving of special praise; we have only done what was our duty" (Lk 17:10).]
QUESTION 19: True
QUESTION 20: *Your answer*

Lesson 7 Self Check Answers

QUESTION 1: True
QUESTION 2: False
QUESTION 3

D. Demas

QUESTION 4: True
QUESTION 5

B. One

QUESTION 6: True
QUESTION 7

C. Not praying

QUESTION 8

B. Romans 12:1-2

QUESTION 9

B. Faith involves leaving your past life to follow God's promises.

QUESTION 10: False

Lesson 8: Called to Be a Steward—Using Wisely All God Entrusts to Me

God is the originator of everything. So everything belongs to Him. According to Isaiah, we are molded by God. In one of his psalms, David marveled at the notice God takes of people. That is a beautiful thing. Not only are we noticed by God, but we also belong to Him and have been created for a purpose. This purpose is to glorify God who has entrusted to us the management of some of what belongs to Him. Because we are stewards, we are accountable to Him.

Sometimes people are hesitant to become Christians because they don't want to spend their time pursuing God's agenda and His purposes. Perhaps they feel this way because they don't quite understand the Christian idea of how God interacts with people. These same people are likely to have lives that are very full with their own agenda such as family and work, and the idea of investing in someone else's agenda isn't appealing to them. But consider this: If our life is so full, why do we spend time trying to accomplish our boss's agenda at work? Perhaps it is because we *need* that job. We may feel that when we are at work, our boss owns us.

The biblical viewpoint is that God owns us and everything we have. However, there are some important differences between God and our boss. God is both our Creator and Savior. Unlike our boss, God also loves us unconditionally. Everything we have has been entrusted to us by God, and He expects us to invest our life and resources in ways that honor Him. We need to remember that the Christian life is a relationship, and when we know that God loves us, it makes sense to honor Him with all that we have.

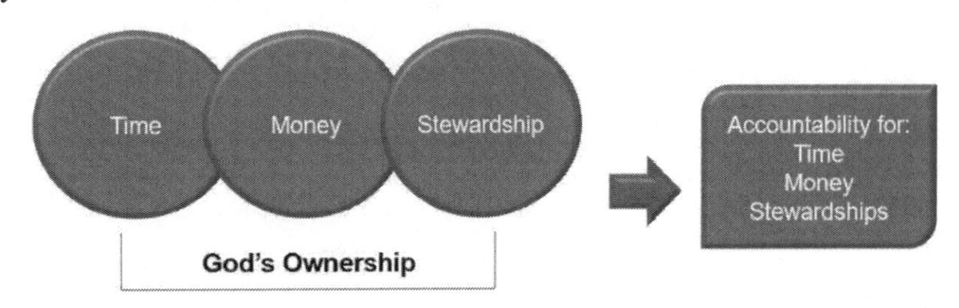

We will look at aspects of what it means to be a good steward in this lesson. In Topic 1, we examine the extent of God's lordship and ownership over us as the foundation for stewardship. We build on this understanding to respond appropriately to its truth. Topic 2 looks at the nature of stewardship: what a steward is, what is expected of one, and some biblical examples. Topics three and four discuss two common aspects of stewardship. Topic 3 discusses the importance of managing our time; time is a precious gift that once used can never be brought back. Topic 4 talks about managing money: what should be our attitude toward it and how do we best use it to testify about God. In Topic 5 we look directly at how we are all accountable to God for the way we live.

Lesson Outline

Topic 1: Recognizing God's Lordship and Ownership

Topic 2: The Nature of Stewardship

Topic 3: Managing Time

Topic 4: Financial Responsibility

Topic 5: Accountability

Topic 1: Recognizing God's Lordship and Ownership

Have you ever given serious consideration to who owns everything you have? After all, we only live once, and it seems like what is ours really ought to be ours. Why would we want to give everything up and live for someone else?

The Bible make it clear that God is both Creator and Savior. Christians are not only God's by creation. We are also God's because Jesus died for us. God has shown us great mercy because Christ personally died for us. Because of God's grace, Christians might sometimes act as though God is not the rightful owner and their Lord just as a child can act as though his parents have no authority over his life. But if they do so, they are acting selfishly and ungratefully because Christ fully gave His life for them. You see, it turns out that 'what is mine' really isn't mine at all.

Christians believe God created everything, as the Bible describes in Genesis 1–2. But they also believe that everything belongs to Him. God makes this claim many times in the Bible (Gen 1:9; Isa 40:28). Psalm 50:10 says, "For every wild animal in the forest belongs to me, as well as the cattle that graze on a thousand hills." Colossians 1:16 tells us that all things, "whether visible or invisible…were created through him and for him." In fact, He alone is *uncreated.*

Christians are not only God's by right of creation, but they belong to Him through Christ by right of redemption. We are purchased with a price and that price was Christ's blood (1 Pet 1:18-19). In effect when we believed we placed ourselves on the cross with Christ and died with Him (2 Cor 5:14). "And he died for all so that those who live should no longer live for themselves but for him who died for them and was raised" (2 Cor 5:15). Therefore, since He was resurrected, we are also in Him and raised to newness of life (Rom 6:4).

QUESTION 1

Christians belong to God both because God is their creator and because Christ is their Savior. *True or False?*

As our Creator, God is the owner of everything we possess, including our lives. In this way He is also Lord of our lives. Read "Lord and Creator" to gain a deeper understanding of God's lordship in our lives. Then answer the questions that follow.

Lord and Creator

It is crucial for every person to acknowledge that God is the Creator; those that do not fall into all kinds of error. Romans 1:18-23 says that God's eternal power and divine nature have been clearly seen through His creation. The unrighteous deny this basic fact and exchange the worship of God for worship of things of this world. Therefore, they are given over to impurity, dishonorable passions, and a depraved mind (Rom 1:24-32).

In Romans 9:20-24 Paul gave God's perspective on His rights as man's Creator. He asked,

> But who indeed are you – a mere human being – to talk back to God? Does what is molded say to the molder, "Why have you made me like this?" Has the potter no right to make from the same lump of clay one vessel for special use and another for ordinary use? But what if God, willing to demonstrate his wrath and to make known his power, has endured with much patience the objects of wrath prepared for destruction? And what if he is willing to make

> known the wealth of his glory on the objects of mercy that he has prepared beforehand for glory –even us, whom he has called, not only from the Jews but also from the Gentiles?

In these passages we see that understanding God as Creator leads to proper humility. This humility is crucial in both responding to the gospel and living our lives in proper submission to God. Christians need to understand that we are God's both by creation and by redemption. We are bought with a price, the precious blood of Christ (1 Cor 7:23).

Based on what Christ has done, what is our proper response? We should offer ourselves as a sacrifice to God. This offering is *voluntary*, not something that is forced by God or given in exchange for salvation. It is our *reasonable* service (Rom 12:1). Paul says it is reasonable based on the mercies of God. He has just spent the first eleven chapters of Romans telling us of the many mercies God has shown toward us as Christians. We have been redeemed from a wasted life in which we either knowingly or unknowingly served Satan and the passing pleasures of this world (Eph 2:2-3). While we were in this unredeemed state, we were under God's wrath and destined for eternity in the lake of fire (Eph 5:6; Rev 20:11-15).

What God asks of redeemed people is simply to recognize the reality of what He has done and to act on that reality. He has redeemed us from our futile way of life and restored us to fellowship with Him. The One who has brought us back into a relationship with Himself is the Creator, Redeemer, and Lord, and it makes sense to treat Him as such.

Christ gave His life to redeem us and also to be an example for us (Heb 10:5-7):

> So when he came into the world, he said, "Sacrifice and offering you did not desire, but a body you prepared for me. Whole burnt offerings and sin-offerings you took no delight in. "Then I said, 'Here I am: I have come – it is written of me in the scroll of the book – to do your will, O God.'"

Though we do not often think about it, Jesus was human just like us; but without a sin nature (Heb 4:15). That means He had a will to live and avoid death (Mk 14:36). Yet He put aside His own feelings and served us by giving His life as a ransom for many (Mk 10:45). The choice Jesus made was irrevocable and the consequences eternal. Jesus made this sacrifice willingly because He considered a relationship with us whom He created to be worth it. We can choose to make a similar sacrifice as our reasonable service (Rom 12:1), laying aside our self-ruled lives because we consider a relationship with Him to be worth it.

QUESTION 2

According to Romans 12:1-2, which of the following is the Christian's proper response to God as seen in Romans 1–11?

A. We are required to offer ourselves as a living sacrifice.

B. We offer ourselves in exchange for our salvation (redemption).

C. Offering ourselves is a reasonable response to Christ's redemption.

D. We offer ourselves out of fear of God.

QUESTION 3

Which passage best explains how human behavior is affected by not believing in God as Creator?

A. Romans 1:18-31

B. Romans 12:1-2

C. Hebrews 10:5-7

D. Revelation 5:9-10

QUESTION 4

Please read Romans 12:1-2. Then open your Life Notebook and record your response to Paul's appeal to present your bodies as a sacrifice to God. Include applications that you want to make to your life.

Topic 2: The Nature of Stewardship

Have you ever considered what primary characteristic God looks for in those who serve Him? Some have suggested it's that they are hard working. While this is important, it may help to consider the most important characteristic you look for in your friends. Perhaps you look for friends who won't give up on you. Perhaps you like friends who are *loyal* to you. That may be especially true during tough times or maybe when you don't think you deserve it. Others appreciate someone who's *faithful*. God values these traits as well.

Good stewards take personal responsibility for managing another's property and money. In Lesson 7, we saw that the main qualification for a steward is faithfulness (1 Cor 4:2). Moses is a good biblical example of a faithful steward because he testified as God asked him to do (Heb 3:2, 5). Of course, Christ is the primary example of someone completely faithful in God's house (Heb 3:1-3):

> Therefore, holy brothers and sisters, partners in a heavenly calling, take note of Jesus, the apostle and high priest whom we confess, who is faithful to the one who appointed him, as Moses was also in God's house. For he has come to deserve greater glory than Moses, just as the builder of a house deserves greater honor than the house itself!

Jesus talked a lot about stewardship when He was on earth. Read "Faithful Stewardship" to see the instruction Jesus gave us in this area.

Faithful Stewardship

Jesus taught that the Christian life is characterized by stewardship. His teachings reveal that Christians will be judged and rewarded by Him on how faithful they are as stewards of God's ministry and gifts. The parable of the Talents in Matthew 25:14-30 is one example of His teaching. In this parable a man summons his slaves before going on a journey. "To one he gave five talents, to another two, and to another one, each according to his ability. Then he went on his journey" (Mt 25:15). The first two each put the money to work and doubled their master's money. But the third dug a hole to keep the money safe, returning the entrusted amount of money back to his master. The first two were praised for their work, put in charge of many things, and entered into the joy of their Master. Meanwhile the latter had all responsibility taken away from him and was thrown into outer darkness (Mt 25:30). A steward is responsible to use whatever has been entrusted to him in the way that pleases his master. We will be held responsible for how we use our money and gifts.

Jesus' teaching about faithful stewardship in Luke 12:35-48 gives other examples of what is expected of us as stewards. He began His teaching by telling us to "get dressed for service and keep your lamps burning" (Lk 12:35).

- Getting dressed for service means that we are to have an attitude of preparedness for whatever we are called to do. We are to prepare ourselves for our work of ministry.
- Keeping our lamps burning refers to patiently waiting and always being ready for the Master's return. That way the light would be on whenever the master came. This is a major responsibility for us while we wait for the imminent return of our Lord. (In another discourse about the end times, we are commanded in the same way with Jesus telling us to "stay alert!" four times in the six verses that end His sermon in Mk 13:32-37.)
- The steward is blessed if his master finds him at work when he returns (Lk 12:43). Jesus added, "I tell you the truth, the master will put him in charge of all his possessions" (Lk 12:44). There is also a warning to the wicked steward who will be caught by surprise by his Master's return and will be removed from his position (Lk 12:46).

Paul viewed his apostleship as a steward of the gospel. He told the Corinthians how they should view his ministry: "One should think about us this way—as servants of Christ and stewards of the mysteries of God" (1 Cor 4:1). Paul pointed out that he was the apostle to the Gentiles and Peter was the apostle to the Jews (Gal 2:8). But Paul was very humble about his apostleship, saying he was unworthy to be called an apostle because he persecuted the church of God (1 Cor 15:9). He claimed that the grace of God compelled him to work harder than all of them (1 Cor 15:10). These balancing forces of God's grace and his determined work were keys to his successful apostolic stewardship.

As with Paul, God's grace has also made us what we are. He has made it possible for us to serve Him in the context of a growing, loving relationship. That grace and love help motivate us to be faithful stewards of all He entrusts to us.

QUESTION 5

The illustration in Hebrews 3:1-3 teaches that Moses is the builder of a house and that Christ is the house. *True or False?*

The illustration in Hebrews 3:1-3 teaches that Moses is the builder of a house and that Christ is the house.

QUESTION 6

In the parable of the talents (Mt 25:14-30), Jesus praised the slave who kept his talents safe, returning the same amount to his master. *True or False?*

QUESTION 7

Please match the following references with the teachings Jesus gave about how to fulfill our responsibilities while we await His return.

Reference	*Teaching*
Mark 13:32-37	Stay alert!
Luke 12:35	Prepare ourselves, patiently wait and always be ready for the Master's return.
Luke 12:43	The wicked steward will be "cut in pieces" and assigned a place with the unfaithful.
Luke 12:44	The steward is blessed if his master finds him at work when he returns.
Luke 12:45-46	The steward will be rewarded for faithful service by being placed in charge of the Master's possessions.

QUESTION 8

Briefly explain the keys to Paul's apostolic success (1 Cor 15:8-11).

Topic 3: Managing Time

Becoming a follower of Christ may mean giving up some things we like to do. This may not be appealing to unbelievers who value the way they currently spend their time. And some believers think they should wait until they're older to start serving the Lord. That way they can live their life as they want and still make it into heaven.

There are several reasons why we should not wait to start serving the Lord. First, we don't know when we will die. Second, there is a great reward we receive in eternity for serving Him while we are on earth, and He wants us to receive our full reward. And third, we would miss out on the great relationship we have with Him.

Yes, it can be difficult to give up some of the things we would really like to do with our life, and this is true for everyone who decides to follow Christ. It's good to be aware that being a follower of Christ involves some changes. This is one of the reasons Christ told Christians who are serious about following Him to understand what they must give up in order to do so.

According to Colossians 4:5, we need to redeem our time, to make the most of it. That's the idea behind a Christian's management of time. We want to consider it as a valuable commodity committed to us, with the understanding that there is a limited amount and we must use it wisely. Once it is gone, we will never get it back. Read "Time Management" to learn more about this.

Time Management

Time is a gift of immeasurable value that can be spent only once. Though everyone is not given the same length of life, all of us are given the same amount of time in each day. Because the time we have is provided by God, we will need to account for how we use it in the same way we will account for how we spend the money the Lord gives us. So how do we manage our time well? The Bible gives us some guidelines.

We are told not to love sleep so that we do not become impoverished (Prov 20:13). Excessive sleeping can be an escape from our duties not only to God but also to our family. Practically speaking it cuts into the time we have available in a day. On the other hand, it is good to wake up rested with enough sleep. Some people try to accomplish more by depriving themselves of some of the sleep they need. Both of these extremes, too much sleep and too little, are examples of poor stewardship of time. Keeping a proper balance is important.

Though the example given refers to physical sleep, the Lord is not concerned simply with physical sleep; He is just as concerned with our spiritual alertness or lethargy. Managing our time is part of the discipline of living the Christian life, and lethargy interferes with a disciplined life. We must remain alert to the opportunities and dangers we may encounter. The Christian life is a moment-by-moment relationship with the Lord, and so we need to avoid spiritual lethargy by doing what we are supposed to do when we are supposed to do it. In Hebrews 5:11-14 the believers became lethargic because they no longer practiced what they knew was right. So, they could no longer discern between good and evil.

The discernment we need does not come immediately; rather it comes through long practice. As comprehensive as the Bible is, it does not address every situation we may face. Often the choices we face are not between clear cut cases of good and evil, but between what is good, better, and best. As our relationship with Christ deepens and we practice making wise choices that please Him, we become better at it. In other words, we mature in the faith.

As we have seen previously, our spiritual responsibility while we await the Lord's return includes staying alert and continuing to work (Mt 25:13, 16; Mk 13:32-37). We must be prepared because He may return at any time. If we are, He will find us when He returns pursuing the mission He has given us.

To grow and mature in the Christian life, we must remain active in our pursuit to fulfill the great commission. Paul compares living Christians to athletes who train diligently and compete purposefully, keeping their eyes on the reward. Similarly, a Christian's diligent pursuit and focus on pursuing God's goals will result in strengthening his Christian life.

When Paul received his calling to be an apostle, he immediately started to do the work of an apostle (1 Cor 15:10). In fact he worked harder at his apostleship than all of the other apostles. Jesus' attitude toward His mission was similar. He told His disciples He had to continue to work as long as He was able, because He would not be on earth forever (Jn 9:4). He worked through exhaustion, hunger, and thirst (Jn 4:31-33). His sustenance came from doing the Father's will (Jn 4:34-35). Both Jesus and Paul knew their mission and were determined to fulfill it. Believers should determine to do the same.

God has given us our great salvation through faith (Jn 6:29-30). But He has a body of work planned for us to do along with that salvation—a mission (Mt 28:18-20). One of the most important resources God has entrusted to us for the fulfillment of that mission is time. As it was with Paul and with Jesus, our time is limited, and once spent, it is gone. To successfully carry out the mission God has given us we need to manage faithfully and wisely the time he has graciously provided.

We will be judged and rewarded for the way we spend our time in the same way we will be judged and rewarded for how we spend our money.

QUESTION 9

The Bible finds it unnecessary to warn its readers against getting too much sleep. *True or False?*

QUESTION 10

Hebrews 5:11-14 talks of believers who were immature because of which of the following?

A. They were carnal.

B. They did not practice doing good.

C. They were new Christians.

D. They were young of age.

QUESTION 11

Please match each reference below with the corresponding teachings.

Reference	*Teaching*
1 Corinthians 9:23	He does all things to participate in the gospel.
1 Corinthians 9:24	He makes his body his slave.
1 Corinthians 9:25	He exercises self-control and looks to the reward.
1 Corinthians 9:26	He competes with a purpose.
1 Corinthians 9:27	Among many participants, he runs to win.

Topic 4: Financial Responsibility

Christian are called to be wise stewards of their financial resources. In Acts we read the story of Ananias and Sapphira, a married couple in the early years of the church (Acts 5:1-11). They lied to God and His church, saying they had sold some of their land and given all of the money to the church. But they really had given only part of the money from that sale to the church, keeping the rest for themselves and lying about what they had done. However, God disciplined them by immediately taking their lives.

While this may sound pretty severe, Christians carry the name of Christ, and He takes that fact very seriously because when Christians sin, God's name is blasphemed among unbelievers (Rom 2:24). In this case God met their public sin with public discipline. Even though they gave some of their money to the church, that money wasn't really theirs. *Everything* Christians have belongs to God and His work, and He wants to be honored by the way we use it.

How we use our money is a good test of how faithful we are. Paul wrote in 1 Timothy 6:10, "For the love of money is the root of all evils. Some people in reaching for it have strayed from the faith and stabbed themselves with many pains." Often people quote this verse incorrectly as saying that money is the root of all evils. But note it says the *love* of money causes problems. Like many other things that are morally neutral in and of themselves, money can be either correctly managed or subjected to abuse.

Believers need to understand what they are called to do with their money. For practical guidelines read "Financial Responsibility" below.

Financial Responsibility

One of the ongoing struggles for many Christians is trying to manage wisely the financial resources God has entrusted to them. Whether they have much or little of this world's wealth, using wisely what they have can be challenging. The Bible has much to say about money, and stewardship is at the heart of its teaching. Since the money a Christian has belongs to God, it makes sense that it should be used in ways that please God. One of the important ways in which God lets us demonstrate that we understand His priorities for our finances is through giving.

The most direct teaching about giving in the New Testament is in 2 Corinthians 8 and 9. Many principles can be seen in these chapters:

- Giving can and should be done with joy (2 Cor 8:2).
- Giving can be done even when the givers are in extreme poverty (2 Cor 8:2-3).
- Giving can be done even beyond one's means (2 Cor 8:3).
- Giving should be done voluntarily (2 Cor 8:3; 9:5).
- Giving increases fellowship with the recipients (2 Cor 8:4).
- Giving should be done by first giving oneself to the Lord (2 Cor 8:5).
- Giving should measure up to the faith and love from which it flows (2 Cor 8:7).
- Giving should follow Christ's example of becoming poor for our sakes (2 Cor 8:9).
- Giving should result in equality between the churches (2 Cor 8:13-15).

Other passages contribute to these principles. 1 Corinthians 16:2 suggests setting aside some income on the first day of the week. This should be done regularly and in proportion to how much God has blessed us.

Jesus taught us to accumulate treasure in heaven, not treasure on earth (Mt 6:19-20). "For where your treasure is, there your heart will be also" (Mt 6:21). He continued, saying, "No one can serve two masters, for either he will hate the one and love the other, or he will be devoted to the one and despise the other. You cannot serve God and money" (Mt 6:24). However, many get caught up in pursuing their own success in this world and that takes them away from serving the Lord.

Maintaining the proper attitude toward giving is important. Everything we have belongs to the Lord with whom we enjoy a relationship. He has supplied it all, so we are only giving back to Him what is already His.

A more proper attitude will also help us to give properly in the right proportion. Paul said that he had to learn what he really needed in life to be content. He said, "But if we have food and shelter, we will be satisfied with that" (1 Tim 6:8). Material wealth is a blessing that God can provide, but some who have more than they need complain too easily about what they do not have. Focusing on non-essential things—such as the pursuit of riches—can weigh us down and keep us from serving God.

A proper attitude toward our brothers and sisters in Christ also helps us give in the right proportion (Jas 2:15-16). As Christians we enjoy not only a relationship with Christ but also with other believers, and so we should be sensitive to the needs of our brothers and sisters. If they lack and we have enough, we must be willing to share. Without this attitude we may be shortchanging them by not meeting their needs and thus hurting the cause of the gospel. As giving should result in equality between the churches, so it should with individuals as we are able to help meet one another's needs (2 Cor 8:13-15).

Spiritually, the most dangerous thing about material wealth is having the attitude of a rich man who views his riches as all-important. Jesus taught that such an attitude keeps us from coming to God. The classic example of this can be seen in the interaction between Jesus and a rich man (Mk 10:17-22). The rich man approached Jesus and asked Him what he must do to inherit eternal life (Mk 10:17). Jesus told him, "Go, sell whatever you have and give the money to the poor, and you will have treasure in heaven. Then come, follow me" (Mk 10:21). In response, "The man looked sad and went away sorrowful, for he was very rich" (Mk 10:22). Jesus explained to His disciples what had just happened by saying, "How hard it is for the rich to enter the kingdom of God" (Mk 10:23). Eternal life can't be bought by giving away riches. Rather, it was a powerful demonstration that following Jesus is more important and more valuable than any amount of wealth. Wealth itself does not make it difficult to follow Christ. The attitude that riches on earth are more important than heavenly riches is what makes it difficult to follow Christ. For unless God steps in, the person with that attitude will have only earthly vision and continue forfeiting heavenly riches (Mk 10:26-27).

The important point is not how much or how little material wealth one has. What is important is that we recognize that whatever we have belongs to the Lord, and that He has given us the privilege of being a faithful steward of what He has entrusted to us.

QUESTION 12

Please match the following references with the corresponding teachings about giving.

Reference	*Teaching*
2 Corinthians 8:2	Giving can be done even beyond one's means.
2 Corinthians 8:3	Giving should be done by first giving oneself to the Lord.
2 Corinthians 8:4	Giving increases fellowship with the recipients.
2 Corinthians 8:5	Giving should measure up to the faith and love from which it flows.
2 Corinthians 8:7	Giving can and should be done with joy.

QUESTION 13

Please match the following references with the corresponding teachings about giving.

Reference	*Teaching*
2 Corinthians 8:2-3	For where your treasure is, there your heart will be also.
2 Corinthians 8:9	Giving should result in equality among the churches
2 Corinthians 8:13-15	Giving can be done even when the givers are in extreme poverty.
1 Corinthians 16:2	We should set aside some income on the first day of the week.
Matthew 6:21	Giving should be according to Christ's example of becoming poor for our sakes.

QUESTION 14

In 1 Timothy 6:8 Paul taught that Christians should be satisfied with which two of the following? *(Select all that apply.)*

A. Clothes

B. Drink

C. Food

D. Gifts

E. Love

F. Shelter

QUESTION 15

Riches are more spiritually dangerous to a person than having an attitude similar to the rich man's attitude. *True or False?*

Topic 5: Accountability

You may have heard of wealthy Christian leaders who emphasize riches and possessions. Some people wonder why God lets these people have all the luxury items that they would love to have. You may also have heard about Christian leaders getting into trouble over money. Why do such leaders fall? Why would they hurt Christ's cause? It can be hard to understand why a Christian leader would get into trouble over money. And it can be very hard to understand why God lets it happen. Why doesn't He either keep them from getting rich or keep them from sinning?

These are difficult questions to answer. Many believers have wondered about Christian leaders who fall. In many cases their fall does not happen overnight. Christians live in bodies of flesh just as non-Christians do. The same temptations that appeal to non-Christians appeal to Christians. When those pleasures are available, some fall to their attractions. God doesn't force Christians to do what is right. He would rather they choose to do so because they love Him. They are being shortsighted because what they are doing is exchanging their fellowship with the Lord for temporary earthly pleasures.

God trusts Christians with a lot. He seems to stake His reputation on what His children do. He gives them a lot of room to use their own judgment and go their own way. He doesn't seem to be looking over their shoulder all the time. But we shouldn't forget that Christians are in a relationship with Christ. The Lord is intimately familiar with everything we do and holds us accountable. But He doesn't always act immediately. Sometimes He waits because He wants us to choose repentance. Sin always gets in the way of a relationship with God, and part of what God's Spirit does for us is to make us aware of sin. The ultimate accountability, of course, will happen after death when there will be a final, just accounting. God is preparing the faithful for something special in His glorious future.

Christians should acknowledge that in addition to God holding us accountable in this life, "we must all appear before the judgment seat of Christ, so that each one may be paid back according to what he has done while in the body, whether good or evil" (2 Cor 5:10). This verse should be a sobering one for Christians. All of us will have to account for what we have done in this lifetime. This account will be given before an all-seeing and all-knowing God.

Not only Christians, but every person will have to give an account for how they lived their lives. People who die during this church age will either appear at Christ's judgment seat if they are Christians or at the Great White Throne if they are not. The article "Accountable to God" takes a more thorough look at what Scripture says about accountability. Read it before answering the questions that follow.

Accountable to God

As we saw in the lesson, everyone will appear before God's judgment seat. It is both a sobering and encouraging thought that God notices and remembers everything we do. He not only remembers every action in detail, but even every thought and intent of our hearts (Mk 7:21; Acts 8:22; Heb 4:12). This truth is sometimes overlooked because of God's longsuffering and mercy (2 Pet 3:9). In fact, an important historical judgment, the judgment of the flood, came on the earth because God saw that "every inclination of the thoughts of their minds was only evil all the time" (Gen 6:5). We should be encouraged as we remember that God cares so much for us that He notices everything we do!

An example of how God sees everything is found in His assessment of the reign of each king of Israel and Judah. Most of the kings of Judah were judged by how they compared with King David, and Israel's kings were compared with their first king, Jeroboam. For example:

- Solomon: Solomon did evil in the Lord's sight; he did not remain loyal to the Lord, like his father David had (1 Kgs 11:6).
- Jeroboam of Israel: Jeroboam still did not change his evil ways; he continued to appoint common people as priests at the high places. He consecrated as priest anyone who wanted the job. This sin caused Jeroboam's dynasty to come to an end and to be destroyed from the face of the earth (1 Kgs 13:33-34).
- Abijah of Judah: He followed all the sinful practices of his father (Rehoboam) before him. He was not wholeheartedly devoted to the Lord his God, as his ancestor David had been (1 Kgs 15:3).
- Asa of Judah: Asa did what the Lord approved as did his ancestor David (1 Kgs 15:11).
- Nadab of Israel: He did evil in the sight of the Lord. He followed in his father Jeroboam's footsteps and encouraged Israel to sin (1 Kgs 15:26).

These detailed assessments continued for each of the kings that reigned: over two hundred years (930–722 BC) for the kings of Israel and almost 350 years for the kings of Judah (930–586 BC). Yes, these were kings, so their deeds stood out for that reason, but God also notices in detail the things that ordinary people do.

- He noticed when Israel's most evil king Ahab showed remorse before Him (1 Kgs 21:29).

- He noticed when a "secret disciple" named Joseph of Arimathea cared for the Lord Jesus' body after He died (Jn 19:38).
- He noticed the lies of Ananias and Sapphira (Acts 5:1-11).
- He noticed when Simon, after he believed, still had a wicked heart, being bitterly envious and in bondage to sin (Acts 8:14-24).
- He noticed Rahab who hid the Israelite spies (Heb 11:31).

Paul expressed concern that even if he fulfilled his mission, he might in some way be disqualified (1 Cor 9:27). His main concern was to exercise self-control in everything (1 Cor 9:25). He knew he would be held accountable not only for fulfilling his mission, but also for how he fulfilled it (1 Cor 9:27).

The Bible warns that it is possible for us to make choices that will keep us from enjoying the blessing God wants to give (Heb 12:17). The example the author gives is Esau: "See to it that no one becomes an immoral or godless person like Esau, who sold his own birthright for a single meal" (Heb 12:16). Though such a choice may be difficult to understand, it is possible for a person to value immediate and temporal satisfaction more highly than the blessings that accompany a relationship with Christ. Esau was hungry, and to satisfy that hunger with one meal, he gave away his inheritance. We can similarly lose out on what God wants to give us, our rewards, by satisfying our carnal desires instead of maintaining "self-control in everything" (1 Cor 9:25). The principle is clearly stated in Galatians 6:7-8.

> Do not be deceived. God will not be made a fool. For a person will reap what he sows, because the person who sows to his own flesh will reap corruption from the flesh, but the one who sows to the Spirit will reap eternal life from the Spirit.

Based on that principle, believers are encouraged to sow wisely by doing good (Gal 6:9-10). Not surprising is the fact that God, with whom we enjoy an intimate relationship, notices everything, both good and bad, and that He holds us accountable and delights to reward our obedience.

QUESTION 16

Only Christians will appear for judgment at the Great White Throne (Rev 20:11-15). *True or False?*

QUESTION 17

Which passages would you use to teach someone that God knows even the thoughts and intentions of our hearts? *(Select all that apply.)*

A. Genesis 6:5

B. Mark 7:21

C. Acts 8:22

D. Hebrews 4:12

E. 2 Peter 3:9

QUESTION 18

Please read the Scripture passages and match the king with the corresponding evaluation of him.

King	*Evaluation*
King Nadab of Israel (1 Kgs 15:25-26)	He "did more evil in the sight of the LORD than all who were before him."
King Omri of Israel (1 Kgs 16:25)	He "made an Asherah pole; he did more to anger the LORD God of Israel than all the kings of Israel who were before him."
King Ahab of Israel (1 Kgs 16:33)	"He followed in his father Asa's footsteps and was careful to do what the LORD approved. However, the high places were not eliminated; the people continued to offer sacrifices and burn incense on the high places."
King Jehoshaphat of Judah (1 Kgs 22:43)	"He did what the LORD approved, just as his father Uzziah had done. But the high places were not eliminated; the people continued to offer sacrifices and burn incense on the high places. He built the Upper Gate to the LORD's temple."
King Jehu of Israel (2 Kgs 10:29-30)	"He did evil in the sight of the LORD. He followed in his father's footsteps and encouraged Israel to sin."
King Jehoash of Judah (2 Kgs 15:34-35)	"Did not repudiate the sins which [other kings] encouraged Israel to commit; the golden calves remained in Bethel and Dan. The LORD said to Jehu, 'You have done well. You have accomplished my will and carried out my wishes with regard to Ahab's dynasty. Therefore, four generations of your descendants will rule over Israel.'"

QUESTION 19

Who did the author of Hebrews use as an example of an Old Testament character who lost his birthright through godlessness (Heb 12:16-17)?

A. Canaan

B. Esau

C. Ishmael

D. King Ahab

QUESTION 20

Please read through Hebrews 12:14-17. Open your Life Notebook and write down some of the blessings you can experience because of your relationship with Christ. Then ask God to make you aware of any actions or attitudes that could keep you from experiencing His blessing and write those down. As you confess these things, thank God for showing you and for holding you accountable.

Lesson 8 Self Check: The Christian Life

QUESTION 1

Christians belong to God both because God is their creator and because Christ is their Savior. *True or False?*

QUESTION 2

According to Romans 12:1-2, which of the following is the Christians' proper response to God as seen in Romans 1–11?

A. We offer ourselves out of fear of God.

B. We offer ourselves in exchange for our salvation (redemption).

C. We are required to offer ourselves as a living sacrifice.

D. Offering ourselves is a reasonable response to Christ's redemption.

QUESTION 3

According to Hebrews 3:1-3 Christ is the builder of the house. *True or False?*

QUESTION 4

Which of the following actions was NOT praised by Jesus in His call to faithful stewardship in Luke 12:35-48?

A. Being at work when He returns

B. Eating and drinking

C. Patiently waiting

D. Staying alert

QUESTION 5

Hebrews 5:11-14 talks of believers who were immature because of which of the following?

A. They did not practice doing good.

B. They were carnal.

C. They were new Christians.

D. They were young of age.

QUESTION 6

The Bible finds it necessary to warn its readers against getting too much sleep. *True or False?*

QUESTION 7

On the subject of giving, the Bible warns believers against giving beyond their means. *True or False?*

QUESTION 8

Having a rich man's improper attitude is more spiritually dangerous than having worldly riches. *True or False?*

QUESTION 9

Only believers will appear for judgment at the Great White Throne (Rev 20:11-15). *True or False?*

QUESTION 10

When God evaluated the reigns of the kings of Judah, whose reign were they usually compared to?

A. Ahab

B. David

C. Jeroboam

D. Rehoboam

Lesson 8 Answers to Questions

QUESTION 1: True

QUESTION 2

C. Offering ourselves is a reasonable response to Christ's redemption. [Notice that this offering is voluntary. God does not force it, nor is it given in exchange for salvation. Paul said it is our reasonable service based on the mercies of God.]

QUESTION 3

A. Romans 1:18-31 [Romans 1:18-23 says that God's eternal power and divine nature have been clearly seen through His creation, but the unrighteous deny this basic fact and "became fools and exchanged the glory of the immortal God for an image resembling mortal human beings or birds or four-footed animals or reptiles" (Rom 1:22-23). Therefore, they are given over to impurity, dishonorable passions, and a depraved mind (Rom 1:24-32).]

QUESTION 4: *Your answer*

QUESTION 5: False [Jesus is the one compared to the builder of a house.]

QUESTION 6: False [The first two were praised for their work, put in charge of many things, and entered into the joy of their Master. Meanwhile the latter had all responsibility taken away from him and was thrown into outer darkness (Mt 25:30).]

QUESTION 7

Reference	*Teaching*
Mark 13:32-37	Stay alert!
Luke 12:35	Prepare ourselves, patiently wait and always be ready for the Master's return.
Luke 12:43	The steward is blessed if his master finds him at work when he returns.
Luke 12:44	The steward will be rewarded for faithful service by being placed in charge of the Master's possessions.
Luke 12:45-46	The wicked steward will be "cut in pieces" and assigned a place with the unfaithful.

QUESTION 8: *Your answer should be similar to the following:*

He claimed the grace of God made him an apostle (1 Cor 15:10). Yet, because of God's grace toward him, he worked harder than all of the others (1 Cor 15:10). These balancing forces of God's grace and his determined work were keys to his successful apostolic stewardship.

QUESTION 9: False [We are told not to love sleep so that we do not become impoverished (Prov 20:13). Excessive sleep can also be an escape from our duties not only to God but also to our family.]

QUESTION 10

B. They did not practice doing good.

QUESTION 11

Reference	*Teaching*
1 Corinthians 9:23	He does all things to participate in the gospel.
1 Corinthians 9:24	Among many participants, he runs to win.
1 Corinthians 9:25	He exercises self-control and looks to the reward.
1 Corinthians 9:26	He competes with a purpose.
1 Corinthians 9:27	He makes his body his slave.

QUESTION 12

Reference	*Teaching*
2 Corinthians 8:2	Giving can and should be done with joy.
2 Corinthians 8:3	Giving can be done even beyond one's means.
2 Corinthians 8:4	Giving increases fellowship with the recipients.
2 Corinthians 8:5	Giving should be done by first giving oneself to the Lord.
2 Corinthians 8:7	Giving should measure up to the faith and love from which it flows.

QUESTION 13

Reference	*Teaching*
2 Corinthians 8:2-3	Giving can be done even when the givers are in extreme poverty.
2 Corinthians 8:9	Giving should be according to Christ's example of becoming poor for our sakes.
2 Corinthians 8:13-15	Giving should result in equality among the churches
1 Corinthians 16:2	We should set aside some income on the first day of the week.
Matthew 6:21	For where your treasure is, there your heart will be also.

QUESTION 14

C. Food

F. Shelter

[Paul said that he had to learn what he really needed in life to be content. He said, "But if we have food and shelter, we will be satisfied with that" (1 Tim 6:8).]

QUESTION 15: False [Spiritually, the most dangerous thing about riches is having a "rich-man" attitude. Jesus taught that such an attitude keeps us from coming to God. The classic example of this is the story of the rich young ruler (Mk 10:17-22).]

QUESTION 16: False [Only nonbelievers will appear before the Great White Throne. But at Christ's judgment seat Christians will have to give an account of how they lived their lives.]

QUESTION 17

A. Genesis 6:5

B. Mark 7:21

C. Acts 8:22

D. Hebrews 4:12

[It is a sobering thought that God notices and remembers everything we do. He not only remembers every action in detail, but even every thought and intent of our heart (Mk 7:21; Acts 8:22; Heb 4:12).]

QUESTION 18

King	*Evaluation*
King Nadab of Israel (1 Kgs 15:25-26)	"He did evil in the sight of the Lord. He followed in his father's footsteps and encouraged Israel to sin."
King Omri of Israel (Kgs 16:25)	He "did more evil in the sight of the Lord than all who were before him."
King Ahab of Israel (1 Kgs 16:33)	He "made an Asherah pole; he did more to anger the Lord God of Israel than all the kings of Israel who were before him."
King Jehoshaphat of Judah (1 Kgs 22:43)	"He followed in his father Asa's footsteps and was careful to do what the Lord approved. However, the high places were not eliminated; the people continued to offer sacrifices and burn incense on the high places."
King Jehu of Israel (2 Kgs 10:29-30)	"Did not repudiate the sins which [other kings] encouraged Israel to commit; the golden calves remained in Bethel and Dan. The Lord said to Jehu, 'You have done well. You have accomplished my will and carried out my wishes with regard to Ahab's dynasty. Therefore, four generations of your descendants will rule over Israel.'"
King Jehoash of Judah (2 Kgs 15:34-35)	"He did what the Lord approved, just as his father Uzziah had done. But the high places were not eliminated; the people continued to offer sacrifices and burn incense on the high places. He built the Upper Gate to the Lord's temple."

QUESTION 19

B. Esau [The implication is that Christians can lose part of their spiritual inheritance by being shortsighted and fleshly.]

QUESTION 20: *Your answer*

Lesson 8 Self Check Answers

QUESTION 1: True

QUESTION 2

D. Offering ourselves is a reasonable response to Christ's redemption.

QUESTION 3: True

QUESTION 4

B. Eating and drinking

QUESTION 5

A. They did not practice doing good.

QUESTION 6: True

QUESTION 7: False

QUESTION 8: True

QUESTION 9: False

QUESTION 10

B. David

Lesson 9: Called to Follow—Making Wise Decisions

Since the Lord is my Shepherd, I need to follow His leading. This lesson will focus on the practical issue of determining God's will for our lives. We will explore principles from Scripture for determining God's will and explore wise decision-making.

Have you ever seriously considered finding God's will in your life? Sometimes we'll hear an older person say that we need to be certain of God's will in our life. They may keep asking us to find what God is calling us to do. They may believe that God calls people to their vocation, that He tell us whom to marry, and specifically how we are to serve the church. While this older person needs to be respected, the trouble is that there are many times when believers haven't heard or felt God call them to any of these things in any specific way.

But how exactly do we find God's will? And once we have found it, how do we follow it? Also, how detailed is God's will?

As you study this lesson, keep in mind that the Christian life is a relationship with Christ; knowing God's will becomes less complex as believers know God more intimately. But many Christians experience some degree of struggle with determining what God's will is for them in a particular set of circumstances.

We will explore in this lesson the nature of God's will as well as some of the practical ways in which God provides guidance to us as we face decisions. We will also look at a few things that might hinder us from knowing God's will.

Lesson Outline

Topic 1: Various Uses of God's Will

Topic 2: Discovering God's Will

Topic 3: The Role of God's Word

Topic 4: The Role of Miraculous Intervention

Topic 5: The Role of Godly Counsel

Topic 6: Hindrances to Guidance

Topic 1: Various Uses of God's Will

Some people think that God wants us to have an exact job in an exact place. And to live in a specific house with a specific person, and so on. As we study God's will, we'll discover that God directs His people in many different ways.

- Biblically there are times that God directs His people in a very detailed way. One famous example of this is Gideon and his fleece (Judg 6:36-40).
- Yet there are other times when God directs only in the most general way. This is how He directed Paul when the Holy Spirit prevented him "from speaking the message in Asia" (Acts 16:6).

- There are other times when God even uses unbelievers to accomplish His will. An example of this is in Ezra 1:1-2 when "the Lord stirred the mind of King Cyrus of Persia…to build a temple for him in Jerusalem."
- There are also times when "God's will" refers to His moral will for the believers who represent Him. "For this is God's will: for you to become holy, you to keep away from sexual immorality" (1 Thess 4:3).

Many more examples could be cited, but you can see how God's will is used in several different ways in the Bible. Examining the context can help us better understand what the term "God's will" means. Let's start learning more about the uses of God's will by reading "God's Will" below.

God's Will

God's Sovereign Will

Christians understand that God is sovereign but knowing that He has supreme authority and power does not guarantee that they will always be comfortable with His sovereignty. Even Jesus had a struggle with God's sovereign will. He knew what the Father's will was: for Him to go to the cross and die for the sins of the world (Heb 10:5-10). Yet we see that in Gethsemane, Jesus, being fully human, struggled to accept what lay before Him in the next twelve hours (Mt 26:36-46). Those hours included betrayal, arrest, trial, denial, scourging, crucifixion, and death (Mt 26:47–27:56). Many feel it also involved broken fellowship with the Father as He bore the sins of the world.

Yet when Jesus was assured that there was no other way to accomplish God's purpose, He was prepared to obey God's sovereign will. He had said, "My soul is deeply grieved, even to the point of death," and He "prayed that if it were possible the hour would pass from him" (Mk 14:34-35). After praying, however, "He said, 'Abba, Father, all things are possible for you. Take this cup away from me. Yet not what I will, but what you will'" (Mk 14:36). For Jesus, submitting to the Father's sovereign will was part of the intimate relationship He enjoyed with the Father.

God's sovereign will is sometimes called His determinative will because whatever He has determined to have happen will happen. Having determined that eleven of the twelve disciples would not be lost, then this came true (Jn 17:12). Since He determines that the waters will go so far and no further, then that is what happens (Job 38:11). His sovereign will cannot be thwarted.

Testing and Approving God's Will

Romans 12:2 tells us that we can test God's will for us. He invites us to discover how good, well-pleasing, and perfect it is.

In this case Scripture is speaking of God's will for our lives rather than a will that cannot be altered. Since we are invited to test God's will, we can either resist or accept it. Though He encourages us to accept it, knowing it is best for us, He doesn't force it on us. In the context God's will is speaking specifically of our response to His work of salvation on our behalf, as detailed in Romans chapters 1–11. In Romans 12:1, Paul wrote that our reasonable service, in light of God's work, is to present our bodies as a living sacrifice to God.

This is a call for us to yield the control we think we have over our lives and to place ourselves in God's hands. For who is better able to have that control? Whether we keep control or give it over to God, we do not know if our lives may be required of us tonight (Lk 12:16-21). Our lives are God's because we are His creation, and as Christians our lives are also God's by redemption. So, the life we now have should be given to God. What God is asking for is that the Christian, who has already trusted Him for salvation, also trusts Him with his earthly life. We should reasonably give it to Him as a living sacrifice.

Personal Holiness Is God's Will

This facet of God's will should be the easiest to understand. God Himself is holy, so He wants us to be holy (1 Pet 1:16).

> For this is God's will: for you to become holy, for you to keep away from sexual immorality, for each of you know how to possess his own body in holiness and honor, not in lustful passion like the Gentiles who do not know God. In this matter no one should violate the rights of his brother or take advantage of him, because the Lord is the avenger in all these cases, as we also told you earlier and warned you solemnly. For God did not call us to impurity but in holiness. (1 Thess 4:3-7)

God's will, in this case, means avoiding sin and doing His will.

Understanding God's will is a function of the Christian's growing relationship with the Lord. As that relationship becomes deeper and more intimate, we should expect that our understanding of what God wants and expects will increase. Because He loves us, He has a will that should impact our lives.

QUESTION 1

Please match each of the following references with the corresponding teaching about God's will.

Reference	*Teaching*
Judges 6:36-40	Gideon laid a fleece out overnight to corroborate God's will.
Ezra 1:1-2	God stirred the mind of Cyrus to build a temple for Him in Jerusalem.
Acts 16:6-10	God prevented Paul from speaking the message in the province of Asia.
1 Thessalonians 4:3	God's will is that we become holy and avoid immorality.

QUESTION 2

Which will of God does He invite us to test in order to see that it is good?

A. His will for our personal holiness

B. His sovereign will

C. His will for our lives

D. The center of His will

QUESTION 3

Please read through Romans 12:1-2. Seriously consider what Paul is urging us to do. Then write out your response to his request in your Life Notebook.

Topic 2: Discovering God's Will

Many of us know God's will for our lives in general terms, yet we are still tempted to go our own way. The question is one of determining how much latitude God gives a person in his life. Suppose an unbeliever who likes to fish is thinking about becoming a Christian. Would he still be able to fish?

These questions can be difficult to answer. Individuals have to discover God's will for their lives for themselves. There's nothing morally wrong with fishing. In many cases people don't fish to earn a living for their family, so it's mainly for recreation. The question to be considered is, 'Does fishing interfere with our relationship with Jesus?' Christians need to use their time wisely so that they do not neglect their spiritual lives. When we become a Christian, we have a relationship with God, so in a sense we would need to know if God wanted to go fishing with us.

Most Christians think they would like to know God's will for all the details of their lives. If they could discover exactly what God wants, then they could have the perfect spouse, job, school, home, and so on. But God wants us to learn to make decisions that reflect His will rather than following it mechanically as though we were robots. So we seek advice from others, pray, study the Word, look to circumstances and do other "spiritual" things to try to discern His will. Looking back on our lives, we can often see how He was working out His plan. But it is often a lot more difficult trying to discern His will in advance.

What would our lives be like if we knew His plan at this detailed level? And if we did, would we willingly follow His plan? Or would we rebel against it? To look at some ways of discovering God's will, read "Finding God's Will."

Finding God's Will

Sometimes people talk about finding God's will as though it were something that had been lost or hidden. But if God were to obscure His will that would be contrary to His character. Discovering His will for a particular situation can be challenging, especially if we do not recognize the parameters of His will and our freedom.

When people speak of God's will, they often mean they want to find out what God wants them to do in a specific situation. For instance, they may want to know whom God wants them to marry. Now God's Word clearly expresses both God's will and our freedom by telling us that we are free to marry anyone we wish, so long as he or she is a believer (1 Cor 7:39). God's will is that we marry a believer; within that one restriction we are free to choose whom we wish.

However, also true is the fact that God, who is sovereign, has known whom each person will marry before that person was born. Whether God has one specific person in mind a Christian should marry, and how He works to bring those people together, is a different question. If something in our life does not work out well, we might believe that we made a decision outside of God's will. Sometimes this evaluation is true. But the flaw in our thinking is that our perception of what constitutes a good outcome is different than God's. We think that if we are spiritual enough, we will always make the right decision and things will always work out for our good. If they do not, we then infer that we must get ourselves back into the center of God's will.

But is this correct? Did everything always work out well for God's people when they made godly decisions? Obviously, the answer to this question is no. Sometimes the mess in which people found themselves was exactly where God wanted them.

- Even though Ezekiel was obedient, his wife passed away; her death served as an illustration of what Judah faced in the Babylonian invasion, namely, defeat (Ezk 24:15-27).
- Even though Hosea did nothing wrong, God told him to marry a prostitute; again their marriage was an illustration to Israel of their deteriorated relationship with God (Hos 1:1-8).
- Even though Stephen testified by the Holy Spirit, he was martyred as he finished his testimony (Acts 7).

We should seek guidance for major decisions through prayer and godly wisdom. But whether everyone must find God's specific will for him and receive specific guidance before making every decision is debatable. Someone may want to know what profession they should be in. Or what courses to take at school. Or whether to make a certain purchase or not. For some of these specific, daily decisions some Christians may find it difficult to discern a specific will of God.

Some believers were called by God to a certain profession even before they were born. Jeremiah's call in Jeremiah 1:4-5 says that God appointed him to be a prophet while he was still in the womb.

Without a doubt Jeremiah was specifically called by God to be a prophet, and therefore in his case God's will was clear. However, the Bible does not tell us that his situation is typical for all believers.

Beyond obedience to God's will in His word, how deliberately should we try to find God's specific will in our lives? When should we step out and make a decision? When should we continue to wait on the Lord? Most Christians find that there are some individual decisions for which it is difficult to discern God's will. Two people in similar circumstances may not receive the same degree of direction. That God is very specific with one person and less so with another does not mean that He is inconsistent. Instead, this is evidence of His grace. Just as children in a family may have differing levels of need for their parents' guidance, so God relates to us as individuals. God desires that we make wise decisions in the light of what He has revealed. He knows us well. If we want to find His will, we need to know Him.

QUESTION 4

According to God's Word, Christians are free to marry any believer they choose (1 Cor 7:39). *True or False?*

QUESTION 5

If a decision we make does not work out in our life, then it is one sure indication that we were out of God's will when we made that decision. *True or False?*

QUESTION 6

Please match the references below with the corresponding teaching.

Reference	*Teaching*
Jeremiah in Jeremiah 1:4-5	God called this man to be a prophet before he was born.
Ezekiel in Ezekiel 24:15-27	The death of this man's wife served as an illustration for his prophecy.
Hosea in Hosea 1:1-8	God called this man to marry a prostitute.
Stephen in Acts 7	This man was martyred after speaking through the Holy Spirit.

QUESTION 7

Think about a time when you had to make a decision, choosing from several options. Remember how you looked at each option and weighed it against the others. Maybe there were two or three choices that would be good. How did you identify the best decision? Write about this decision in your Life Notebook. Would you have done anything differently?

Topic 3: The Role of God's Word

Let's discuss further the question raised at the beginning of Topic 2 as to whether fishing for recreation is an acceptable activity for Christians. One very important question to consider is: "How can we know how much fishing is too much?" One guideline is to recognize when it interferes with something that's more important in our life. For example, something is too much if it means we don't get our tasks done around the house. Or if we don't get to spend enough time with our family. Or most importantly, we shouldn't go if it takes away from my relationship with God or our ability to serve Him. Of course, we may think it would be easier if He just told us at the time whether we could go. Otherwise it may seem difficult to determine whether it's the right thing to do today.

In the Old Testament the Jews had a highly developed set of rules. Under the Law of Moses, the Jews had 613 laws to follow. But when Jesus was asked which law was most important, He summarized the law in two simple statements—to love God wholeheartedly and love your neighbor as yourself (Mt 22:34-40). That's a lot less complex, but it requires some decision-making. He expects believers today to make decisions at the level of an adult son enjoying a relationship with his Father. He has given us room to make good decisions based on His Word.

We've already looked at the importance of God's Word in the Christian's relationship with the Lord. Even some unbelievers look on the Bible as God's comprehensive guide to how a person should live his life before Him. So, when we seek to find God's will, there is no better place to begin than in the Bible.

What role does God's Word have in our daily decision-making? A thorough knowledge of God's Word is vital to making godly decisions. Read "God's Word" to find out what the Word has to say about God's will.

God's Word

Because God speaks through His Word, He wants His people, and particularly leaders, to know His Word thoroughly. For example, after Moses died God prepared Joshua for leadership by giving him the following instructions:

> Make sure you are very strong and brave! Carefully obey all the law my servant Moses charged you to keep! Do not swerve from it to the right or to the left, so that you may be successful in all you do. This law scroll must not leave your lips! You must memorize it day and night so that you can carefully obey all that is written in it. Then you will prosper and be successful. (Josh 1:7-8)

Similarly, the Law of Moses required all the kings of Israel and Judah to make a copy of the Law (Deut 17:18). That was as much of the Scripture as existed at that time. Today this includes all the Scriptures that have been added since that time. Of course, if someone personally made a copy of the entire Law, they could not plead a lack of knowledge of it. If this instruction would have been obeyed, it could have ensured that each king had a thorough knowledge of God's Word. What a difference this would have made in Israel's history! To be spiritually successful during our time, we need this same thorough knowledge of Scripture.

God could have individually guided each king's decision-making without requiring them to study God's Word. However, God expected the kings to have full knowledge of the Scriptures and to base their decisions on that knowledge. In other words, He expected them to show maturity in making wise decisions. When Israel's leaders needed specific guidance, God would still give it through His prophets (Jer 34:6), Urim and Thummim (Ezra 2:63), an angelic messenger (Judg 6:22), or any of the many other methods He used (Heb 1:1). But for most decisions throughout the day the king was expected, just like us, to apply the godly knowledge he had from his study of the Word to make wise decisions.

The Holy Spirit uses God's Word to guide believers. For us to live as the spiritual people we are called to be (1 Cor 2:13), we need to know God's Word. It must become part of the knowledge base from which we can explain spiritual things to spiritual people. We should also use God's Word as the basis for making good decisions. The graphic below shows the steps of decision-making from Hebrews 5:11-14.

As maturing Christians, we are all expected to have enough knowledge of God's Word to be teachers, if necessary (Heb 5:12). We learn by doing, and so the godly decisions we have made in the past help equip us to make godly decisions in the future. Our "perceptions are trained by practice to discern both good and evil" (Heb 5:14). We learn to discern God's will for our lives in future decisions from making good decisions now, as well as having made them in the past.

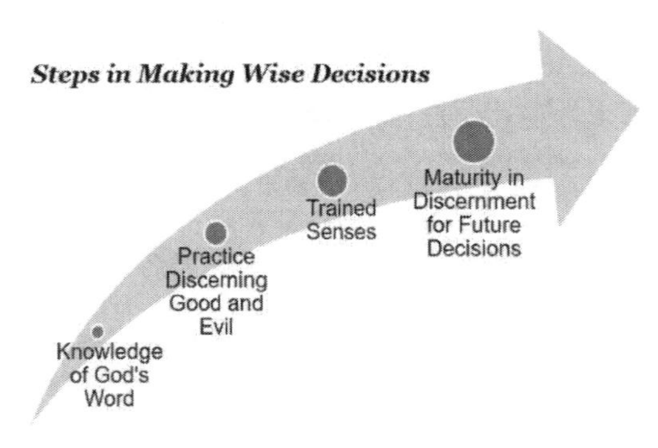

This process of learning to make godly decisions also helps to develop our conscience; in this verse this process is translated "perceptions" (Heb 5:14). We need to be aware that this learning process works in the opposite direction as well. If we ignore God's will or fail to put into practice His Word, we damage our conscience. The Bible describes it as having our consciences seared as with a hot iron (1 Tim 4:2). By making spiritually poor decisions now we hinder ourselves from making wise decisions in the future. Knowing God's Word and letting it affect the decisions we make will help us grow in our ability to recognize God's will.

QUESTION 8

Which of the following instructions about the Law did God give to Joshua when he became the leader of Israel (Josh 1:7-8)? *(Select all that apply.)*

A. Do not swerve from it to the right or the left.

B. Make a copy of it.

C. This law scroll must not leave your lips.

D. You must memorize it day and night.

QUESTION 9

Which of the following instructions did God give to Israel's future kings in the Law of Moses (Deut 17:18)?

A. Do not swerve from it to the right or the left

B. Make a copy of it

C. This law scroll must not leave your lips

D. You must memorize it day and night

QUESTION 10

What did God expect the kings of Israel and Judah to use for the majority of their decision-making?

A. Angelic messages

B. Their study of the Word

C. Prophets

D. Urim and Thummim

QUESTION 11

Please put these steps in making wise decisions based on God's Word (Heb 5:11-14) in the order they develop.

Order	*Step*
Number 1	Knowledge of God's Word
Number 2	Practice discerning good and evil
Number 3	Trained senses
Number 4	Maturity for discernment of future decisions

Topic 4: The Role of Miraculous Intervention

Making good decisions may seem like a lot of work, especially when we remember Bible stories that sound spectacular. We recall the apostle Paul who was struck blind and called to follow Christ (Acts 9:1-19). And Gideon who put out a fleece to see whether it got wet in order to determine God's will (Judg

6:36-40). And Moses who talked with God at the burning bush (Ex 3). Believers understand there have been times when God has led dramatically and miraculously.

However, even in the case of those leaders God did not miraculously lead them for every decision in their lives. The one exception may be Moses. After he was chosen to lead God's people out of Egypt, God clearly led him to accomplish his tasks. There have been others too, like David and Elijah. When God led in this way, it was spectacular. This also tends to happen most at times when God moves His people in a new direction.

Miraculous intervention is the most spectacular way to get guidance from God. This is the method the Jews habitually sought in order to confirm a message from God. The Scripture testifies that "Jews demand miraculous signs and Greeks ask for wisdom" (1 Cor 1:22). There is a place for this miraculous guidance and we'll explore some of the more common times that God led in this way. Please read "Miraculous Interventions" to start exploring those times.

Miraculous Interventions

Gideon's Fleece

One of the most renowned incidents involving miraculous intervention in decision-making is that of Gideon and his use of a fleece (Judg 6:36-40). This is an interesting story in which Gideon asked for the presence or absence of moisture on the fleece compared to the surrounding ground to indicate God's will. However, from this incident Gideon did not really learn anything new about God's will. He should already have known because God had already told him: "You have the strength. Deliver Israel from the power of the Midianites! Have I not sent you?" (Judg 6:14). Each additional step he took to confirm this call served only to erase his doubt about his call and to bolster his faith. God was graciously confirming His will that He had already revealed to Gideon.

The Urim and Thummim

The Urim and Thummim are another curious and unique way God revealed His will (Lev 8:8). In Israel, these stone-like objects were placed in the high priest's breast piece (Ex 28:30). Though not much is known about them, it seems they somehow revealed God's will in some circumstances when Israel was under the Mosaic Law (Num 27:21; 1 Sam 14:41-42; 28:6; Ezra 2:63). The two stones could have indicated a positive or negative response to the question asked or they may have been used to cast as lots.

The most famous incident that describes their use is in 1 Samuel 14:41-42, in which lots are cast. Saul used this method to determine a guilty person. If the result was Urim, he and Jonathan were guilty. If the result was Thummim, the Israelites were to blame. Then to further determine whether it was Jonathan or Saul who was guilty, another lot was cast, and it showed that Jonathan was guilty.

Surprisingly, the replacement for Judas was determined by the casting of lots (Acts 1:12-26). Of course, this was before the coming of the Holy Spirit, and this method of determining God's will is never suggested after Pentecost.

Miraculous Leading in the New Testament

Most of the New Testament examples of miraculous leading are recorded in the book of Acts. Paul's calling as an apostle on the Damascus Road is probably the most dramatic (Acts 9:1-31). But the dramatic nature of it and the fact that it was so out of the ordinary makes it less likely that it is meant as a normative method of finding God's will. No one else was called in quite the same way as Paul, just as no one other than Moses encountered God at a burning bush. Occasionally God intervened and led through a dream or vision as He did with Peter in Acts 10. God, being sovereign, can do what He wants, when He wants, how He wants, and with whom He wants. To insist that He must use—or that He cannot use—miraculous intervention is to place human limitations on the infinite God. His occasional use of the miraculous shows the extent to which He can go to bring someone to Him when He so chooses.

Decision-Making in the New Testament

In contrast to the miraculous, the decision of the Jerusalem Council seems more normative. There the apostles relied on their experience with God's Word to make their decision. Peter noted that in salvation God had made no distinction between the Jews and the Gentiles, He gave grace and the Holy Spirit to both groups (Acts 15:8-11). Then Barnabas and Paul explained all the miraculous deeds God had done among the Gentiles through them (Acts 15:12-14). Next, they turned to the prophetic Word to verify that their work was according to predictive Scripture (Acts 15:15-18). Then out of respect for Moses' followers, they added four rules to guard against unduly offending Jewish sensibilities (Acts 15:19-21). Then they said, "It seemed best to the Holy Spirit and to us not to place any greater burden on you than these necessary rules" (Acts 15:28). As God guided them in the whole process, they also relied on their experience, the Word of God, the Holy Spirit, and godly counsel.

Miraculous Guidance with a New Message

On another occasion God chose to communicate miraculously an important direction to Paul about whether to go to Macedonia or the province of Asia (Acts 16:7, 9):

> When they came to Mysia, they attempted to go into Bithynia, but the Spirit of Jesus did not allow them to… A vision appeared to Paul during the night: a Macedonian man was standing there urging him, "Come over to Macedonia and help us!"

Keep in mind that Paul was an apostle on an important pioneering mission. Also notice that God sovereignly controlled the method. Paul had not sought miraculous guidance; God chose to intervene in that way.

God often used the miraculous to announce a new message at the beginning of a new frontier in the advance of the gospel: "While God confirmed their witness with signs and wonders and various miracles and gifts of the Holy Spirit distributed according to his will" (Heb 2:4). God may well use the miraculous to bring someone to Christ or to lead a believer in a certain direction. However, when God has made a clear statement, it is unbelief to keep asking for signs (Lk 11:29). God's power is no less evident in His Word than it is in His miraculous acts. If we are enjoying a growing and intimate relationship with the Lord, we will not insist that the method He uses meet our expectations. Rather, we will be ready to listen, familiar with His Word, however He chooses to lead. God has demonstrated His ability to use the miraculous. Whether He chooses to do so with us is not important; knowing Him with increasing intimacy is.

QUESTION 12

Gideon's use of the fleece was primarily a way of discovering a new revelation of God's will. *True or False?*

QUESTION 13

In 1 Samuel 14:41-42 who was determined to be guilty through the use of Urim and Thummim?

A. Jonathan

B. Saul

C. Israel

D. Samuel

QUESTION 14

Please match the references below from the Jerusalem Council with the corresponding discussion or conclusion (Acts 15).

Reference	*Teaching*
Acts 15:8-11	They gave four rules to guard against unduly offending Jewish sensibilities.
Acts 15:12-14	In salvation God had made no distinction between the Jews and the Gentiles.
Acts 15:15-18	They verified that their work was according to predictive Scripture.
Acts 15:19-21	The apostles and the Holy Spirit determined not to burden their audience with additional rules.
Acts 15:28	Barnabas and Paul explained all the miraculous deeds God had done among the Gentiles.

QUESTION 15

Consider some of the reasons that God might choose to use—or not use—miraculous intervention. Open your Life Notebook and reflect on those factors. If you have experienced God's miraculous intervention, describe how it impacted you and others.

Topic 5: The Role of Godly Counsel

When you need advice, who do you ask? Perhaps friends, family, or neighbors? Christians? Non-Christians? The kinds of people from whom we seek advice may influence the responses we get.

Where Christian values come into play, it's best for a Christian to get advice from another Christian. The most important thing in the life of believers should be their relationship with the Lord. Other Christians, because they share that value, will look at some things differently than non-Christians. That's why it's important to seek the advice of another Christian who understands that we want to please the Lord.

Seeking advice is a natural way to handle a problem when it arises. What does the Bible say about receiving advice?

> When there is no guidance a nation falls, but there is success in the abundance of counselors. (Prov 11:14)

Plans fail when there is no counsel, but with abundant advisers they are established. (Prov 15:22)

For with guidance you wage your war, and with numerous advisers there is victory. (Prov 24:6)

These proverbs show the importance of seeking counsel for important decisions. Few presidents and kings, even worldly ones, try to run their countries by themselves. They have ministers that specialize in education, health, security, finance, and other important areas of expertise. They do not have to accept all the ideas that are suggested, but they do have opportunity to hear them and share their ideas with others.

Through studying other aspects of God's will, we have already touched on the key role godly counsel plays. Psalm 1:1 says, "How happy is the one who does not follow the advice of the wicked, or stand in the pathway with sinners, or sit in the assembly of arrogant fools!" We as Christians want to befriend unbelievers without adopting their lifestyle or following their ungodly counsel. We want to influence them without being negatively influenced by them. Please read "Godly Counsel" before continuing with the questions.

Godly Counsel

Words Well Spoken

"Like apples of gold in settings of silver, is a word fitly spoken" (Prov 25:11). Our words are powerful. Have you ever been in a situation where you've felt bad and someone said the perfect word to lift you up? Do you remember how good it felt? The same thing can happen during a time of controversy. Sometimes someone says the perfect word to settle the conflict. That is what this verse is talking about—using the tongue in a positive way to accomplish good.

Jesus was a master at using His words to accomplish good. His counsel was always valuable, and He knew how to use His words in a way that silenced many of His opponents. He refused to give into conflict. In Mark 12, the Pharisees asked Jesus if they should pay taxes to Caesar. He responded by asking whose image was on the coin. They said that Caesar was pictured on it. Jesus simply answered, "Give to Caesar the things that are Caesar's." The Pharisees did not reply because were too amazed to speak (Mk 12:17).

Believers today can also encourage each other with kind words as a way to counsel them in a decision. Paul mentions the importance of encouraging each other several times throughout his letters to different churches. When one of our fellow believers is feeling bad, an encouraging word builds them back up (1 Thess 5:11). Words of encouragement can also prevent a believer from being hardened by sin (Heb 3:13). Using our words for the glory of God is important; James wrote that our speech controls the direction that a person goes, comparing it to a horse's bit or ship's rudder (Jas 3:3-6).

The Downfall of Kings

Sometimes the tongue's ability to do damage is cloaked as advice. Ungodly, inexperienced counsel can contribute to the downfall of kings. Rehoboam's example illustrates this principle. When he became king over Israel and Judah, before the countries separated, he heard godly counsel from his elders on how to respond to the concerns of his people (1 Kgs 12:6-8). Yet he rejected that advice in favor of the ungodly advice from the young advisors he had grown up with (1 Kgs 12:9-11). When Israel heard his decision, they left Judah and formed the separate kingdom of Israel (1 Kgs 12:16). As a result, Rehoboam permanently lost his rule over ten of the twelve tribes of Israel. Rejecting godly advice in order to follow the advice of his companions cost him severely.

In a later incident good King Jehoshaphat of Judah foolishly formed an alliance with wicked King Ahab of Israel. But before joining him in war against the Syrians he wisely asked for counsel from a prophet of the Lord (1 Kgs 22:4-5). Unfortunately, Jehosaphat did not follow the advice and he still went with Ahab to attack Ramoth Gilead (1 Kgs 22:29-40). He survived the battle because of his God-fearing reign (2 Chron 20:32). However, he put himself in grave danger by joining with Ahab, one of Israel's most ungodly kings.

Joash is an example of a king who prospered early in his reign because he had the right godly counselor. "Joash was seven years old when he began to reign. He reigned for forty years in Jerusalem… Joash did what the Lord approved, throughout the lifetime of Jehoiada the priest" (2 Chron 24:1-2).

> After Jehoiada died, the officials of Judah visited the king and declared their loyalty to him. The king listened to their advice. They abandoned the temple of the Lord God of their ancestors and worshiped the Asherah poles and idols. Because of this sinful activity, God was angry with Judah and Jerusalem. (2 Chron 24:17-18)

These new advisors gave Joash ungodly advice, which he followed with tragic results. God became his enemy, sending the Syrian army against him and ultimately taking his life (2 Chron 24:25-26).

The Salvation of People

In the book of Esther, Mordecai is an example of a good counselor who did good for his people and his niece, Queen Esther. He was her advisor on how to advance the cause of her people. When the Jews in Babylon were targeted for extinction, Mordecai told her, "Don't imagine that because you are part of the king's household you will be the one Jew who will escape. If you keep quiet at this time, liberation and protection for the Jews will appear from another source, while you and your father's household perish. It may very well be that you have achieved royal status for such a time as this!" (Est 4:14). Esther took Mordecai's godly counsel to heart, and as a result, God used her to accomplish salvation for the Jews (Est 4:15-17).

As we saw in an earlier topic, the Jerusalem Council received godly counsel from several apostles and church leaders that led to their wise decision about whether salvation required keeping the Jewish Law (Acts 15:1-35). The godly counsel they received and followed protected the simple clarity of the gospel that separated the practices of Judaism from the way of salvation. This allowed Jews and Gentiles to be saved in the same way, making no distinction (Acts 15:9-11).

God has given Christians the privilege and responsibility of helping one another with our words. Because our desire is to please the Lord, the advice we give must be consistent with God's Word. For the same reason, when we receive advice, it must be measured with God's Word and God's character. Counsel that does not reflect His Word and His character is not godly counsel.

QUESTION 16

Which of the following kings lost his rule over ten of the tribes of Israel because he listened to the ungodly counsel of young advisors?

A. Ahab

B. Jehoshaphat

C. Joash

D. Rehoboam

QUESTION 17

Queen Esther had a godly adviser in Mordecai, who encouraged her to allow God to save her people through her. *True or False?*

QUESTION 18

Open your Life Notebook and describe a time when you sought counsel from somebody else. How could you tell if the counsel you got was godly or not?

Topic 6: Hindrances to Guidance

What kind of rules do you have to follow in your church? You may be asked this question by non-believers, or even by people who attend another church. Sometimes this question is motivated by the perception that Christianity seems to be a negative religion because Christians have a list of things they cannot do.

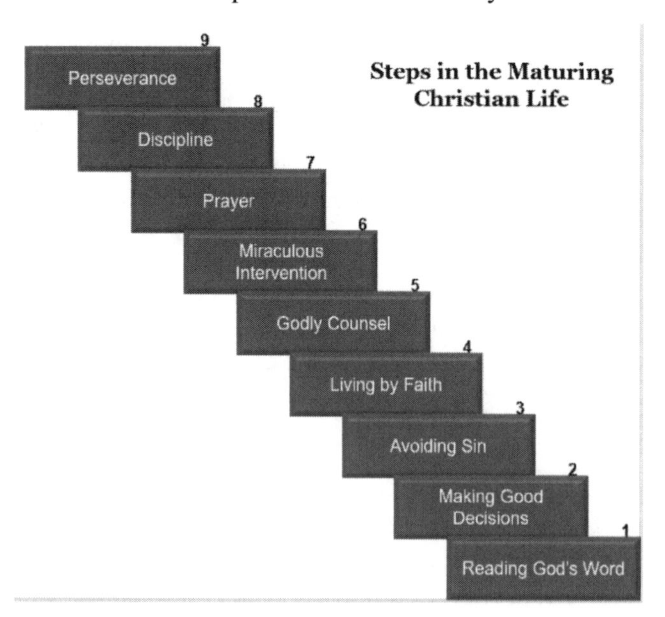

When answering this question, it is important to keep in mind that Christianity is a relationship with the Lord rather than a list of rules. In spite of this, there are Christians whose approach to spirituality involves following many rules. In their defense, they try to avoid offending God by sinning. Avoiding sin is important because God is holy, and sin gets in the way of the relationship.

Just as one takes positive steps to enhance his chances of making wise decisions, also one may make unwise choices that can hurt him. We have seen many things we can do to make wise decisions, and it is now time to look at some dangers in decision-making.

As we have seen, the Bible presents the maturing Christian life as a process that takes time. It is a lot of small steps faithfully taken daily, as illustrated in the graphic above. These small steps, not listed in any particular order, involve being in the Word, in prayer, and making good decisions. Occasionally we may take a fairly large step when we learn to step out in faith.

Before continuing with the questions below, read "Hindrances."

Hindrances

The Path to Destruction

The things that interfere with a relationship with God and hinder growth in the Christian life can also block God's guidance to us. That principle may not seem either fearsome or important, but it is. The life of King Saul gives us a sobering example of a man who both drifted from God and ceased to hear from Him. Saul started well in walking with the Lord. But he drifted farther away from the Lord as he continued in his reign. Eventually the Lord refused to answer him to give him guidance (1 Sam 28:4-6). He became so desperate for God's Word that he sought it through a medium commonly known as the witch of Endor (2 Sam 28:7). His seeking guidance from an ungodly source led to his destruction (1 Sam 28:18-19).

Hindrances to Knowing God's Will

As Christians, we want to continue to grow in our relationship with the Lord. We need to avoid the kinds of things that will interrupt our growth and distance us from the Lord. Because growth in the Christian life happens in a series of small steps, perseverance is important. That is one of the things the readers of the epistle to the Hebrews were missing. They had not practiced making wise decisions; therefore, their perceptions were not "trained by practice for discerning both good and evil" (Heb 5:14). In Hebrews 12 the author gave them practical advice that would help them avoid things that would hinder both their growth and their ability to perceive God's will. Consider how this advice would impact your relationship with Christ and your recognition of His will.

- To rid themselves of sin and endure through the race (Heb 12:1).
- To keep their eyes fixed on Jesus, who disregarded the shame of the cross (Heb 12:2).
- To endure like Jesus, to not grow weary in their souls and give up (Heb 12:3).
- To remember that they had not resisted to the point of bloodshed in their struggle against sin (Heb 12:4).
- Not to scorn the Lord's discipline or give up when He corrects them as His sons (Heb 12:5-10).
- To accept the Lord's discipline, knowing that later it produces peace and righteousness (Heb 12:11-13).
- To pursue peace and holiness and not become immoral or godless (Heb 12:14-24).
- To be careful not to refuse the Lord (Heb 12:25-29).

The Bottom Line

The bottom line in following God's will is to know that finding it is primarily a result of an increasingly intimate relationship with the Lord. As we have seen, the Christian life is simple; but simple does not necessarily mean easy. There is no shortcut to a mature relationship with God. Neither is there a shortcut to knowing God's will for our lives. But there is a great reward for having this type of relationship with Him.

The movie "Chariots of Fire" is the true story of the Olympic runner, Eric Liddell. In a scene in the movie, Eric explains his decision to delay going to the mission field. He said, "I believe God made me for a purpose, but He also made me fast. And when I run, I feel His pleasure." Finding out what pleases God enables us to feel His pleasure as we do His will.

Paul is an example of a Christian who had reached the point in His relationship with Christ where he could feel God's pleasure. Remarkably he was at this point despite the fact that his personal circumstances were dire. In prison and anticipating the possibility of his death, he described what it was like to the Christians at Philippi. He said:

> But even if I am being poured out like a drink-offering on the sacrifice and service of your faith, I have joy and rejoice together with you. And in the same way, you also should be glad and rejoice together with me. (Phil 2:17-18)

To feel God's pleasure is a great thing. We get to experience the kind of relationship with the Lord in which we can know what He wants.

QUESTION 19

Please match the following references with the corresponding teachings.

Reference	*Teaching*
Hebrews 12:1	Accept and endure the Lord's discipline.
Hebrews 12:2	Get rid of every sin and run with endurance the race set out for us.
Hebrews 12:3	Do not grow weary and give up but endure like Jesus.
Hebrews 12:4	Keep your eyes focused on Jesus who disregarded the shame of the cross.
Hebrews 12:5-10	Pursue peace and holiness and do not become immoral or godless.
Hebrews 12:14-24	Take care not to refuse the Lord.
Hebrews 12:25-29	Remember that some had not yet shed blood in resisting sin.

QUESTION 20

Please look through the teachings from Hebrews 12 from the previous question and choose the three that you feel most apply to you. Then write out how you can apply these teachings to your life in order to demonstrate progress in your relationship with the Lord.

QUESTION 21

From the graphic *Steps in the Maturing Christian Life* please list as many of the small steps as you can that Christians can take.

QUESTION 22

The key to understanding God's will for our lives is primarily a result of an increasingly intimate __________ with the Lord.

Lesson 9 Self Check: The Christian Life

QUESTION 1

In Romans 12:2 Paul invited us to test God's will to see that it is good. *True or False?*

QUESTION 2

In Acts 16:6-10, God prevented Paul from going into Macedonia and instead directed him to go into the province of Asia. *True or False?*

QUESTION 3

When decisions we make work out well in our lives, that is a sure sign that we made the decision according to God's will. *True or False?*

QUESTION 4

Whose wife's death was used to illustrate his prophecy?

A. Hosea
B. Ezekiel
C. Jeremiah
D. Stephen

QUESTION 5

Which of the following instructions did God give to the kings of Israel in the Mosaic Law?

A. Do not swerve from it to the right or the left
B. Make a copy of it
C. This law must not leave your lips
D. You must memorize it day and night

QUESTION 6

Which of the following determined that Saul's son Jonathan was guilty of the offense recorded in 1 Samuel 14:41-42?

A. Through an angelic messenger
B. Through observation
C. Through prophecy
D. Through Urim and Thummim

QUESTION 7

According to Hebrews 2:4, how did God confirm the new message of the apostles in the early days of the church?

A. By casting lots
B. Through an angelic messenger
C. Through prophecy
D. Through signs and wonders

QUESTION 8

Which part of the body is compared to a ship's rudder and a horse's bit in James 3:1-12?

A. The tongue

B. The eye

C. The ear

D. The hand

QUESTION 9

Who was Queen Esther's godly counselor in the book of Esther?

A. Haman

B. King Ahasuerus

C. Mehuman

D. Mordecai

QUESTION 10

The key to understanding God's will for our lives is primarily a result of an increasingly intimate relationship with the Lord. *True or False?*

Unit 3 Exam: The Christian Life

QUESTION 1

Someone who sings a new song in Scripture has personally experienced the event described by the song. *True or False?*

QUESTION 2

David humbly accepted Michal's criticism for dancing before the Lord in 1 Samuel 6:12-23. *True or False?*

QUESTION 3

Who does Paul say deserted him because he loved this present age (2 Tim 4:10)?

A. Timothy

B. Mark

C. Epaphrus

D. Demas

QUESTION 4

Believers who no longer meet together tend to fall away from their confession (Heb 10:25). *True or False?*

QUESTION 5

Which of the following did Jesus say was the disciples' error when they failed to cast out the demon in the boy in Mark 9:14-29?

A. They lacked authority.

B. Jesus said that He must be present with them.

C. They were not praying.

D. They were not abiding.

QUESTION 6

According to 1 Corinthians 4:2, what is the character requirement for a Christian steward?

A. Alert

B. Faithful

C. Industrious

D. Ready

QUESTION 7

Which of the following verses would be best to use to urge a fellow believer to give his life to God as a proper response to Christ's redemptive work on his behalf?

A. Isaiah 55:8-9

B. Romans 12:1-2

C. 1 Corinthians 4:12

D. Philippians 4:12-13

QUESTION 8

We will have reason to boast only after we have done everything God has asked of us. *True or False?*

QUESTION 9

Christians belong to God both because God is their creator and because Christ is their Savior. *True or False?*

QUESTION 10

In the parable of the talents (Mt 25:14-30) Jesus praised the slave who kept his talents safe, returning the same amount to his master. *True or False?*

QUESTION 11

The illustration in Hebrews 3:1-3 teaches that Moses is the house and that Christ is builder of the house. *True or False?*

QUESTION 12

One thing Jesus told believers to do while they wait for His return is to stay alert. *True or False?*

QUESTION 13

Hebrews 5:11-14 talks of immaturity that comes from which of the following?

A. They did not practice doing good.

B. They were carnal.

C. They were new Christians.

D. They were young of age.

QUESTION 14

In 1 Timothy 6:8 Paul taught that Christians should be satisfied with food and __________.

A. Clothes

B. Drink

C. Love

D. Shelter

QUESTION 15

On the subject of giving, the Bible warns believers against giving beyond their means. *True or False?*

QUESTION 16

All Christians will appear for judgment at the Great White Throne (Rev 20:11-15). *True or False?*

QUESTION 17

When God evaluated the reigns of the kings of Judah, with whose reign were they usually compared?

A. Ahab

B. David

C. Jeroboam

D. Rehoboam

QUESTION 18

Why did Gideon lay out his fleece in Judges 6?

A. To defy God's will

B. To discover God's will

C. To confirm God's will

D. To approve God's will

QUESTION 19

In Acts 16:6-10 God prevented Paul from going into Macedonia and instead directed him to go into the province of Asia. *True or False?*

QUESTION 20

When decisions we make work out well in our lives, it is a sure sign we made the decision according to God's will. *True or False?*

QUESTION 21

Which of the following men did God call before he was born?

A. Ezekiel

B. Hosea

C. Jeremiah

D. Stephen

QUESTION 22

In 1 Samuel 14:41-42 who was determined to be guilty through the use of Urim and Thummim?

A. Israel

B. Jonathan

C. Samuel

D. Saul

QUESTION 23

Which of the following instructions did God give to the kings of Israel in the Mosaic Law?

A. Do not swerve from it to the right or the left.

B. Make a copy of it.

C. This law scroll must not leave your lips.

D. You must memorize it day and night.

QUESTION 24

Which of the following kings lost his rule over ten of the tribes of Israel because he listened to the ungodly counsel of the young advisors he had grown up with?

A. Ahab

B. Jehoshaphat

C. Joash

D. Rehoboam

QUESTION 25

The key to understanding God's will for our lives is primarily a result of an increasingly intimate relationship with the Lord. *True or False?*

Lesson 9 Answers to Questions

QUESTION 1

Reference	*Teaching*
Judges 6:36-40	Gideon laid a fleece out overnight to corroborate God's will.
Ezra 1:1-2	God stirred the mind of Cyrus to build a temple for Him in Jerusalem.
Acts 16:6-10	God prevented Paul from speaking the message in the province of Asia.
1 Thessalonians 4:3	God's will is that we become holy and avoid immorality.

QUESTION 2

C. His will for our lives

QUESTION 3: *Your answer*

QUESTION 4: True

QUESTION 5: False

QUESTION 6

Reference	*Teaching*
Jeremiah in Jeremiah 1:4-5	God called this man to be a prophet before he was born.
Ezekiel in Ezekiel 24:15-27	The death of this man's wife served as an illustration for his prophecy.
Hosea in Hosea 1:1-8	God called this man to marry a prostitute.
Stephen in Acts 7	This man was martyred after speaking through the Holy Spirit.

QUESTION 7: *Your answer*

QUESTION 8

A. Do not swerve from it to the right or the left.

C. This law scroll must not leave your lips.

D. You must memorize it day and night.

QUESTION 9

B. Make a copy of it [If this instruction had been obeyed, it would have ensured that each king had knowledge of God's Word.]

QUESTION 10

B. Their study of the Word

QUESTION 11

Order	*Step*
Number_1	Knowledge of God's Word
Number_2	Practice discerning good and evil
Number_3	Trained senses
Number_4	Maturity for discernment of future decisions

QUESTION 12: False [Each additional step he took to confirm this call helped erase his doubt about his call and to bolster his faith.]

QUESTION 13

A. Jonathan

QUESTION 14

Reference	*Teaching*
Acts 15:8-11	In salvation God had made no distinction between the Jews and the Gentiles.
Acts 15:12-14	Barnabas and Paul explained all the miraculous deeds God had done among the Gentiles.
Acts 15:15-18	They verified that their work was according to predictive Scripture.
Acts 15:19-21	They gave four rules to guard against unduly offending Jewish sensibilities.
Acts 15:28	The apostles and the Holy Spirit determined not to burden their audience with additional rules.

QUESTION 15: *Your answer*

QUESTION 16

D. Rehoboam

QUESTION 17: True

QUESTION 18: *Your answer*

QUESTION 19

Reference	*Teaching*
Hebrews 12:1	Get rid of every sin and run with endurance the race set out for us.
Hebrews 12:2	Keep your eyes focused on Jesus who disregarded the shame of the cross.
Hebrews 12:3	Do not grow weary and give up but endure like Jesus.
Hebrews 12:4	Remember that some had not yet shed blood in resisting sin.
Hebrews 12:5-10	Accept and endure the Lord's discipline.
Hebrews 12:14-24	Pursue peace and holiness and do not become immoral or godless.
Hebrews 12:25-29	Take care not to refuse the Lord.

QUESTION 20: *Your answer*

QUESTION 21: *Your answer should be similar to the following:*

Those listed in the graphic are: Reading God's Word, making good decisions, avoiding sin, living by faith, godly counsel, miraculous intervention, prayer, discipline, and perseverance.

QUESTION 22: Relationship [There is no shortcut to a mature relationship with God; neither is there a shortcut to knowing God's will for our lives. But there is a great reward for having this type of relationship with Him.]

Lesson 9 Self Check Answers

QUESTION 1: True
QUESTION 2: False
QUESTION 3: False
QUESTION 4

B. Ezekiel

QUESTION 5

B. Make a copy of it

QUESTION 6

D. Through Urim and Thummim

QUESTION 7

D. Through signs and wonders

QUESTION 8

A. The tongue

QUESTION 9

D. Mordecai

QUESTION 10: True

Unit 3 Exam Answers

QUESTION 1: True
QUESTION 2: False
QUESTION 3
   D. Demas
QUESTION 4: True
QUESTION 5
   C. They were not praying.
QUESTION 6
   B. Faithful
QUESTION 7
   B. Romans 12:1-2
QUESTION 8: False
QUESTION 9: True
QUESTION 10: False
QUESTION 11: True
QUESTION 12: True
QUESTION 13
   A. They did not practice doing good.
QUESTION 14
   D. Shelter
QUESTION 15: False
QUESTION 16: False
QUESTION 17
   B. David
QUESTION 18
   C. To confirm God's will
QUESTION 19: False
QUESTION 20: False
QUESTION 21
   C. Jeremiah
QUESTION 22
   B. Jonathan
QUESTION 23
   B. Make a copy of it.
QUESTION 24
   D. Rehoboam
QUESTION 25: True

Unit 4: Faithfulness—Trusting God in Life's Challenges

Unit Introduction

It's been said that if it wasn't for the resurrection of Jesus, life wouldn't be worth living. Would you agree?

Paul says in 1 Corinthians 15:19 "For if only in this life we have hope in Christ, we should be pitied more than anyone." Christ alone gives us hope through the power of His resurrection. Jesus said "in me you may have peace. In the world you have trouble and suffering but take courage—I have conquered the world." (Jn 16:33). No matter what circumstances we find ourselves in, or what difficulties life throws our way, our hope should reside in Christ, and in Him alone.

The Christian life is a dangerous journey. Many Christians throughout history and in many parts of the world have been martyred for their faith. Some of us are sheltered from this reality, but most are aware that thousands of Christians lose their lives every year simply because they are Christians who seek to be loyal to Christ. Other believers when faced with persecution are reluctant to let their faith in Christ be known. That is why the Bible continually exhorts us to remain faithful until the end. Paul rejoiced at the end of his life saying, "I have competed well; I have finished the race; I have kept the faith!" (2 Tim 4:7).

The lessons in this unit will deal with the challenges of living the Christian life as an alien in a non-Christian world. At the end of our lives we want to echo Paul's testimony and say, "we have kept the faith." Lesson 10 examines the reality of suffering in the Christian's life. We are not guaranteed a life free from suffering. We will look at what the Bible says, and even though we may not see the reason God allows pain in our lives, we will try to make sense of suffering. Lesson 11 looks at how believers must live their lives as aliens in this world to deal successfully with temptation. We no longer belong to the world, which is one of our three enemies. We will explore what God's Word says about how to overcome temptation. Lesson 12 examines how to live the victorious Christian life in the midst of the spiritual battle. We will look at the sacrifices it takes to achieve victory and the rewards that are promised to the overcomer.

Unit Outline

Lesson 10: Trusting God when Life Hurts—Making Sense of Suffering

Nobody likes suffering, but it is an inescapable reality in our earthly lives. God has not guaranteed that Christians will be free from suffering in this life. He has promised to "wipe away the tears from every face," but that promise will not be ultimately fulfilled until "he will swallow up death permanently" (Isa 25:8). Until then, He will continue to wipe our tears as we continue to experience pain. In fact, God's Word tells us to expect persecution because of our faith. Jesus told His disciples, "If they persecuted me, they will also persecute you" (Jn 15:20). We follow a grand tradition. Jesus also pointed out to the Pharisees in Matthew 23:34-36 that His followers would be persecuted:

> I am sending you prophets and wise men and experts in the law, some of whom you will kill and crucify, and some you will flog in your synagogues and pursue from town to town, so that on you will come all the righteous blood shed on earth, from the blood of righteous Abel to the blood of Zechariah son of Barachiah, whom you murdered between the temple and the altar. I tell you the truth, this generation will be held responsible for all these things.

Suffering is not wasted. This lesson focuses on God's ability to use suffering in the lives of His people regardless of what caused that suffering. Topic 1 explores some of the causes of suffering that are similar to the ones that cause sin: the world, the flesh, and the devil. Topic 2 looks at some of the dangers to the Christian from suffering. Two of these dangers are the possibility of shrinking away from Christ and of returning to the world. Topic 3 looks at how God uses suffering in the Christian's life; through it the Christian is trained, he is made like his Savior, and he receives many benefits. Topic 4 addresses the opportunity to minister to those who are suffering. We look at how God Himself chose not to avoid personal suffering. Instead, He became flesh and opened Himself up to suffering. We also see how suffering leads to comfort, especially in the arms of God. Topic 5 explores the importance of being prepared for suffering. We will look at an example from Scripture of one who suffered intensely and see some of the things that prepared Him to endure successfully the experience of suffering.

Lesson Outline

Topic 1: The Causes of Suffering

Topic 2: The Dangers of Suffering

Topic 3: How God Uses Suffering

Topic 4: Ministering to the Suffering

Topic 5: Preparing for Suffering

Topic 1: The Causes of Suffering

Other people often look down on Christians or treat them unfairly. Even in stories if there is a Christian character, that person sometimes is pictured as a fool or a hypocrite or a source of problems. It doesn't seem fair.

A Christian's values are often in conflict with those of the world in which he lives, so living as a Christian can have its challenges. Of course, it helps when we remember that Jesus was persecuted for His behavior. Even His own family thought He was out of His mind. Jesus taught His followers to expect to suffer persecution just like He did. So if we want a relationship with Christ, we're not exempt from suffering persecution. Interestingly the apostle Paul saw the persecutions he had suffered as badges of honor and proofs of his apostleship. Of course, that doesn't make it any easier to accept the world's characterization of Christians. Apparently they don't like it that we're no longer part of their world.

Christians are sometimes subjected to ridicule and suffering from people in the world. We know that Christians can expect to suffer. Suffering is not a surprise to us because Christ Himself predicted we would suffer for His sake (Jn 15:20). The world hates us because it hated Him first, and as His followers we belong to Him and not to the world (Jn 15:18-19).

Read:"Three Aspects of Suffering." This article will help you to understand some of the reasons Christians suffer.

Three Aspects of Suffering

1. We Do Not Belong to the World

The primary reason the world hates Christians is that they no longer belong to it (Jn 15:19). When you became a Christian, your allegiance shifted from the world and its values to Christ. Of course, the leader of this world, Satan, is the king of hatred and rebellion toward anything of God (Jn 12:31; Eph 2:2). Because the Christian belongs to the Lord and not to the world, that antagonism to anything of God is aimed at the Christian as well. Unredeemed people, often without thinking about what they are doing, naturally follow the course of this age (1 Cor 2:6). They expect that everyone else will adopt and live by the same beliefs and goals they have. Since Christians do not conform to that expectation, they become targets.

2. Satan

The root of the persecution of Christians lies in Satan's hatred of God. When humanity rebelled against God, they followed the desires of their flesh, which were evil (Eph 2:2-3). The problem for Satan is that he cannot directly attack God and succeed. Instead he must watch for vulnerability in those who represent Him. For example, when Jesus walked the earth in a body of flesh, Satan tempted Him (Mt 4:1-11). When Jesus did not fall to his temptations, Satan turned to those closest to Jesus. One example of this shift in Satan's target is when Peter attempted to turn Jesus away from the cross (Mt 16:21-23). Now, Satan turns his attention to Christians in general, especially the ones "who want to live godly lives in Christ Jesus" (2 Tim 3:12).

In Revelation 12:1-6, which describes the vision of the woman, the Child, and the dragon, we see how Satan attacks God indirectly through areas of vulnerability in God's people. While the vision is highly symbolic, John's readers would probably have been able to identify the characters. The main characters in this vision can be identified as follows:

- The woman represents God's people Israel.
- The dragon represents Satan.
- The stars that are swept away are probably angels who followed Satan in his rebellion.
- The child is Jesus.

In this illustration Satan starts out persecuting Israel. Through the Israelites other nations had learned about God since the time He brought Israel out of Egypt (Ezk 20:9; 39:7). That message could be compromised if Israel's leaders were unfaithful. Therefore, Satan attacked their leaders with whatever accusations he could make (e.g., Zech 3:1-5).

Then, after Israel gave birth to the Christ child, Satan immediately persecuted Him and attempted to destroy Him. One example of this was the attempted murder of the Christ child along with the actual murder of all the children under age two in the area of Bethlehem (Mt 2:1-18). However, after Christ finished His work on the cross, "her child was suddenly caught up to God and to his throne" (Rev 12:5). Since Christ was now beyond Satan's reach, Satan once again turned to indirect attacks by targeting God's people. In the vision the woman, representing God's people Israel, flees into the wilderness to escape the intensified persecution that will come during the tribulation (Rev 12:6, 12). While Satan's eventual defeat is assured, he continues to target those who are faithful to the Lord (Rev 12:17).

As we have seen, Satan is always opposing God by attacking those who are faithful to the Lord. Since at the present time, both God the Father and Jesus are beyond Satan's direct reach, Satan again turns his attention to God's representatives on earth, the church (2 Cor 5:20). Along with the church, the Jews are also targeted as a former and future representative of God (Rom 9–11).

3. Our Own Sin

Suffering can also be caused by our own sinful flesh and consequent unrighteousness in this world (1 Pet 3:17). This is a completely different kind of suffering than the honorable suffering we do for being godly. Peter wrote that how it is better to "suffer for doing good, if God wills it, than for doing evil." Though the world may persecute us just for being Christians, the world authorities, in general, do not persecute lawful citizens (Rom 13:1-7). Most of the time, though there are exceptions, world governments tend to support those who pursue peace and righteousness. Christians who choose to do wrong invite their own unnecessary suffering. If Christians suffer, it should NOT be for doing evil. If we suffer for doing wrong, then our suffering is the deserved consequence of our own decisions and actions.

QUESTION 1

The world hates Christians because they no longer belong to it. *True or False?*

QUESTION 2

When in the Bible did Satan tempt the Son of God?

A. Before the creation of the world

B. When Satan first rebelled against God

C. When Jesus came into the world in the flesh

D. After Jesus was resurrected and ascended to the Father

QUESTION 3

According to the vision in Revelation 12, who will flee into the wilderness to escape Satan's persecution?

A. Israel during Jesus' ministry on earth
B. Israel during the tribulation
C. People without the sign of the beast
D. The church

QUESTION 4

According to 1 Peter 3:17, it is better to suffer for doing wrong than to suffer for doing good. *True or False?*

Topic 2: The Dangers of Suffering

Why would people want to follow Christ when they know it will make them stand out as different in the world's eyes? And why would anyone willingly suffer? Naturally we want to avoid suffering at almost any cost.

It's true that it can be extremely painful to suffer as a Christian. Christian beliefs may cost us our friendship with some people. As soon as they find out we are Christians, they may want nothing to do with us. Others with whom we think we could have a good relationship obviously keep us at a distance. At work, the boss may warn us in a threatening manner not to share our faith and not to try to convert anyone. But our relationship with Christ is too important to set aside. What kind of Christians would we be if we denied knowing the One who willingly gave His life for us? The suffering Christ faced didn't keep Him from giving Himself on the cross so that we could have a relationship with Him. We shouldn't want to let the suffering that we may experience get in the way of that relationship either.

Suffering can lead to many good things in the Christian life including endurance, hope, and mutual comfort (e.g., Rom 5:3-4; 2 Cor 1:6). But in spite of those benefits, suffering can also be dangerous for the Christian (e.g., Heb 10:32-39). If persecuting Christians and making them suffer was never an effective tactic, then their enemies would try a different strategy. But because suffering is unpleasant, it sometimes accomplishes the purpose of the enemies who inflict it. The intention of our enemies is to impede Christians from living a godly life and being an effective witness for Christ. However, God wastes nothing, and even intense suffering, if we properly responded to it, can make us a stronger and more effective for Christ. Notice the apostles in Acts 5:40-42 before the Jewish council:

> [40] and they summoned the apostles and had them beaten. Then they ordered them not to speak in the name of Jesus and released them. [41] So they left the council rejoicing because they had been considered worthy to suffer dishonor for the sake of the name. [42] And every day both in the temple courts and from house to house, they did not stop teaching and proclaiming the good news that Jesus was the Christ.

Though suffering can produce good things in the Christian life, it is also a dangerous path for the Christian to navigate. In the previous topic we saw that godly Christians can expect to suffer. Read "Dangers in Suffering to learn more about the dangers Christians face.

Dangers in Suffering

Return to the World

When suffering comes to a Christian, whatever the cause, it carries with it the temptation to turn back to the world in rebellion against God and to turn away from an intimate relationship with the Lord. If the suffering is in the form of an attack, its goal is to interrupt the Christian's godly behavior and witness of Christ. This is the world's way of wooing the Christian, who once belonged to it, back into the world again (Jn 17:9, 14-15). Faithful Christians must continue to willingly desert worldly pleasures, choosing instead to follow the Lord and to continue growing in Him (2 Pet 2:18). Those worldly pleasures, while fleeting, are a real attraction to their flesh.

Practicing faithfulness can make the battle easier. By faithfully following God's will we may find our desire for former pleasures reduced. Instead of returning to a pattern of sin, we find ourselves in effect blazing a new path through the wilderness in our walk with the Lord (see Heb 5:11-14). Once we do that, the journey the next time becomes easier.

The New Testament provides examples of Christians who returned to the world (the present age) because of the pleasures they found in it. One clear example is in 2 Timothy 4:10 where Paul says, "For Demas deserted me, since he loved the present age, and he went to Thessalonica." Now Paul had previously called Demas his "colaborer" when he wrote to Philemon and also sent greetings from him to the Colossians (Phm 24; Col 4:14). So, at one time he was well thought of for his Christian work. He was not the only one who pulled back from a strong witness during persecution, Paul mentioned that almost everyone deserted him in his imprisonment. He said, "Only Luke is with me" (2 Tim 4:11).

This possibility of pulling back from a strong testimony also existed in the Old Testament. For example, Jezebel's persecution drove a hundred prophets of the Lord to hide in a cave (1 Kgs 18:4). We can see how persecution and threats can affect God's people and cause them to shrink away from their testimony (Heb 10:38).

Shrinking Away from Christ

Not only our testimony is affected. Suffering can put distance between the Christian and Christ. Jesus warned His followers against shrinking away from Him because of shame.

- In Mark 8:38 He said, "For if anyone is ashamed of me and my words in this adulterous and sinful generation, the Son of Man will also be ashamed of him when he comes in the glory of his Father with the holy angels." When He spoke these words, Jesus had just announced His mission to the disciples for the first time. It would not be a mission of immediate glory as Peter expected when he committed to follow the Messiah. Instead it was the shocking message "that the Son of Man must suffer many things and be rejected by the elders and the chief priests and the experts in the law and be killed and after three days rise again" (Mk 8:31).
- John echoed the same concern saying, "And now, little children, remain in him, so that whenever he appears we may have confidence and not shrink away from him in shame when he comes back" (1 Jn 2:28). Contextually, John was encouraging his readers to stand strong in their testimony to who Jesus is in spite of opposition.
- A third author expressed the same concern, saying, "But my righteous one will live by faith, and if he shrinks back, I take no pleasure in him" (Heb 10:38). Contextually the author of Hebrews was encouraging his readers to remain strong in their Christian lives

and not shrink back; for they were in danger of denying Christ by lapsing back into the temple sacrifices of Judaism. They wanted to live by the familiar spiritual reality of the temple cult and its sacrifices instead of by faith in Christ's finished work.

The believers in the above situations faced persecution and therefore the danger of shrinking away from Christ. Since this was a concern of so many authors of the New Testament, we also need to pay attention to their warning.

Even the apostle Peter, faced with the opposition of those who had arrested Jesus, took the easy way out and denied that he knew Christ. Despite being warned that he would deny his Lord, he denied Him three times the night before Jesus was crucified (Mt 26:75). Christians face the danger that they may fall to the pressures of suffering and persecution. If they do, they risk the danger of harming their mission to tell the world about Christ along with their ability to make disciples (Mt 28:18-20). Along with that, if we are tempted away from our testimony, we can lose what God has planned for us as a reward (1 Cor 9:24-27). Not only can their mission and testimony be harmed, but our relationship with Christ suffers if we begin to distance ourselves from Him. A fearsome prospect is that a Christian might harm his relationship with the One who gave Himself for him (2 Tim 2:8-13). Imagine how Peter felt after denying Jesus (Lk 22:60-62):

> But Peter said, "Mister, I do not know what you are talking about!" Immediately, while he was still speaking, a rooster crowed. Then the Lord turned and looked at Peter, and Peter remembered the word of the Lord that he had said to him, "Before a rooster crows today, you will deny me three times." So Peter went out and wept bitterly.

Suffering brings both the danger of harming our relationship with Christ and the potential to draw us closer to Him. How we choose to respond to suffering determines the difference.

QUESTION 5

Persecutions by the world can pose dangers to Christians. *True or False?*

QUESTION 6

According to 2 Timothy 4:10, the co-laborer with Paul who deserted him because "he loved this present age" is named __________.

QUESTION 7

Please match the following passages with the corresponding reason the believers were tempted to shrink away from Christ.

Passage	*Reason*
Mark 8:38	They were ashamed of Jesus and His words.
Hebrews 10:38	They will not live by faith.
1 John 2:28	They were not abiding in Christ.

QUESTION 8

Please read Luke 22:21-62. Then open your Life Notebook and put yourself in Peter's place in this story of denial. What warnings did he receive about the sin he was about to fall into? What attitudes did he have that contributed to his falling into this sin? In what ways did Peter show that he misunderstood either Jesus' teachings or the situation he was in? From your observations about Peter's denials, write out what application you can make in your life that will help you avoid this sin.

Topic 3: How God Uses Suffering

Have you ever noticed there seems to be a lot of people who believe in God, but they are mad at Him?

It's true that God gets blamed for many things. For example, a lot of people consider themselves Christians until someone close to them dies. Often, it's when a person's mother or father or another close relative dies at an unexpectedly young age. The one who died usually was very important in that person's life.

It is a very difficult experience to suffer that kind of loss. Our parents and family members are a gift from God and losing them hurts. But one of the consequences of living in a sinful world is that every one of us is vulnerable to death at any time.

> Indeed, my plans are not like your plans, and my deeds are not like your deeds, for, just as the sky is higher than the earth, so my deeds are superior to your deeds, and my plans superior to your plans. (Isa 55:8-9)

God's plans, and methods, are truly different than ours. After all, who among us would think of using suffering to accomplish maturity—sanctification—in the Christian life? Yet the suffering that comes into our lives plays a key role in our spiritual development and maturity in the faith (Rom 5:3-5).

The Bible tells us there are not any guarantees from God about how long we will live (Ps 90:10). God did not initiate death; His rebellious people did (Rom 5:12). Experiencing the death of a loved one is no less painful for faithful Christians but trusting a sovereign God who loves them helps. Christians can count on the "God of all comfort" to be by their side in the midst of suffering (2 Cor 1:3). They also know that God does not waste the pain they experience, and what happens to them will work out for good for those who love and trust God (Rom 8:28). Also, if we know a person's destiny is in heaven, we do not mourn in the same way an unbeliever would, or as Paul put it, "you will not grieve like the rest who have no hope" (1 Thess 4:13).

Though many non-Christians do not understand that pain can be useful, suffering has a constructive purpose for the Christian (Rom 5:3). Please read "Uses of Suffering" to gain insight into the purposes of suffering for Christians.

Uses of Suffering

Many immature Christians center their lives on seeking pleasure and avoiding suffering (Heb 12:2-4). The growing Christian can benefit from suffering because it becomes a tool in the hands of God to draw us closer to Him (Heb 12:5-13). One of the purposes that suffering can accomplish is to train the Christian and make him godly. The maturing process that makes us like Christ is a necessary part of our practical sanctification (Rom 8:28-30).

Training for the Christian

> So, since Christ suffered in the flesh, you also arm yourselves with the same attitude, because the one who has suffered in the flesh has finished with sin, in that he spends the rest of his time on earth concerned about the will of God and not human desires. (1 Pet 4:1-2)

This is an amazing passage that tells us that suffering keeps us from sin because it helps us focus on the will of God, not our fleshly desires. This is the opposite of indulging the flesh and reaping destruction (Gal 6:8). It seems comparable to the way exercise is essential to training an athlete for a competition. The training is not always fun or pleasant, but it prepares the athlete (1 Cor 9:24-27). In a similar way, suffering trains a Christian to fully rely on God.

"And let endurance have its perfect effect, so that you will be perfect and complete, not deficient in anything" (Jas 1:4). The endurance James talks about in this context is the enduring of trials. He relates the enduring of trials, which often involve suffering, to our maturing in the faith. Paul's letter to Timothy tells us to take our share of sufferings as a good soldier of Jesus Christ (2 Tim 2:3). As a soldier takes on unpleasant duties as a matter of course in his profession, likewise taking on suffering is a part of what we should expect when we agree to follow Christ. Like a soldier we endure suffering while staying focused on the goal of a growing relationship with Christ. Peter agreed, saying that we were called for doing good, suffering, and enduring, "since Christ also suffered for you, leaving an example for you to follow in his steps" (1 Pet 2:21). When suffering draws us closer to the Lord, it accomplishes what God intends.

Produces Results in Eternity

Paul acknowledged the reality of suffering in this life in 2 Corinthians 4:7-11, 14-18. Though the kind of suffering described in these verses is severe, Christians should persevere through it because such suffering carries the promise of eternal reward. In Revelation, believers are told that they will not suffer the second death in the lake of fire (Rev 2:11). Believers will instead receive blessings from the Father and enjoy fellowship with the Lord (Rev 2:17, 28; 3:5, 21).

Through suffering, "the life of Jesus" is seen in us, which helps us carry out our Great Commission—to take God's message to the nations (Mt 28:18-20). In the face of suffering we are to take heart because:

- God who raised Jesus will also raise us.
- Our suffering is momentary and light compared to eternity.
- Suffering produces an eternal weight of glory.
- We are rewarded for our faithfulness during suffering.

Produces Results Now

The church of Smyrna is evaluated in Revelation 2:8-11. They were a good church, suffering persecution. The name "Smyrna" means "bitter," and the name itself has the root of the word "myrrh" a common perfume in Bible times sometimes used to embalm dead bodies (Ps 45:8; Mt 2:11; Mk 15:23). Putting it under pressure (or "distress" in Rev 2:9) was the best way for its manufacturers to release its fragrance from the plant in its raw state. Therefore, Jesus' point was that these believers would also give off their best fragrance under the pressure of persecution. The Lord's encouragement to them, and therefore to us, was not to escape or evade the suffering, but to remain faithful in spite of and in the midst of the suffering (Rev 2:10).

Helps Us Identify with Christ

Paul's goal was not to avoid suffering but rather to share in Christ's sufferings—even to the point of sharing in His death (Phil 3:10-11).

The author of Hebrews said the same thing but from a different perspective. Moses regarded suffering for God to be greater wealth than the treasures of Egypt (Heb 11:24-26). Moses, who purposely chose to decline the earthly comforts of Egyptian royalty was like Paul who chose to share in the sufferings of God's people. Not that they enjoyed or valued suffering for its own sake, but rather when they faced the choice of remaining faithful to the Lord or avoiding suffering, they chose the Lord.

"But remember the former days when you endured a harsh conflict of suffering after you were enlightened" (Heb 10:32). In this passage the readers of Hebrews demonstrate a danger that applies to us also. They started well in enduring sufferings, but when those sufferings continued for an extended period of time they started pulling away from their faith in Christ. Continued suffering took a toll on their faithfulness to the Lord, and they became ineffective followers of Christ. We also can get worn down, which makes us more vulnerable to the temptation to seek release from our sufferings, compromising our testimony. Yet like them, we have probably "not yet resisted to the point of bloodshed in your struggle against sin," which is the temptation to depart from a clear testimony (Heb 12:4). The writer of Hebrews encouraged his readers not only to "remember the former days when we endured a harsh conflict of suffering" (Heb 10:32), but also to remember the joy with which that suffering was accepted because their focus was on a "better and lasting possession" (Heb 10:34). Like them we need to remember both the endurance and joy as we stay focused on a relationship with the Lord that will last forever.

QUESTION 9

Which of the following are reasons Christians endure suffering? *(Select all that apply.)*

A. It becomes fun after a while.

B. It is part of our calling as a Christian soldier.

C. It makes an end to sin for us.

D. It places us in Christ's footsteps.

E. It strengthens our flesh.

F. It trains us in the Christian life.

QUESTION 10

According to 2 Corinthians 4:17, how does our suffering now compare to how it produces "for us an eternal weight of glory"? *(Select all that apply.)*

A. Extended

B. Light

C. Momentary

D. Shared

QUESTION 11

According to Revelation 2:9, how would believers give off their best fragrance for Christ?

A. By reading God's Word daily
B. Doing things in love
C. Through denying the flesh
D. While under distress

QUESTION 12

The readers of the epistle to the Hebrews had suffered in their struggle against sin to the point of shedding their blood. *True or False?*

QUESTION 13

Recall a time when you experienced suffering or witnessed it in someone else's life and God used that suffering to accomplish His purposes. Open your Life Notebook and describe both the suffering and how God used the suffering to produce good.

Topic 4: Ministering to the Suffering

Sometimes a person's suffering can benefit somebody else. Have you ever noticed that the people who have suffered the most also have the ability to comfort the most?

There was once a widow who went to her neighbor's house after the neighbor's child died in an accident. The widow went over to comfort the mother of the child. When she returned home, her daughter asked her how she was able to help the neighbor. She said that she sat with the mother, held her hand, and cried with her.

That widow had experienced grief and likely knew what the mother needed. The loss of her husband made her better able to comfort people when they suffer. When we experience suffering, we are drawn toward people who have had similar experiences because they are better able to comfort us. People who haven't lived through similar circumstances are less able to understand.

> Remember your word to your servant, for you have given me hope. This is what comforts me in my trouble, for your promise revives me. (Ps 119:49-50)

God is the source of all comfort; He encourages the downhearted (see 2 Cor 1:3-4; 7:6). These verses tell us that God often gives comfort through His people. We are God's representatives on earth, and as such, we have the privilege and responsibility to pass along His comfort to others. One of the ways God equips us for that task is to allow us to experience suffering and to comfort us in the process, often through other people.

Suffering often leads to opportunities to minister to others who are suffering. Christ Himself is a powerful example of the connection between suffering and ministry. Read "Ministry in Suffering" and consider the example of Jesus, who has both suffered and ministered.

Ministry in Suffering

You would think that if anyone was immune from suffering it would be God. After all, He is holy and separate from His creation (Jn 1:1-3; Eph 1:4; Col 1:15). He is also separate from all sin and evil of every kind (Heb 7:26). Not only that, He is self-existing (Ex 3:14). This means that He does not depend on anyone else for His survival or satisfaction and He is all-powerful and all-knowing. If He chose to do so, God could prevent anything from causing Him suffering, and yet amazingly, He chose a path marked with intense suffering. Instead of remaining apart from His needy and troubled creation, He voluntarily sent His Son into this world to give His life as the atoning sacrifice for our sin (Rom 8:3; 1 Jn 4:10). When the path on which God leads us includes suffering, He is not asking us to do anything He has not willingly done Himself.

God Became Flesh

God sent His Son into the world to live as a human. Sometimes we have difficulty understanding what was involved in the incarnation but consider it from God's point of view (Phil 2:5-11). Jesus was carried in the womb for nine months and then born by a natural human birth to His mother (Lk 1:35). He grew up with natural human limitations, suffering from hunger and thirst, as well as enduring both mental and physical pain (Mt 4:2; Jn 4:6-7; 11:33-36; Lk 23:36). One of the insults He endured even suggested that His birth was the result of His mother's sexually immoral behavior (Mk 6:3; Jn 8:41). He not only endured extreme mental pain (Mk 14:34), but He also endured extreme physical pain. The flogging He received on the morning He went to the Cross weakened Him physically (Mt 27:32). This led to the Roman soldiers forcing Simon of Cyrene to carry His cross the rest of the way to Golgotha.

Godly Suffering Leads to Comfort

What was the purpose of all that suffering? God saw humanity, people He had created and loved, suffering in a sinful world, and He saw their need for a divine Savior (1 Jn 4:9). Though He was transcendent and apart from His creation, He voluntarily entered the world He had created because of His love and compassion for His lost people (Heb 10:5-10). His suffering made possible our redemption. Christ's suffering not only brings salvation but also brings compassion and comfort to those of us who are already Christians (2 Cor 1:5). God's intention is that we who have suffered and been comforted should in turn bring comfort to those we meet who suffer and need comfort. Those who suffer the most are usually the ones who can bring the most comfort to others (see 2 Cor 1:3-11).

God's Arms Are the Ultimate Comfort

In this world we see suffering people all around us. Christ is the only source of true comfort the world can experience, and Christians—we who have received His comfort—are called to bring that comfort to others (2 Cor 1:3-5). Though people may search for an answer to suffering in other places, ultimate comfort is found only in God's arms, and Christians are His connection, His chosen method of delivering that comfort to a lost world.

QUESTION 14

Through Christ, God voluntarily put Himself in a position to experience suffering. *True or False?*

QUESTION 15

Please match the references below with the corresponding factors that contributed to Jesus' suffering.

Reference	*Contributor to Suffering*
Luke 1:35	He grieved deeply to the point of death
Matthew 4:2	He was born by natural human birth.
John 4:6-7	He wept in empathy with friends' pain.
John 11:33-36	He suffered hunger.
Mark 14:34	He became tired and thirsty.
John 8:41	He endured insults (e.g., some said His conception was from sexual immorality)

QUESTION 16

God's offer of comfort extends only to those who are believers. *True or False?*

QUESTION 17

Ultimate comfort is found in God's arms, and Christians are His __________ to the lost world.

QUESTION 18

Open your Life Notebook and respond to the following question. Think of a time when somebody else comforted you. What experiences in that person's life helped prepare them to offer you comfort? What experiences of suffering in your life might God use to help you offer comfort to someone else?

Topic 5: Preparing for Suffering

Many people can identify with the desire to avoid suffering, but avoidance is not always possible. Jesus told His disciples to expect trouble. He said, "In the world you have trouble and suffering" (Jn 16:33). But He also declared His intent that the disciples experience His peace, even in the presence of suffering. In the fallen world in which we live, we will encounter suffering. While we cannot always avoid it, we can handle it in ways that do not destroy our joy.

Few people seek out suffering, and so when it comes, those who suffer often do not feel ready for it. If the experience is intense, they may feel overwhelmed. But God has graciously promised that we will not be tried beyond our ability to endure (1 Cor 10:13). No matter what the source of the suffering may be, believers need to be ready to deal with it. To learn more about how to be ready for suffering, read "Prepared" before answering the questions that follow.

Prepared

Job had no idea that disaster was about to strike. He was not a party to the conversation that led up to the startling series of losses that would be enough to crush most people. His story, told in the Old Testament book that bears his name, reveals the depth of his pain. But when the story ends, Job's relationship with God is intact, and he is praying for his critics. That one could suffer to such a degree and survive with his faith stretched but not broken may seem improbable, but Job's experience gives us some practical clues for surviving suffering in our own lives.

Integrity

Job was an extraordinary individual, not only because of his wealth, but even more because of his character. When we first meet Job, he is described as "pure and upright, one who feared God and turned away from evil" (Job 1:1). To make sure that we do not miss this important description, God repeated it when He described Job (Job 1:8; 2:3). Job's upright character makes his suffering more difficult to understand from a human perspective. His friends repeatedly assumed that his suffering was the result of his own personal sin and therefore deserved. Eliphaz, for example, made that assumption in Job 4:7-9, and Bildad expressed his opinion that the death of Job's children was God's judgment of their sin. They, of course, were wrong.

While Job's character makes his suffering more difficult for his friends explain, it helped him to endure it. Adversity has the potential to erode faith, and even Job's wife was ready to give up on God and told Job to curse God and die (Job 2:9). Believers do not face much of a challenge to fear God when He is showering blessings on their lives; however, in the midst of adversity it is more difficult. Job would not easily abandon his pattern of shunning sin and trusting God, and so he rejected his wife's advice (Job 2:10).

Adversity will test our character and commitments. Maintaining a habit of godliness developed over time is easier than to try to create that habit in the midst of suffering.

Gratitude

Job recognized that God is the source of the blessings he had experienced. He did not take those blessings for granted. Even after suffering the loss of his children, his wealth, and his health, Job acknowledged that God is the One who had given them. His answer to his wife (Job 2:10) echoed his earlier statement that God was the source, the One who gave (Job 1:21). Job had a better understanding than most people of the nature of stewardship. All the good things Job once had and now had lost had been given by God and entrusted to Job. That realization enabled Job to say that the Lord gives and the Lord takes away (Job 1:21).

Many people are thankful while enjoying blessings God has provided but maintaining an attitude of gratitude in the face of deep suffering is difficult. Giving thanks while consumed with one's losses is no easy task. Job himself was no stranger to that struggle, and when he began to speak to his friends, he said he wished that he had never been born. Obviously, such a wish does not express gratitude, but when a thankful heart can rise above the pain of loss, then that pain is a bit easier to bear. Thankfulness in the midst of suffering is our expression of trust in God despite circumstances.

The apostle Paul, who also experienced much suffering, encouraged the Christians at Thessalonica to give thanks in everything (1 Thess 5:16-18). He was not endorsing the worship of pain, but rather encouraging believers to keep being thankful even when the circumstances of life are painful. He understood from his own experience the power of gratitude in the face of suffering.

Eternal Perspective

In the midst of his suffering Job began to understand that he had been created for eternity. Early in the conversation with his friends, Job looked on death as desirable because it would mean the end of his pain. His understanding of death is expressed in terms of what it is not—no pain, no consciousness, no turmoil, and even no friends (see for example Job 3:11-13; 7:8-10). But as he began to anticipate his own death, his understanding began to deepen. In Job 14:14-15 Job raised the possibility of life after death and of God's desire for an eternal relationship with His creation. By the nineteenth chapter Job expressed a stirring affirmation of eternal life, declaring his expectation of seeing God after his skin is destroyed (Job 19:25-27). Even with the advances of modern medicine, the destruction of one's skin is a sure route to death. But Job, anticipating that his now rotting skin would lead to death, looked forward to seeing God.

If life is limited to no more than the span from birth to death, then hope dies long before we do. But for the Christian, life is much more than that. Believers are able to look forward to eternity in God's presence, and when they do, their perspective on their current suffering changes. Suffering is limited and will eventually be left behind. In the context of eternity, the suffering we experience now, no matter how painful it may be at the moment, is temporary. Paul described it as "light and momentary" (2 Cor 4:17, NIV). From a purely human perspective, we probably would not choose those words to describe Paul's suffering. But from the perspective of eternity, they are the words Paul chose.

Maintaining an eternal focus while living in time can be a challenge, but this challenge needs to be met. When we do so, we are much better equipped to make sense of suffering.

Knowing God

Knowing God and having a relationship with him should help prepare people for suffering. Sadly, for some people suffering has been a catalyst for rejecting God. Not understanding how a good God can allow bad things to happen, they accept the reality of their experience but reject God. Job was a worshipper of God before tragedy struck. Already he knew something of God's love and power. He would learn more in the midst of his pain. His suffering produced a lot of questions, many of which remained unanswered for him, but he did not reject his relationship with God. He discovered a hunger to understand and enjoy that relationship more deeply. When a person chooses to remain faithful to God in the midst of suffering, it is not uncommon for them to experience such a deepened hunger.

Eventually Job and his friends ran out of things to say, and God spoke. When he did, it was not to explain to Job why he was suffering. Instead, God focused Job's attention on Himself. With a series of questions God redirected the conversation so that the focus was on who He is and what He has done. The questions left Job speechless; he was unable to respond except with silence and repentance (Job 40:3-5; 42:1-6).

At first glance it might seem harsh for God to severely question a man who is suffering without ever revealing the reason for his suffering. But God's answer is a manifestation of His grace; He gave Job exactly what Job needed. Knowing God is a powerful resource when times of suffering come. God reminded Job of who He is, and when He did, even though Job's suffering continued, his questions ceased. The sovereign God who loved him had revealed Himself to Job, and that was enough. God reactivated Job by calling on him to minister in his pain to his friends by praying for them, and Job did so while he was still suffering (Job 42:7-10).

The great danger in suffering is that a person becomes so focused on the suffering his relationship with the Lord begins to wither. But in the midst of suffering our relationship with the Lord and our need to listen to Him is most obvious. God's desire to enjoy a relationship with us is not diminished because we suffer. Our desire and need for that relationship must stay strong as well. The more intimately we know Him, the better equipped we will be to endure whatever may come.

QUESTION 19

Which of the following did Jesus tell His disciples about suffering in this world? *(Select all that apply.)*

A. Because He loved them, they would not experience suffering.

B. They should expect trouble and suffering in this world.

C. Jesus had conquered the world.

D. He wanted them to experience peace.

QUESTION 20

Which of the following accurately describe the character of Job? *(Select all that apply.)*

A. Pure

B. Poor

C. Upright

D. Lucky

E. Fearing God

F. Turning away from evil

QUESTION 21

When God spoke to Job, what is the focus of what He said?

A. He answered Job's questions.

B. He explained why Job was suffering.

C. He agreed with Job's friends.

D. He focused on His own character and works.

E. He revealed when Job's suffering will end.

QUESTION 22

Which of the following help prepare Christians for times of suffering? *(Select all that apply.)*

A. Integrity

B. Gratitude

C. Eternal perspective

D. Knowing God

In spite of the fact that nobody likes to suffer, and few people would knowingly choose it, all of us encounter times of suffering in our lives. For Christians, such times can become an opportunity to deepen their relationship with Christ. When suffering has that result, it accomplishes God's purpose, and it also helps equip them both for ministry to others who suffer and for successfully navigating possible future times of suffering. Because we enjoy a relationship with Christ, we face the potential for suffering not alone, but with a sovereign God whose love is unending.

QUESTION 23

Please open your Life Notebook and record your thoughts about what is the Christian's proper response to suffering. Are there any changes you need to make to your life?

Lesson 10 Self Check: The Christian Life

QUESTION 1

According to the vision in Revelation 12, who flees into the wilderness to escape Satan's persecution?

A. The church

B. People without the sign of the beast

C. Israel during the tribulation

D. Israel during Jesus' ministry on earth

QUESTION 2

According to 1 Peter 3:17, it is better to suffer for doing good than doing wrong. *True or False?*

QUESTION 3

Even intense persecution can make a Christian a stronger witness. *True or False?*

QUESTION 4

Why were the believers in the book of Hebrews tempted to shrink away from Christ?

A. They were ashamed of Jesus and His words.

B. They were not living by faith.

C. They were not remaining in Christ.

D. They were threatened by the Jewish council (the Sanhedrin).

QUESTION 5

According to Revelation 2:9, under what circumstances would believers give off their best fragrance for Christ?

A. While under distress

B. When they successfully endured until the end

C. By reading God's Word daily

D. By doing things in love

QUESTION 6

The original readers of the epistle to the Hebrews were being martyred in their struggle against sin. *True or False?*

QUESTION 7

Jesus wept over which of the following?

A. When empathizing with His friends' pain

B. When He was exhausted

C. When His mother was insulted as a fornicator

D. When suffering hunger and thirst

QUESTION 8

Christians are called to minister Christ's comfort to others. *True or False?*

QUESTION 9

How does Paul describe the Christian's suffering when he talks about an eternal perspective in 2 Corinthians 4:16-18?

A. Momentary and light
B. Painful and purifying
C. Unnecessary and avoidable
D. Deep and lasting

QUESTION 10

When God spoke, He explained to Job the reason for his suffering. *True or False?*

Lesson 10 Answers to Questions

QUESTION 1: True

QUESTION 2

C. When Jesus came into the world in the flesh

QUESTION 3

B. Israel during the tribulation

QUESTION 4: False [Suffering can also be caused by our own sinful flesh and consequent unrighteousness in this world (1 Pet 3:17). This is a completely different kind of suffering than the honorable suffering we do for being godly.]

QUESTION 5: True [Because suffering is unpleasant, it sometimes accomplishes the purpose of the enemies who inflict it. The intention of our enemies is to impede Christians from living a godly life and being an effective witness for Christ.]]

QUESTION 6: Demas [Paul had previously called Demas his co-laborer when he wrote to Philemon and also sent greetings from him to the Colossians (Col 4:14; Phm 24). So he, at one time, was well thought of for his Christian work.]

QUESTION 7

Passage	***Reason***
Mark 8:38	They were ashamed of Jesus and His words.
Hebrews 10:38	They will not live by faith.
1 John 2:28	They were not abiding in Christ.

QUESTION 8: *Your answer*

QUESTION 9

B. It is part of our calling as a Christian soldier.
C. It makes an end to sin for us.
D. It places us in Christ's footsteps.
F. It trains us in the Christian life.

QUESTION 10

B. Light
C. Momentary

QUESTION 11

D. While under distress [The name "Smyrna" contains the root of the word "myrrh," which was a common perfume in Bible times. Putting it under pressure (or "distress" in Rev 2:9) was the best way for its manufacturers to release its fragrance in its raw state. Therefore, Jesus' point was that these believers would also give off their best fragrance under the pressure of persecution.]

QUESTION 12: False [The readers had "not yet resisted to the point of bloodshed in [their] struggle against sin" (Heb 12:4). The author encouraged his readers not only to "remember the former days when [they] endured a harsh conflict of sufferings" (Heb 10:32), but also to remember the joy with which that suffering was accepted because their focus was on a "better and lasting possession" (Heb 10:34).]

QUESTION 13: *Your answer*

QUESTION 14: True

QUESTION 15

Reference	*Contributor to Suffering*
Luke 1:35	He was born by natural human birth.
Matthew 4:2	He suffered hunger.
John 4:6-7	He became tired and thirsty.
John 11:33-36	He wept in empathy with friends' pain.
Mark 14:34	He grieved deeply to the point of death
John 8:41	He endured insults (e.g., some said His conception was from sexual immorality)

QUESTION 16: False [Though He was transcendent and separate from His creation, He voluntarily entered the world He had created because of His love and compassion for His lost people (Heb 10:5-10).t]

QUESTION 17: Connection

QUESTION 18: *Your answer*

QUESTION 19

B. They should expect trouble and suffering in this world.

C. Jesus had conquered the world.

D. He wanted them to experience peace.

[Jesus told His disciples to expect trouble: He said, "In the world you have trouble and suffering" (Jn 16:33). But He also declared His intent that the disciples experience His peace, even in the presence of suffering.]

QUESTION 20

A. Pure

C. Upright

E. Fearing God

F. Turning away from evil

[When we first meet Job, he is described as "pure and upright, one who feared God and turned away from evil" (Job 1:1). To make sure that we do not miss this important description, God repeats it when He describes Job (Job 1:8; 2:3).]

QUESTION 21

D. He focused on His own character and works.

QUESTION 22

A. Integrity

B. Gratitude

C. Eternal perspective

D. Knowing God

QUESTION 23: *Your answer*

Lesson 10 Self Check Answers

QUESTION 1

C. Israel during the tribulation

QUESTION 2: True

QUESTION 3: True

QUESTION 4

B. They were not living by faith.

QUESTION 5

A. While under distress

QUESTION 6: False

QUESTION 7

A. When empathizing with His friends' pain

QUESTION 8: True

QUESTION 9

A. Momentary and light

QUESTION 10: False

Lesson 11: Trusting God in the Face of Temptation—Living as an Alien

In this lesson, we will examine the reality of temptation in the life of the Christian. When you became a Christian, your citizenship changed. Now you are a citizen of heaven instead of a citizen of this world. But in this life, you still live day-by-day in a world to which you no longer belong, and you continue to face temptations to return to values and practices that are incompatible with your heavenly citizenship.

We will look at three avenues through which temptation comes: the world, the flesh, and the devil. These three are related. The world we live in is under the influence of Satan, and it still appeals to our sinful nature even though our citizenship has changed. Satan desires to destroy our relationship with Christ, and while he is a defeated foe, his sentence has not yet been carried out.

Because we live as maturing Christians in enemy territory, we wage a constant battle against these enemies. In this lesson we will look closely at the ways in which temptation comes and then apply what the Bible teaches about how we can resist temptation.

Lesson Outline

Topic 1: Living in a Fallen World

Topic 2: Battling the Old Nature

Topic 3: The Third Enemy

Topic 4: Resisting Temptation

Topic 5: Coming to the Throne

Topic 1: Living in a Fallen World

We may not always fully understand our struggles with temptation and the avenues through which that temptation can come. While many people might not see anything wrong with complaining about a difficult person, we should be concerned about such scriptural guidelines as Colossians 4:6, "Let your speech always be gracious..." Graciousness and gossiping do not easily mix. Values that the world considers normal, or at least neutral, can lead to sin and are often much different from God's values. The world's values interfere with a healthy relationship with the Lord.

The problem is that we live in a fallen world. When Adam and Eve sinned, the consequences of their sin affected not only them but the world in which they lived as well. The world that God had created was now subject to God's judgment as was mankind itself (Gen 3:16-19).

Please read "Living in a Fallen World" to further explore what it means to live our lives in this world.

Living in a Fallen World

One of the challenges of the Christian life is that we live in a fallen world. Both the physical creation itself and the world system through which it is perceived have been affected by man's sin. Paul vividly describes the impact of the fall on creation in Romans 8:19-23:

> For the creation eagerly waits for the revelation of the sons of God. For the creation was subjected to futility—not willingly but because of God who subjected it—in hope that the creation itself will also be set free from the bondage of decay into the glorious freedom of God's children. For we know that the whole creation groans and suffers together until now. Not only this, but we ourselves also, who have the firstfruits of the Spirit, groan inwardly as we eagerly await our adoption, the redemption of our bodies.

Creation groans and suffers not because of its own sin, but because of man's sin. A world that was created for us cannot fully fulfill its purpose because of our sin.

A relationship stands between fallen people and a fallen world. Human sin has lessened the goodness of a creation that God declared to be good. That fallen world becomes a catalyst for sin. The world, Scripture declares, is in the power of the evil one (1 Jn 5:19).

Consider the unsavory description of life in this fallen world in Ephesians 2:1-3. Fallen people are described not only as dead in sin, but also as living in that dead state according to the world's present path. The simple and sad truth is that this fallen world is friendly to sin—and that is the world in which Christians, who have been redeemed from sin, live. The world makes sin easy, and that is a problem.

Not only do we live in a world that makes sin easy; we also live in a world that is hostile to Christians. It would be a challenge enough if it were just a case of living in a world where sin was easy, but it is more than that. The world presses us to conform to its ungodliness. Romans 12:2 encourages us to avoid that pressure to conform to the world. Instead we are to change the way we think, to be transformed by the renewing of our minds.

We Christians are aliens in this world; we do not belong. Jesus made this clear in His prayer for the disciples in John 17:14-16. Like Jesus, Christians do not belong to the world and are hated by it. We live in a world that has no interest in supporting our relationship with Christ. We live in a dangerous environment, and so Jesus prays that His followers will be kept safe. Living in a dangerous and hostile environment can make unfaithfulness to Christ look attractive. Compromising one's commitment and accepting the ungodly values and practices of the world may seem easier than remaining committed to Christ. If we yield to the temptation of such a compromise, we damage our relationship with Christ and we damage the effectiveness of our testimony. We also act in a way directly contrary to Jesus' prayer in John 17.

When we choose the world over our relationship with Christ, we are choosing the temporal instead of the eternal. But the world will not last. In 2 Peter 3:6-13 Peter gave the ultimate answer to the question, *What is the world coming to?* God who created it will destroy it in gracious judgment and replace it with a new heaven and a new earth, "in which righteousness truly resides." Our knowledge that the world is destined for destruction, Peter wrote, should motivate us to lead lives marked by holiness and godliness.

Though we live in a fallen world, we do not have to live as worldly people. We are aliens; our citizenship is in heaven, and one day we will be home.

QUESTION 1

All of creation is groaning and suffering because of man's sin. *True or False?*

QUESTION 2

How are fallen people described in Ephesians 2:1-3? *(Select all that apply.)*

A. Dead in sins

B. Living according to the world's path

C. Unable to be redeemed

D. Children of wrath

QUESTION 3

What did Jesus pray for His disciples in John 17:14-16?

A. That they would be kept safe in the world

B. That they would be taken out of the world

C. That they would belong in the world

D. That they would be loved by the world

QUESTION 4

Please open your Life Notebook and share your thoughts on the following question: How does your knowledge that this world is destined for destruction affect the way you live your life now?

Topic 2: Battling the Old Nature

Have you ever wondered why you no longer value certain things because you are a Christian, yet they are still attractive to you?

The Christian life would be much easier if what we wanted was always in line with what God wants. But we are still human beings, and sometimes what we know is sin looks very attractive. So when we feel weak, we need to rely on Christ to lead us away from those temptations.

Sometimes we may think it would be a lot easier if God made sin unattractive. Why doesn't God just make us immune to sin? Here we need to remember that Christianity is a relationship. God doesn't turn Christians into robots; He has preserved our ability to choose to be faithful to Him. That doesn't mean we always make the right choice, but we always have that opportunity. Sometimes it's a struggle for us to deal with the impulses and desires of our old nature.

Being a Christian does not guarantee either freedom from temptation or consistent victory over temptation. Though a Christian's old nature has been crucified, it does not always act like it is dead. In the previous topic we looked at how the world is our enemy. Now we need to see how our own sinful nature can threaten to damage our relationship with Christ and draw us away from Him. Read "Battling the Old Nature" as you begin to explore this important topic, and then answer the questions that follow the article.

Battling the Old Nature

The Christian life involves a wonderful transformation. Paul described in dramatic terms the change that takes place. Writing to the Christians at Corinth, he described the Christian as a "new creation" (2 Cor 5:17). The "old" self has passed away to be replaced with new life in Christ. The imagery Paul used in Romans is even more dramatic. There he wrote that the "old man" was crucified with Christ. The Christian can consider himself to be dead to sin but alive to God (Rom 6:6-11).

This change is indeed a wonderful thing, and in terms of our standing before Christ, the transaction is complete and final. The outcome has been determined; we are redeemed and members of His family. But in practice, as we continue to live in a fallen world, we struggle between our sin nature that does not want to give up and our new nature in Christ. The old nature, even though crucified, does not always act as though it is dead because we do not always treat it as dead. As long as we live in the flesh, we will continue to face these battles and the need to make critical choices that will affect whether we allow the old nature to regain control in our lives.

Choosing to Die and to Live

This battle with the flesh begins in the heart and the mind. Paul told Christians to consider themselves dead to sin (Rom 6:11). That decision to consider yourself dead to sin must be made again and again, every time your old nature wants to yield to the allure of sin. Christ has set us free from the power of sin, but we must keep choosing to live in that freedom. Sometimes that choice is difficult, but it is always worth it.

The choice to which we are called is not only to consider ourselves dead to sin, but also to consider ourselves alive to God. This choice impacts the way in which we view the world. If we live by the flesh, then the things of the flesh will shape the way we view life (Rom 8:5-8). We have been brought into a relationship with a holy God. It is far better to live by His Spirit than to yield to our old sin nature and damage our relationship with Him. God wants us to enjoy a relationship with Him in Christ Jesus.

Choosing to Serve

The sin nature does not easily yield its control of our lives. Sometimes Christians are tempted to think that they can tame the sin nature and rule their own lives, but this is an illusion. Christians need to understand that we cannot live as the master of our own sin. If we try to do so, we will find that sin has become our master. Such a situation is contrary to God's grace (Rom 6:14). Scripture makes clear that we will either serve sin or serve the Lord. Paul made that choice clear as he followed up his encouragement to the Romans to consider themselves dead to sin with a call to not let sin reign in their bodies (Rom 6:12-14). We are to avoid presenting ourselves as servants of sin and instead to present ourselves to the Lord as those who are alive in Him and as instruments of righteousness.

Paul made the reality of this choice poignantly clear in the following chapter as he pointed to himself as an example of one who struggles with the sin nature. He described this struggle in Romans 7:18-25. The battle is not a matter of philosophy for intellectual debate; it is painfully practical and constantly present. The will to sin is not easily conquered, but there is hope, and that hope rests in Christ (Rom 7:24-8:2).

Choosing to Put Off the Deeds of the Flesh

Sooner or later our battle with the old nature comes down to decisions about specific actions. Will I break that promise, will I tell that lie, and countless other questions will need to find their answers in our actions. Scripture repeatedly encourages us Christians to separate ourselves from sinful deeds that once might have been a normal part of our lives. Colossians 3:5-10 makes this encouragement clear. The lists of "old nature" deeds in verses 5 and 8 are not exhaustive and will vary from person to person, but most of us can find ourselves within those lists.

Because of the fall, sin comes naturally to us; our old nature finds it easy to sin. We have the ability to choose our actions and to say no to the desires of the flesh. This passage in Colossians reminds us again that the battle begins in the mind (Col 3:2). Where the mind dwells the body is likely to follow. We need to keep distancing ourselves from the sinful acts of the old nature. Tolerating compromise with the flesh will lead to failure. Romans 13:14 warns us to make no provision for the sinful desires of the flesh.

Choosing the Fruit and Deeds of the Spirit

Successfully battling the flesh is not just a matter of fleeing from its desires and denying its lures. There is a positive side to the battle as well. Instead of choosing the deeds of the flesh we can choose the actions and attitudes that flow out of a relationship with Christ. Having told the Colossian believers to put off the deeds of the flesh, Paul goes on to encourage them to be characterized by qualities that are in sharp contrast to those deeds of the old nature (Col 3:12-17). These qualities—mercy, kindness, humility, gentleness, patience, forbearance, forgiveness, love, peace, thankfulness—are choices for believers.

They are also part of what God's Spirit desires to produce in our lives. A similar passage in Galatians contrasts the works of the flesh with the fruit of the Spirit (Gal 5:16-25). The positive qualities are described as fruit of the Spirit that will produce actions that please the Lord rather than works of the flesh that give in to the desires of the old nature. If this kind of spiritual fruit is to characterize our lives, then we need to cooperate with rather than work against what God's Spirit desires to produce in us.

Battling the old nature is not easy. Nor is that battle avoidable if we want to continue to grow a deeper relationship with the Lord. As long as we live in this life, we will face the need to battle the flesh day by day. The good news is that God makes success in these battles possible when we choose to follow God.

QUESTION 5

How should Christians think of themselves in relationship to their old sin nature?

A. They should consider themselves to be sin's ruler.

B. They should consider themselves to be sin's servant.

C. They should consider themselves to be dead to sin.

D. They do not need to be concerned about the sin nature since they are redeemed.

QUESTION 6

Occasionally indulging the flesh is not a problem as long we do not make a habit of it. *True or False?*

QUESTION 7

In Romans 7 Paul described a struggle within himself in which he wanted to do good but was unable to because of the sin that lived in him. *True or False?*

QUESTION 8

Putting to death the deeds of the body is a decisive once-for-all action that cannot be repeated. *True or False?*

QUESTION 9

Romans 6:11 encourages us to be dead to sin but alive to God. As you consider this encouragement and Paul's testimony of his own struggle in the following chapter (Rom 7), open your Life Notebook and reflect on what it means to be "alive to God." How would you explain this concept to somebody else?

Topic 3: The Third Enemy

Does it ever seem to you that some Christians think they are perfect? They act like they are better than other people and not capable of sinning. We need to take responsibility for our own sin, even though it may have arisen in part by temptation from the devil. Satan is very real, and he is a factor in causing Christians to sin.

So, whose fault is it when we sin, ours or the devil's? Satan can tempt us, but we are still responsible for choosing how to respond to the temptation, and for our choices and actions. The source of the temptation doesn't remove our responsibility. Whether the temptation comes from the world, from within ourselves, or from the devil, if we sin, we bear the responsibility for that sin.

It may seem that dealing with temptation that comes from other people, and especially from the devil, is hardly a fair fight. However, we need to keep in mind that Jesus is stronger than Satan. Satan can tempt us, but he can't make us sin; that is up to us.

In the first two topics of this lesson, we looked at the world and the flesh as avenues through which temptation comes. In this topic we will look at the third enemy, Satan. Satan's name means *adversary* or *accuser*, and that is a good description of the way he relates to believers. We should never assume that Satan does not exist. That is one of several common false assumptions that people make about the devil. The devil would like us to believe this lie. The truth is that he is real, he is our enemy, and we need to understand his tactics.

The Bible has much to tell us about Satan. Read "The Third Enemy" to explore some of what Scripture says about the devil's character and the ways in which he works.

The Third Enemy

Christians can easily understand the temptations that come from the world and from the flesh. We live in a world that we have come to know well, and we have had lots of experience dealing with our old sin nature, even though that nature is deceptive. Satan's role in temptation can be a bit more difficult for us to grasp accurately. Gaining a greater understanding of who he is and how he works can help us be more successful in resisting him.

His Character

Satan is not God. While that statement may seem obvious, it is important. People tend to make two common errors in thinking about the devil. Either they wrongly decide he does not exist, or they wrongly think he is equal to God. Both views are incorrect. Scripture makes it abundantly clear that he is real, and Isaiah 14:12-15 describes in poetic language Satan's failed attempt to make himself like God.

Satan is limited. When the Lord and Satan talked about Job, God placed specific limits on what Satan could do (Job 1:12; 2:6). God, not Satan, is sovereign. Satan is powerful but not omnipotent, clever but not omniscient. Some Bible scholars view Ezekiel 28, which is a prophecy against the king of Tyre, as also including an accurate description of Satan. He is described as created, an angel in Eden, whose pride led to his fall.

Satan's intent is to damage the Christian's relationship with the Lord. By enticing Adam and Eve to sin in the Garden of Eden, Satan destroyed the fellowship they had enjoyed there with God (Gen 3:8-10). In the case of Job, Satan's desire was to induce Job to curse God (Job 1:11, 2:5). Satan even boldly tried to tempt Jesus to honor him instead of the Father (Mt 4:8-10). Satan still wants to disrupt the relationship between the Lord and His people; if we are wise we will take note of his tactics.

His Tactics

In a conversation with unbelieving Jews, Jesus described Satan as a murderer and a liar (Jn 8:44). Jesus said there is no truth in Satan. When the devil appeared in the Garden of Eden, he cast doubt on the truth of what God had said to Adam and Eve (Gen 3:1-5). Satan is still a liar and still tries to cast doubt on God's truth. Enticing people to believe a lie is an effective way of drawing them away from Christ, who described Himself as "the truth" (Jn 14:6). Each time Satan tempted Jesus, He responded with the truth of Scripture (Mt 4:1-11). Truth, both knowing and using it, is crucially important in countering the temptations of Satan.

One manifestation of Satan's fundamental dishonesty is his ability to appear as an angel of light (2 Cor 11:14). He is deceptive; that deceptiveness often has taken the form of movements or religions that at first glance seem to be of God, but which on closer examination turn out to deny the essential truth about the character and work of Jesus Christ. Because Satan in a master deceiver, we must discern wisely what we encounter, always being ready to evaluate things on the basis of the truth of God's Word.

Revelation 12:10 describes Satan as the accuser of the brothers. He carries out this role of accusing constantly, day and night. Christians need to understand that Satan is *never* on their side; he is *always* opposed to them. While Satan's accusations will never intimidate God, they sometimes intimidate us. But even when we sin, we have an advocate before the Father in the person of Christ (1 Jn 2:1). Because of the work of Jesus Christ, the accusations of Satan cannot stand.

One of the more frightening images of Satan in Scripture is the word picture painted by Peter (1 Pet 5:8). He described Satan as a roaring lion looking for someone to devour. Facing a roaring lion is no more appealing today than it would have been for Daniel in Persia (Dan 6). Intriguingly, Peter does not encourage believers to flee from this "roaring lion." Instead, his counsel is to be sober (or self-controlled), alert, and to resist Satan (1 Pet 5:8-9). We do not need to resign ourselves to being devoured by this roaring lion.

When encouraging the Ephesians to lead holy lives, Paul told them not to give the devil an opportunity (Eph 4:27). Satan is opportunistic. He is more likely to attack us at a point of weakness than at a point of strength. Giving in to a temptation that comes from the world or from our flesh gives Satan an opportunity to do further damage to our fellowship with Christ.

His End

We need to remember that Satan's fate is determined, and his influence will end. God's judgment of Satan was declared in the Garden of Eden with the promise that Christ would crush the serpent's head. Satan is dangerous, but he has been defeated. When we give in to him, we give in to a defeated enemy. The ultimate fulfillment of God's promised judgment of Satan appears in Revelation 20:10, which states that the devil will be cast into the lake of fire forever. The temptations of Satan are limited and will end; our relationship with Christ is for eternity.

QUESTION 10

Which of the following is true of Satan? *(Select all that apply.)*

A. He is omniscient but not omnipotent.
B. He tried to make himself like God.
C. He is powerful.
D. He can do whatever he wants.
E. He is not sovereign.

QUESTION 11

Please match the references below with the corresponding teachings about Satan's characteristic methods of temptation.

Reference	*Teaching*
John 8:44	He is a murderer and a liar from the beginning.
2 Corinthians 11:14	He and his agents appear as angels of light.
1 Peter 5:8	He is "like a roaring lion…on the prowl looking for someone to devour."
Revelation 12:10	He operates as an accuser of the brethren.

QUESTION 12

When we give in to Satan, we are giving in to a defeated foe. *True or False?*

QUESTION 13

Review the tactics of Satan in the above article "The Third Enemy." Then open your Life Notebook and describe some examples of how you have encountered these tactics of Satan in your life. How did you respond?

Topic 4: Resisting Temptation

Have you ever wondered why life as a Christian is joyful, yet we find ourselves fighting temptation all the time? As long as we live in a fallen world, temptation will be a reality for us. The real issue, though, is not the temptation, it's what we do about it.

In this life we will face temptation. Whether it comes from the fallen world in which we live, from our own sin nature, or from the influence of Satan, we have to deal with temptations that threaten to distance us from Christ. How we respond to those temptations is important. When we yield to sin, we hurt that relationship.

Christians need to have a workable strategy for dealing with temptation. We saw in the previous topic some of the tactics that Satan uses. We too need to develop tactics for responding to temptation when we encounter it. God has not left us without guidance in this area. Many passages in Scripture can help us, and we will look at some of these as we seek to sharpen our ability to respond to temptation without yielding to it. Read "Responding to Temptation" and then answer the questions that follow the article.

Responding to Temptation

Certain moments in life demand a response. If someone drops a brick from above your head and you do not respond by moving, disaster will strike. If you are on the banks of a river that is about to flood and do not respond, the least that will happen is that you will get wet. If you find yourself in the path of temptation—and you will—and do not respond appropriately, you risk falling into sin and damaging your relationship with Christ. Understanding the nature and risks of temptation and knowing how to respond will help you deal with it successfully without falling into sin. A variety of possible responses are given in God's Word and believers need to seek His guidance for which response fits for their temptation. One response may be successful for one temptation but not another, so seeking God's will each time you face temptation is important.

Happy Is the One Who Endures

James provided some very practical help in faithfully enduring temptation in James 1:12-18. He reminded us at the outset that happiness is the result of enduring through temptation. Then he dug a little deeper and helps us understand what is involved:

- *Our motivation* (Jas 1:12): In this verse James holds out a future reward, a crown of life, as a motivation for faithfully enduring temptation, often synonymously translated as testing or trial. He also says that our love for God is another motivating factor in enduring temptation.
- *The source of sin* (Jas 1:13-14): James clarifies that temptation to evil does not come from God, and he points out the important role of our old nature in luring us toward sin.
- *The birth of sin* (Jas 1:15): James tells us that when we give in to our evil desires—for there is a moment when we must choose—they conceive and give birth to sin.
- *The ripening of sin* (Jas 1:15): When sin is full grown, it gives birth to death.
- *The source of good* (Jas 1:17): Every perfect gift is from the Father of lights above.
- *The purpose of our new birth* (Jas 1:18): We are to be "a kind of firstfruits of all he created."

In the face of temptation, we can easily lose sight of the fact that happiness lies in successfully resisting temptation rather than in yielding to sin.

Finding a Way Through

Paul wrote wonderfully encouraging words to the Corinthians about dealing with temptation. In 1 Corinthians 10:13 he made several crucial points. First, he reminded us that the temptation we face is not unique. Often when people face temptation, the temptation may seem unique to them and they may think that the temptations others have faced are irrelevant. Paul corrected this error and stated that "no trial has overtaken you that is not faced by others."

I can learn from others because they may have experienced a temptation similar to what I am facing. In the verses immediately preceding this statement, Paul cited the experiences of the Israelites, reminding us that those experiences are examples for us. He listed some of their sins from which we can learn:

- Idolatry (1 Cor 10:7).
- Immorality (1 Cor 10:8).
- Putting Christ to the test rather than trusting Him (1 Cor 10:9).
- Complaining (1 Cor 10:10).

It is, of course, far less painful to learn from the mistakes of others than to fall into those sins ourselves.

A second important reminder in 1 Corinthians 10:13 is that God is faithful. In the midst of temptation, it can be easy to begin doubting, or to simply lose sight of, God's faithfulness. When we doubt God's faithfulness, it becomes easier for us to drift into sin. Having a firm grasp of the character of God before temptation comes helps to equip us to endure the temptation successfully.

A fourth important encouragement is that with the trial, God "will also provide a way through it so that you may be able to endure." It is important to understand that God is not guaranteeing freedom from temptation itself. What He is promising is that when temptation comes, there will be a way for us to endure it without giving in to it. He does not promise that the way through will be easy, and it would be presumptuous for us to assume that to be the case. Enduring—the "way through"—may be difficult and painful, but there will always be a way through.

Flee

Two words of instruction are important resources for us in finding a way to respond successfully to temptation. The first of those words is *flee*. Particularly for temptations that involve the world or the flesh, the repeated command of Scripture is to flee. We are foolish if we choose to remain in the presence of temptation when that is not necessary. Consider the following exhortations from Scripture:

Immediately after the encouragement of 1 Corinthians 10:13 and his mention of the Israelites sins, Paul urged the Corinthian Christians to "flee from idolatry." Rather than yield to the temptation to give to anything else the allegiance and honor that belongs to God, we are told to flee. When we find ourselves in the presence of things or people that attract our old nature and could take God's place in our lives, we need to remove ourselves. When we find ourselves ready to give our loyalty to an ungodly worldly philosophy, we need to separate ourselves from that influence. "Flee" is good advice.

A few chapters earlier, Paul had told these same Christians to "flee sexual immorality" (1 Cor 6:18). There is perhaps no area of temptation where the wisdom of fleeing is easier to see than the area of sexual temptation. The human sexual appetite, which is a God-given gift, can be a powerful force. When it is misdirected, it becomes a powerful force for evil. When we find ourselves in circumstances that are sexually tempting, we need to remove ourselves from those circumstances. In that kind of situation, to flee is not a sign of weakness; it is an indication of strength.

When Paul wrote to Timothy, he gave him similar encouragement to distance himself from the sources of temptation. In 1 Timothy 6:9-11 the context is a lusting after material wealth. Paul noted the danger of such temptation and recognized that it can even lead a person away from their faith. Then he told Timothy to stay away from those things. Material wealth in itself is not bad, but the misguided and uncontrolled appetite for it is bad. Paul accompanied the call to "keep away" with the encouragement to pursue instead the kind of things that support a relationship with Christ: righteousness, godliness, faithfulness, love, endurance, gentleness.

A similar "keep away" and "pursue" combination appears in 2 Timothy 2:22. Here the encouragement is to keep away from youthful passions. To the instruction to pursue righteousness, Paul added the valuable ingredient of fellowship with other believers. The company of like-minded believers is a valuable resource as we deal with and flee from temptation.

Resist

The second important word of instruction is *resist*. While we are told to flee temptations that appeal to the old nature, Scripture repeatedly encourages us to resist when the temptation is coming from Satan. Consider these scriptures.

Peter describes Satan as a roaring lion, a dangerous image (1 Pet 5:8-9). But instead of telling his readers to flee from Satan, Peter says, "Resist him." Resisting Satan is neither hopeless nor lonely. This instruction follows closely the encouragement to cast our cares on the Lord who cares for us. When we take a stand in resisting the devil, we do not stand alone; we stand with Christ who has conquered Satan. Fear sometimes can keep a believer from resisting Satan. But the issue is not whether Satan is more powerful than us; the point is that Christ, who stands with us, is more powerful than Satan.

James also addressed the need to resist Satan (Jas 4:7). His instruction to resist is coupled with a promised result: "Resist the devil and he will flee from you." Christians are not the ones who should flee; Satan himself should flee as Christians resist him. Appropriately the command to resist immediately follows the exhortation to submit to God. Sometimes it seems that Christians get these two exhortations confused and end up resisting God and submitting to Satan. Resisting Satan and submitting to God go hand in hand. If we are rebelling against God, it will be difficult for us to resist Satan. Effectively resisting Satan requires that we are living in submission to the Lord.

The Context: A Relationship

In responding to temptation, we need to remember that the context for our response is a continuing and growing relationship with Christ. That is why the exhortations to resist and to flee cannot be isolated. We are called to flee from temptation, but to pursue a growing relationship with the Lord. Recall that as soon as Paul has told Timothy to keep away from youthful passions, he tells him to pursue that which God wants to produce in his life—righteousness, faithfulness, love, peace (2 Tim 2:22). Similarly, Peter's encouragement to resist Satan immediately follows the reminder to cast our cares on the Lord who cares for us, and precedes a reminder of our eternal relationship with the Lord (1 Pet 5:6-10).

> Temptation can be a bold attack intended to damage a believer's relationship with the Lord. Responding to temptation by intentionally seeking to strengthen that relationship is a bold and appropriate response. Paul reminded the Romans of that choice in Romans 6:13, "do not present your members to sin…present yourselves to God…" and by doing so we can choose righteousness instead of sin.
>
> As Christians we can expect to experience temptation. We need to be prepared to respond appropriately in ways that will not only keep us from falling into sin but will also strengthen our relationship with Christ.

QUESTION 14

The temptations that a Christian faces are unique to that individual. *True or False?*

QUESTION 15

Please match the items below with the corresponding explanations (based on Jas 1:12-18).

Item	*Explanation*
Our motivation	To be a kind of first fruits of all He created
The source of sin	When sin is full grown it gives birth to death
The birth of sin	When we give in to our evil desires
The ripening of sin	The Father of lights above
The source of good	A crown of life for faithfully enduring temptation
The purpose of our new birth	Never God, but rather our own evil desires

QUESTION 16

Please match the following references with the corresponding example of Israel's sin in the wilderness.

Reference	*Israel's Sin*
1 Corinthians 10:7	So do not be idolaters, as some of them were. As it is written, "The people sat down to eat and drink and rose up to play."
1 Corinthians 10:8	Let us not be immoral, as some of them were, and twenty-three thousand died in a single day.
1 Corinthians 10:9	Do not complain, as some of them did, and were killed by the destroying angel.
1 Corinthians 10:10	Let us not put Christ to the test, as some of them did, and were destroyed by snakes.

QUESTION 17

Which of the following is taught in 1 Corinthians 10:13? *(Select all that apply.)*

A. God provides us a way through our trials without sinning.

B. God limits the trials we face.

C. God will remove temptation if we ask Him.

D. God is faithful.

QUESTION 18

Open your Life Notebook and explain how you are resisting (or have resisted) temptation by fleeing, by resisting, and by pursuing righteousness. Be sure to comment on each of these three strategies.

Topic 5: Coming to the Throne

Non-Christians as well as Christians face temptation. For all of us there can be a battle within ourselves between right and wrong. Since that's true, then when it comes to temptation, what's the difference between Christians and non-Christians?

There is an important difference. When become a Christian, the power of sin is broken. That doesn't mean we don't sin, but it does mean that we don't have to. Now when we face temptation, we don't face it alone. We can come to Jesus in prayer asking Him for His help. After all, He experienced temptation and endured it without sinning. So, He knows how to help us too.

But what happens if we give in to the temptation anyway? Wouldn't that make it worse if we have asked for help and then still fail? Of course, there are times when that happens. We wish we were always successful in dealing with temptation. When we're not, we need to go back to Him in prayer, not so much to ask for help with the temptation, but to confess our sins and receive His forgiveness. And the wonderful thing is that God lets you do that! It's also true that sin always has consequences. That's why Jesus died. And yes, God is gracious, and Christians have experienced that grace.

Many people think that God created the world and humanity but then stepped back and left us on our own. That type of a god is not the God the Bible describes. The God of the Bible desires an intimate relationship with us. He desires that relationship not only when our lives are free from trials, but also when we are tempted. God graciously invites us as Christians to come to His throne to receive all the help we need. Since He also suffered temptation and faithfully endured it, this promise from our sympathetic High Priest is trustworthy.

Prayer is an important component of our response to temptation. In prayer we can seek God's help when we face temptation, and in prayer we can seek His forgiveness when we fail. In lesson six we looked at prayer in some detail; now we want to consider its role in our lives when we deal with temptation. Before continuing with this topic, please read "Coming to the Throne."

Coming to the Throne

The Command to Pray

It had been a long and draining day. They had prepared and shared the Passover meal, listened and talked with the Master, and now they had come to Gethsemane with Jesus, invited by Him to stay while Jesus prayed. Before Jesus withdrew to pray by Himself, and knowing what lay ahead, He gave His disciples something to do. "Pray," He said, "that you will not fall into temptation" (Lk 22:40). This was good advice, but the disciples did not follow it. Jesus moved away from them and agonized in prayer (Lk 22:41-44). His disciples—who must have been physically, mentally, and emotionally exhausted—took a nap. When Jesus returned to them, they were sleeping. In spite of their exhaustion, Jesus repeated His counsel: "Get up and pray that you will not fall into temptation!" (Lk 22:46).

That repeated command was one of the last instructions the disciples would hear from Jesus before His crucifixion. *Pray that you may not fall into temptation.* With those repeated words, Jesus erased any possible doubt about the importance of prayer when facing temptation.

Earlier Jesus had singled out Simon Peter and told him of Satan's intention to target them all (Lk 22:31-34). The image Jesus used was that Satan demanded to sift them like wheat. "I have prayed for you," Jesus told Peter, "that your faith may not fail." Peter's response was one of misplaced self-confidence. He believed that he was ready to face prison and death, but he was wrong. To hear Jesus predict that Peter would repeatedly deny knowing Him must have come as a surprise to Peter. He was less ready for temptation than he thought. When Peter realized his failure, his response was bitter weeping (Lk 22:61-62).

Because Satan targets our weaknesses, it is often true that we are not as ready for temptation as we think we are. Jesus' words to His disciples fit us as well. We need to pray that we may not fall into temptation.

A Great High Priest

The writer of Hebrews reminds us that we have an open invitation to come before the Lord in prayer. He describes Jesus as a great High Priest who intercedes on our behalf, and he shows how much better Jesus is in that role than any other priest. His description of Jesus in the first two chapters of Hebrews is impressive and encouraging when we remember that Jesus is interceding for us. These chapters point out that Jesus, the Son of God, is the Father's final word and that His message must not be rejected. He is unique—the Heir, Creator, and Sustainer of all things. He is immeasurably superior to the angels, and yet He became fully human, suffered, and was tempted, and ultimately gave His life on our behalf.

When we face temptation, it is encouraging to remember who He is. This great High Priest offers us help. No one is more qualified to intercede for us.

Jesus Understands

We have already seen that the temptations we face are not unique; they are common to man and have been experienced by others (1 Cor 10:13). It is encouraging to know that others have faced what we are facing. What is even more encouraging is to know that Jesus has faced what we are facing. Hebrews 4:15 lays out that staggering truth. Jesus is able to fully sympathize with our weaknesses because He has walked where we are walking. He has felt what we feel. He has been tempted with what tempts us, and He has endured without sin.

It can be difficult to talk about a challenge or a struggle with someone who has no experience with that particular struggle. We tend to seek out people who we think will have some personal understanding of what it is we face. Talking with people who have faced similar circumstances can be helpful. When we approach the throne room of our great High Priest Jesus, we are coming before One who knows exactly what we are facing much more intimately than we could imagine. Hebrews 2:18 puts it this way: "Since he suffered and was tempted, he is able to help those who are tempted." None of our temptations will surprise Jesus; He has been there.

Mercy and Grace

In light of who Jesus is, the writer of Hebrews encouraged us to confidently approach the throne of grace (Heb 4:16). We have noted before in this course the importance of understanding something of God's grace, and we need again to take note of its importance here. His throne is one of *grace* to which we are invited. When we are aware of temptation in our lives, we can often easily see our own inclination to sinning. That awareness of sin might discourage us from approaching the Lord in prayer. But when we face temptation, we need to pray, and the God who invites us to approach Him is a God of grace. We may not deserve His help in temptation, but He graciously offers it to us anyway. The invitation is to "find grace whenever we need help."

Sometimes we approach the throne too late to receive help in temptation because we have already failed. At the throne of grace, we can also receive mercy. But once again we might be reluctant to pray, discouraged perhaps by our own sin and aware of our unworthiness. Remember, however, that the adventure of the Christian life began when you approached God in prayer for salvation and received His mercy. His character hasn't changed, and He still welcomes you with the same gracious mercy.

Prayer should not be a last resort in temptation; it should be your first response. "Pray," Jesus said, "that you may not fall into temptation." They did not pray, and soon they had scattered in fear. We do not have to make their mistake. We too are invited to pray. *Let us confidently approach the throne of grace to receive mercy and find help whenever we need help.*

QUESTION 19

Read Hebrews 1–2. Open your Life Notebook and make a list of the truths about Jesus in these chapters that make Him our ideal High Priest.

QUESTION 20

How did Jesus tell His disciples to prepare for temptation in the Garden of Gethsemane?

A. By letting Jesus pray for them

B. By fleeing from the temptation

C. By quoting Scripture

D. By praying themselves that they not fall into temptation

QUESTION 21

Jesus did not experience the same kinds of temptation we face. *True or False?*

QUESTION 22

Which of the following correctly describe the role of prayer in responding to temptation? *(Select all that apply.)*

A. Because of our sin, we should be hesitant to pray when we are facing temptation.
B. God welcomes us into His presence and offers us mercy even when we have sinned.
C. Praying guarantees that we will successfully resist the temptation.
D. Prayer should be our first response when facing temptation.
E. We can find both grace and mercy at God's throne.

Temptation is going to come to all of us, but there are things we can do to be ready to handle it successfully. It's not easy, but Christians are better equipped to handle temptation because of their relationship with the Lord. Our relationship with Christ makes it possible for believers to be equipped and ready to handle temptation successfully. Recognizing temptation for what it is and having a plan to respond will help us. With that in mind, thoughtfully and prayerfully answer the next question.

QUESTION 23

Open your Life Notebook and write out a personal plan for responding to temptation. Identify the common temptations you face and their sources and describe your plan to handle the temptation to sin. Keep in mind the resources that you have studied in this lesson.

Lesson 11 Self Check: The Christian Life

QUESTION 1

What are the three avenues through which temptation comes?

A. The world, God, Satan
B. The flesh, the church, the world
C. The devil, the flesh, the world
D. Satan, the old nature, God

QUESTION 2

How did Jesus pray for His disciples in John 17:14-16?

A. That they would be kept safe in the world
B. That they would be taken out of the world
C. That they would belong in the world
D. That they would be loved by the world

QUESTION 3

Christians live in a world that is hostile to them and that makes it easy to sin. *True or False?*

QUESTION 4

How should Christians think of themselves in relationship to their old sin nature?

A. They should consider themselves to be sin's ruler.
B. They should consider themselves to be sin's servant.
C. They should consider themselves to be dead to sin.
D. They do not need to be concerned about the sin nature since they are redeemed.

QUESTION 5

Putting to death the deeds of the body is a decisive once-for-all action that cannot be repeated. *True or False?*

QUESTION 6

Which of the following is NOT true of Satan?

A. He is limited.
B. He is dangerous.
C. He is powerful but limited.
D. He is sovereign and can do whatever he wants.

QUESTION 7

How did Jesus describe Satan in John 8:44?

A. A murderer and a liar
B. An angel of light
C. A roaring lion
D. A false god

QUESTION 8

Scripture tells us to flee from temptation but to resist Satan rather than to flee from him. *True or False?*

QUESTION 9

Which of the following is NOT taught in 1 Corinthians 10:13?

A. God is faithful.

B. God will limit our trials.

C. Sometimes we encounter temptations that are unique to us.

D. God provides a way through our trial without sinning.

QUESTION 10

Prayer should be our first response in temptation. *True or False?*

Lesson 11 Answers to Questions

QUESTION 1: True

QUESTION 2

A. Dead in sins

B. Living according to the world's path

D. Children of wrath

QUESTION 3

A. That they would be kept safe in the world

QUESTION 4: *Your answer*

QUESTION 5

C. They should consider themselves to be dead to sin.

QUESTION 6: False [Tolerating compromise with the flesh will lead to failure. Romans 13:14 warns us to make no provision for the sinful desires of the flesh.t]

QUESTION 7: True [He asked, "Wretched man that I am! Who will rescue me from this body of death? Thanks be to God through Jesus Christ our Lord! So then, I myself serve the law of God with my mind, but with my flesh I serve the law of sin" (Rom 7:24-25).]

QUESTION 8: False [As long as we live in the flesh, we will continue to face these battles and the need to make critical choices that will affect whether we allow the old nature to regain control in our lives.]

QUESTION 9: *Your answer*

QUESTION 10

B. He tried to make himself like God.

C. He is powerful.

E. He is not sovereign.

QUESTION 11

Reference	*Teaching*
John 8:44	He is a murderer and a liar from the beginning.
2 Corinthians 11:14	He and his agents appear as angels of light.
1 Peter 5:8	He is "like a roaring lion…on the prowl looking for someone to devour."
Revelation 12:10	He operates as an accuser of the brethren.

QUESTION 12: True

QUESTION 13: *Your answer*

QUESTION 14: False [Often when people face temptation, it may seem that the temptation is unique to the individual and that the temptations others may have faced are irrelevant. Paul corrected this error and stated that "no trial has overtaken you that is not faced by others" (1 Cor 10:13).]

QUESTION 15

Item	*Explanation*
Our motivation	A crown of life for faithfully enduring temptation
The source of sin	Never God, but rather our own evil desires
The birth of sin	When we give in to our evil desires
The ripening of sin	When sin is full grown it gives birth to death
The source of good	The Father of lights above
The purpose of our new birth	To be a kind of firstfruits of all He created

QUESTION 16

Reference	*Israel's Sin*
1 Corinthians 10:7	So do not be idolaters, as some of them were. As it is written, "The people sat down to eat and drink and rose up to play."
1 Corinthians 10:8	Let us not be immoral, as some of them were, and twenty-three thousand died in a single day.
1 Corinthians 10:9	Let us not put Christ to the test, as some of them did, and were destroyed by snakes.
1 Corinthians 10:10	Do not complain, as some of them did, and were killed by the destroying angel.

QUESTION 17

A. God provides us a way through our trials without sinning.
B. God limits the trials we face.
D. God is faithful.

QUESTION 18: *Your answer*
QUESTION 19: *Your answer*
QUESTION 20

D. By praying themselves that they not fall into temptation [Before Jesus withdrew to pray by Himself, and knowing what lay ahead, He told the disciples, "Pray that you will not fall into temptation" (Lk 22:39-40).]

QUESTION 21: False [Hebrews 4:15 lays out that staggering truth. Jesus is able to fully sympathize with our weaknesses because He has walked where we are walking. He has felt what we feel. He has been tempted with what tempts us, and He has endured without sin.]

QUESTION 22

B. God welcomes us into His presence and offers us mercy even when we have sinned.
D. Prayer should be our first response when facing temptation.
E. We can find both grace and mercy at God's throne.

QUESTION 23: *Your answer*

Lesson 11 Self Check Answers

QUESTION 1

C. The devil, the flesh, the world

QUESTION 2

A. That they would be kept safe in the world

QUESTION 3: True

QUESTION 4

C. They should consider themselves to be dead to sin.

QUESTION 5: False

QUESTION 6

D. He is sovereign and can do whatever he wants.

QUESTION 7

A. A murderer and a liar

QUESTION 8: True

QUESTION 9

C. Sometimes we encounter temptations that are unique to us.

QUESTION 10: True

Lesson 12: Trusting God in the Spiritual Battle—Living as a Victor

Battles are never easy, whether they are physical or spiritual. In preparing for either kind of battle, it helps to be well trained and well equipped for whatever we face. Like physical battles, spiritual battles are dangerous, but it's a different kind of danger. We always need to be ready for spiritual battles.

For the Christian, life on earth will always be a spiritual battle. We are used to the idea of conflicts in the physical realm in which we live. We can understand battles between nations or coworkers or friends or family members. The battle of the Christian life can be more difficult to grasp because it is spiritual and not limited to the physical realm. In the previous lesson we learned how to recognize and respond to the enemies of the Christian life. In this lesson we will review the nature of the battle and take inventory of the equipment available to us in our fight. We know that the Christian life is a relationship with Christ, and our goal is to continue following Him faithfully even in the midst of battle with the assurance through Christ of ultimate victory.

In this lesson we look at a broader view of the spiritual battle and focus more on living the Christian life in a proactive manner. There are things we can do to prepare ourselves ahead of time in order to be ready for spiritual attacks. Topic 1 of this lesson teaches us to equip ourselves for the battle. We will explore the nature of the battle and discover the resources God makes available to us for the battle. In Topic 2 we will fix our eyes on Jesus. We will consider the ways in which He dealt with the spiritual battle. Topic 3 discusses the need for believers to remain faithful to the end. We will look at examples in the Bible of some who remained faithful and others who did not. Topic 4 continues to examine the victorious Christian life by looking in the book of Revelation at the promises to the one who conquers. Topic 5 looks at the role of every Christian. Not all are called to face battles as dramatic as martyrdom, but because they are related to Christ who is the ultimate victor, ordinary Christians can be victors as well.

Lesson Outline

- Topic 1: Preparing for the Battle
  - The Nature of the Battle
  - Equipping for the Battle
- Topic 2: Following the Example of Jesus
- Topic 3: Remaining Faithful
- Topic 4: Promises to the Conqueror
- Topic 5: Ordinary Victors
- Topic 6: Conclusion

Topic 1: Preparing for the Battle

The Nature of the Battle

The battle Christians fight is a spiritual battle against spiritual foes. Because we are used to living as physical people in a physical world, we do not always accurately perceive the nature of our battle. Dealing with an enemy in the spiritual realm is not the same as dealing with a physical enemy. Unlike a physical battle that can be perceived through our senses, spiritual battles are fought in the heart and mind of the believer. Though that reality may sometimes seem frightening, let us understand two certain truths that you have already read in the title of this lesson. First, it is possible, and from God's perspective, normal, for Christians to live as victors in this battle. We do not need to give up when the battle gets intense and difficult. Second, that victory depends on trusting God. He has not left us to fight the battle alone.

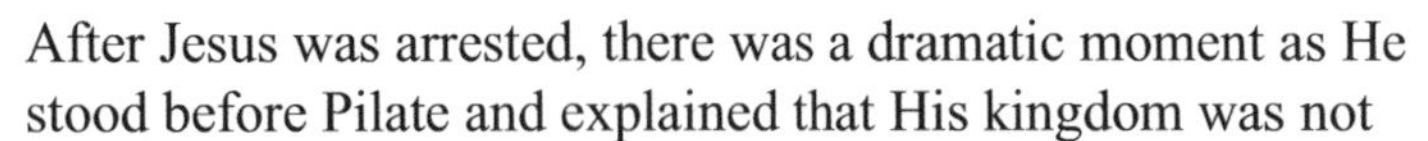

After Jesus was arrested, there was a dramatic moment as He stood before Pilate and explained that His kingdom was not in the physical realm (Jn 18:36). Had His kingdom been of this world, then He and His servants would have been engaged in a physical battle with those who opposed Him. Other than Peter's attack of the high priest's servant when Jesus was arrested, there was no such physical battle (Jn 18:10-11). The battle that was taking place was being waged in a spiritual realm of which Pilate was unaware.

Paul reminded the Ephesian Christians that before they became Christians, when they were spiritually dead, they were living "according to the ruler of the kingdom of the air" (Eph 2:1-3). Unbelievers, though they may not know it, are operating in a realm of spiritual darkness. Later he reminds these same believers that their battle is a spiritual one and their foe is a spiritual foe (Eph 6:10-12).

QUESTION 1

Open your Life Notebook and write down some of the differences you perceive between a physical battle and a spiritual one.

Equipping for the Battle

To be effective in a battle, one must first understand the nature of that battle and then adequately prepare for it. Scripture often uses the metaphor of a battle for the Christian life, and it makes clear that we need to be prepared for the battle. Read 2 Timothy 2:4-5 in which Paul used the images of military service and an athletic contest to point out the need to be ready for the particular battle.

Both soldiers and athletes need to understand the nature of their battle and then prepare for that battle by exercise and self-discipline. The soldier's commander and the athlete's coach play key roles in guiding them to victory, and the Lord, who is a trustworthy commander and coach, guides Christians to spiritual victory. Like the soldier and the athlete, the Christian must understand the nature of his battle and prepare himself for spiritual warfare by depending on Christ and deepening his relationship with Him.

Before continuing with the questions below, please read "Equipped for Battle."

Equipped for Battle

Wise and careful preparation is important in many areas if one expects a successful outcome. In the spiritual battle Christians face, such preparation is essential. When Paul wrote to the Christians at Ephesus, he gave them a clear and graphic description of the preparation they would need if they were to succeed in the battle. Read Ephesians 6:10-18 and then meditate on this essential passage for spiritual warfare.

Paul began with an encouragement to be strengthened in the Lord (Eph 6:10). Earlier in this letter Paul had prayed that they would know the greatness of God's power in their lives and reminded them that that power was at work in them (Eph 1:17-19, 3:30). Now at the outset of this discussion of preparation for spiritual battle, he reminded them that God's strength in them will enable them to triumph.

He then encouraged the Ephesians, and us, to clothe ourselves with the full armor of God so we can stand against the devil's schemes (Eph 6:11). Recognizing who the enemy is (Satan) and what he is like (scheming) should motivate us to use the resources God provides. He reminds us our struggle is not against flesh and blood but against the spiritual forces of evil in the heavens (Eph 6:12). Spiritual battles require spiritual resources and he again exhorted us to put on the full armor of God, which will enable us to stand firm during temptation (Eph 6:13).

The goal and the command here is to stand firm in the battle (Eph 6:14). In order to do so, we will need the equipment that Paul described:

- **The belt of truth** (Eph 6:14). It is interesting that the first piece of armor Paul mentions is truth. Keep in mind that Jesus identified Satan as a liar and the father of lies (Jn 8:44), and Jesus identified Himself as the truth (Jn 14:6). Jesus Himself is truth and His word is truth; we need to take our stand with Him (Jn 17:17). Spiritual warfare is not so much a power encounter as a truth encounter; it is a battle over truth. Basic to our success is that we gird ourselves with truth. For the Roman soldier of old, his belt kept the rest of his armor in place; it was of foundational importance, and so it is for us. We cannot expect to triumph in the spiritual battle apart from truth.
- **The breastplate of righteousness** (Eph 6:14): The righteousness of which Paul wrote is not earned by keeping the Law; it is given by God and comes to us at salvation as a result of Christ's atoning work (Phil 3:8-9). Scripture is clear that our righteousness is not achieved by our own work but is a result of God's grace (Rom 4:3-5). For us to actually use the breastplate means that we must live up to the righteousness we have been given. If we choose to live sinfully, then we are laying down our breastplate and leaving our vital organs exposed in the spiritual battle. The breastplate of righteousness is best seen through living righteously by seeking God and His will. When this is our regular practice, we are better protected from the schemes of the enemy.
- **Fitting your feet with the preparation that comes from the good news of peace** (Eph 6:15): No wise Roman soldier would have gone into battle with bare feet, and nor should we. Our feet are fitted with preparation, and that preparation comes from the good news of peace. Paul seems to have in mind here Isaiah 52:7, which says it is wonderful to see a messenger with good news, announcing deliverance and peace, and declaring that God

reigns. Paul pointed out that Christians engaged in spiritual battle need to be such messengers, proclaiming the gospel of Christ, announcing deliverance, and declaring that God reigns. Satan seeks to obstruct the message of the gospel; we need to be prepared to continue proclaiming it.

- **The shield of faith** (Eph 6:16): The Roman soldier's shield was a large one, covered in leather that could be soaked in water so as to extinguish the flaming arrows of the enemy. Paul likened that shield to our faith. From the time of Adam and Eve, Satan has sought to cast doubt on what God has said. We need to trust God, because by doing so our faith becomes a protective shield the enemy cannot penetrate. Hebrews reminds us that faith is essential if we are to please God (Heb 11:6). Often in battle Roman soldiers would raise their shields side by side, providing a greater area of protection. In our spiritual battles our faith raised in fellowship with others, can minister to them as well as protect us.
- **The helmet of salvation** (Eph 6:17): It would be hard to overemphasize the importance of the Christian's mind; Scripture is sprinkled with many references to our minds and the way we think. Romans 12:2, for example, encourages us to be "transformed by the renewing of your mind." If the enemy can cause us to doubt our salvation, then he can make us ineffective in the spiritual battle. Our salvation is fundamental to our effectiveness, and that salvation needs to be worn as protection for the mind.
- **The sword of the Spirit, which is the Word of God** (Eph 6:17). Up to now the pieces of the armor have been defensive in nature, designed to protect us in the battle. A sword, however, is an offensive weapon that is able to neutralize the effectiveness of the enemy. This single offensive weapon is the Word of God. As we saw in previous lessons, even in the Old Testament knowledge of God's Word was necessary for spiritual success (e.g., Josh 1:7-8). Jesus demonstrated the importance of this weapon when Satan tempted Him. To each of the three temptations Jesus responded with Scripture (Mt 4:1-11). The third time Jesus also told Satan to go away when He quoted Scripture, and Satan did leave. Countering the enemy with the truth of God's Word is powerful and effective. We should strive to be like Ezra who "had given himself to the study of the law of the Lord, to its observance, and to teaching its statutes and judgments in Israel" (Ezra 7:10).
- **Pray** (Eph 6:18). After describing these specific pieces of the believer's equipment for spiritual battle, Paul encouraged them to pray. The disciples experienced a dramatic example of the importance of prayer when they were unable to cast out an evil spirit from a boy. The boy's father had asked them, and they had failed. After Jesus cast out the evil spirit, the disciples asked Him why they had not been able to do so. Jesus answered, "This kind can come out only by prayer" (Mk 9:29). Prayer is absolutely essential to our success in spiritual battle and admitting our dependence on the Lord to guide us through the battle. Interestingly Paul did not focus on their need to pray for their own spiritual success. He told them to pray "for all the saints" (Eph 6:18). We are not engaged in a spiritual war as isolated soldiers. We are part of an army of believers who can support one another in prayer. In the next two verses Paul made himself the subject of their prayers; "Pray for me" he wrote (Eph 6:19). A healthy practice is to pray for the spiritual battles of others and to invite them to pray for us.

God has not left us defenseless in the battle. He has repeatedly told us to stand firm, and He has prepared us to stand firm by giving us armor. Properly and prayerfully using that armor makes victory possible in our spiritual battles.

QUESTION 2

Which of the following did Paul mention repeatedly in Ephesians 6:10-13? *(Select all that apply.)*

A. Our struggle

B. Strength

C. The full armor of God

D. The need to stand

QUESTION 3

In both Ephesians 6:13 and Ephesians 6:14, before detailing the armor of God, Paul encourages us to do what?

QUESTION 4

Please match the following references with the corresponding teachings about the armor of God.

Reference	*Teaching*
Ephesians 6:14	The helmet of salvation and the Word of God
Ephesians 6:15	The belt of truth and breastplate of righteousness
Ephesians 6:16	Feet prepared with the good news of peace
Ephesians 6:17	The shield of faith
Ephesians 6:18	Praying in the Spirit for all the saints

QUESTION 5

Review prayerfully the resources for spiritual battle given in Ephesians 6:10-18. Spend some time talking to God about these resources in your own life. Which would you like to strengthen? Then open your Life Notebook and write a summary of your conversation with the Lord.

Topic 2: Following the Example of Jesus

You may be wondering how we can be ready for a spiritual battle when we can't even see the enemy. Because our spiritual enemy is unseen, that makes it even more important to be ready. We would do well to remember that we are fighting a battle that has been fought before. We probably all have a friend, or know of a senior person in our church, who has been through a spiritual battle. We can learn a lot from them. And most importantly, we have a Friend in Jesus who has already fought this battle for us, and He is the victor. Jesus won that spiritual battle. And this means that Satan has already been defeated.

Expert help is a good thing, and there is no better expert when it comes to spiritual battles than Jesus. Even though Jesus is not present with us in human form, His expertise in spiritual battle has much to teach us. In this topic we will look more closely at Jesus and learn how He handled spiritual battles. Start by reading "Jesus Our Example" and then answer the questions below.

Jesus Our Example

Living the Christian life is a challenge and an adventure. Since it involves engaging in a spiritual battle, it is dangerous. Jesus did not leave His disciples ignorant about how to live that life and how to succeed in the battle. He modeled this life, and He repeatedly invited His disciples to follow His example.

The miracle of the incarnation means God in the person of Jesus Christ became human, taking on the limitations, weaknesses, and struggles of humanity. This means He also faced the same kinds of spiritual battles we face. Though He experienced the same kind of temptations we do, He did not give in to sin. He emerged from spiritual combat as a victor. We can learn much from His example.

Follow Me

As Jesus began His public ministry, He invited His future disciples to join Him (e.g., Jn 1:35-43). What began as exploration on their part would become a life-changing radical commitment. When Jesus invited simple fishermen to catch people instead of fish, they left everything and followed Him (Mk 1:16-20; Lk 5:9-11). When Matthew, the tax collector, heard a similar invitation from Jesus, he too followed Him (Mt 9:9).

In following Jesus, these men embarked on a learning adventure that would turn their lives upside down. Jesus taught them to live differently from the way they were used to living. Their actions and their values changed, and they developed an ability to do battle with the spiritual forces of evil and succeed. Eventually Jesus would send them out with others to minister to people. When they returned, they told Him that even the demons submitted to them in His name (Lk 10:17-20). Their authority to engage the enemy and triumph did not originate with them; it was the authority of the One they followed.

Following the example of Jesus would eventually become a habit in their lives, but like most people, they needed reminders. After Jesus' resurrection He addressed Peter's failure and renewed the invitation and challenge to follow Him. This was a challenge that Peter would later pass on to others (1 Pet 2:21).

Paul likewise repeated the reminder to follow Christ to the believers to whom he wrote. He told those at Corinth that Christ was his pattern: "Be imitators of me just as I also am of Christ" (1 Cor 11:1). In a similar way he reminded the Ephesians that they had a divine example to follow: "Be imitators of God… live in love, just as Christ also loved us" (Eph 5:1-2). To the Colossian Christians he urged, "continue to live your lives in him, rooted and built up in him and firm in your faith" (Col 2:6-7).

Jesus and the Battle

Since Jesus is our example, it is wise for us to see how He handled the spiritual battle. We know already that Jesus was a man of prayer. He sought opportunities for fellowship with His Father, so when times of spiritual conflict came, Jesus already enjoyed close communication with the Father. A close relationship with the Lord is important preparation for times of spiritual battle. While on earth, Jesus' relationship with the Father was one of dependence on the Father's guidance, strength, and will.

That relationship is evident in the descriptions of Jesus' temptations recorded in Matthew 4:1-11 and Luke 4:1-13. We are told that at the outset of this time of temptation, Jesus was "full of the Holy Spirit" and "led by the Spirit" (Lk 4:1). He did not face the battle alone, and nor should we.

For forty days Jesus endured the temptations of the devil without falling into sin. He was as spiritually ready for battle as it is possible to be. The time we spend with the Lord in prayer is not wasted as we learn to listen to Him, respond to His leading, and depend on His strength.

Scripture gives us specific examples of the temptations Jesus experienced. The first was aimed at a weakness. After forty days of fasting, Jesus was famished, and Satan appealed to His physical hunger (Lk 4:2-3). The enemy will regularly attack at a point of perceived weakness, and that is what Satan did. An awareness of one's weaknesses and the ability to exercise control over one's appetites, in dependence on the Spirit, makes victory more certain.

The record of these temptations clearly indicates that Jesus countered each temptation with Scripture. He was demonstrating, as Paul would later teach, that God's Word is an effective response to temptation. Obviously, Jesus did not pull out a scroll so that He could read from the Pentateuch to Satan. He had committed Scripture to memory and used it appropriately. In a sense we have an advantage over Jesus in that we have the New Testament Scriptures available to us in addition to the Old Testament Scriptures Jesus quoted. Memorizing Scripture makes it available to us whenever we find ourselves in a battle.

Jesus had absolute authority and responded to Satan by stating truth with that authority and without fear. Eventually Jesus even told Satan to go away (Mt 4:10). This same fearless authority characterized Jesus when He confronted evil spirits in other people. Both the evil spirits Jesus encountered and the people who witnessed those encounters recognized His authority (e.g., Lk 4:33-36). Sometimes Jesus acted in situations that others considered dangerous. On the east side of the Sea of Galilee Jesus delivered a possessed man who was considered sufficiently dangerous that he was kept chained and guarded (Lk 8:26-35). Jesus understood the enemy's strength, but He also understood the enemy's limits. He knew the truth that John later declared: "The one who is in you is greater than the one who is in the world" (1 Jn 4:4).

The Battle of the Cross

The disciples had many opportunities to see how Jesus handled spiritual battles, but no battle they witnessed would be more intense than the events culminating in His crucifixion. Yet here, too, Jesus' participation in the battle was marked by prayer, truth, and His authority. To the disciples, Jesus' crucifixion must have seemed the ultimate defeat. Only later when confronted with the reality of His resurrection would they fully realize that it was the ultimate victory that guaranteed their own victory.

At Gethsemane Jesus drew on His habit of prayer, agonizingly aware of the spiritual battle in which He would soon give His life. Through the mockery, interrogation, and torture that followed His arrest, He spoke only truth, and always with authority. Some of His followers would face their own life-threatening battles, and having learned from Jesus, were able to respond as He did.

Handling spiritual battles the way Jesus did becomes possible when we are willing to follow Him. He acted out of a close relationship with His Father, in the power and confidence of the Spirit. We can enter the battle in the power of the Spirit with a close relationship with the Lord. He used the truth of Scripture to combat the enemy. So can we. He acted with fearless authority. We, too, can act in the authority He has given us, knowing that He has already secured the ultimate victory.

QUESTION 6

Which of the following changed for the disciples because they followed Jesus? *(Select all that apply.)*

A. Their actions

B. Their values

C. Their ability to succeed in spiritual battles

D. Their identity as Jews

QUESTION 7

Match the Scripture references below with the encouragements they give to follow Christ.

Scripture	*Encouragement*
1 Peter 2:21	Be imitators of me just as I also am of Christ.
1 Corinthians 11:1	Christ also suffered for you, leaving an example for you to follow in His steps
Ephesians 5:1-2	Continue to live your lives in Him rooted and built up in Him.
Colossians 2:6-7	Live in love just as Christ also loved us.

QUESTION 8

Jesus' spiritual battle was limited to three specific temptations in the wilderness. *True or False?*

QUESTION 9

With which of the following did Jesus handle spiritual battles? *(Select all that apply.)*

A. Prayer

B. Fear

C. Memorized Scripture

D. Authority

E. Truth

QUESTION 10

Open your Life Notebook and summarize what you can learn about handling spiritual battles from the example of Jesus. What do you see in His example that is most helpful to you in facing spiritual battles at this point in your life?

Topic 3: Remaining Faithful

Faithfulness is a choice, but when it comes to our relationship with the Lord, sometimes it can be a difficult choice. When the spiritual battles come, it can seem easier simply to give in than remain faithful. But giving up in the face of difficulty or failure underestimates what God can do. It also wrongly equates today's spiritual conflict with the entire battle. Because we continue to experience spiritual conflict, we can become weary in the battle.

One common biblical metaphor for the Christian life is a race. Paul encouraged the Corinthian believers to "run to win" this race (1 Cor 9:24-27). The writer to Hebrews tells us to "run with endurance" (Heb

12:1). Nobody wins a race by dropping out. In the spiritual battles we face in the Christian life, it is important to remain faithful. Please read "Remaining Faithful" and then answer the questions that follow.

Remaining Faithful

Spiritual battles are an unavoidable reality in the Christian life. However, they do not exist as single isolated events; Christians are engaged in an ongoing struggle with the enemy. While we might like to think the end of one particular battle means our struggle is over, that is usually not the case. Not even Jesus was immune to repeated attacks. After a forty-day period in which he tempted Jesus, Satan left but not permanently. Luke's account of those events says that Satan "departed from him until a more favorable time" (Lk 4:13).

The idea of a continuing battle with repeated attacks should not come as a surprise to us. The enemy targets the relationship we enjoy with Christ. Relationships are not single events. By their very nature relationships exist over a period of time, and so attacks on a relationship will also exist over a period of time until either the relationship or the enemy is destroyed. The Christian life is not a short sprint; it is a long-distance marathon in which we need to remain faithful. If we are not faithful, the relationship suffers. Faithfulness by its very nature requires consistency over time. The idea of inconsistent or intermittent faithfulness is a contradiction in terms.

Avoiding Shipwrecks

We can find plenty of examples in the Bible of people who did not remain faithful. Not surprisingly, their relationships with the Lord suffered. By withdrawing from the battle before it was over, they let the enemy win. In encouraging Timothy to hold on to faith and a good conscience, Paul said those who reject these have suffered shipwreck in regard to the faith (1 Tim 1:18-20). Paul had lived through multiple literal shipwrecks, and he wanted to steer Timothy away from any possibility of a spiritual shipwreck. He then named two individuals, Hymenaeus and Alexander, who had suffered such a shipwreck by not only dropping out of the battle, but also turning their backs on their faith. Hymenaeus is again singled out in Paul's second letter to Timothy and described, along with Philetus, as having strayed from the truth (2 Tim 2:16-18).

In this second letter to Timothy, Paul commented on several people, consistently encouraging Timothy to remain faithful (e.g., 2 Tim 3:14-15). Several people had left Paul for a variety of reasons. Among them was Demas, whose reason for leaving involved a shipwreck; he loved the present age (2 Tim 4:10). Paul had called Demas a colaborer (Phm 24). He became a dropout, and when he dropped out, his failure affected more than just himself. His decision had a ripple effect that touched the lives of others, including Paul. A sobering fact is that our failure in a spiritual battle can give the enemy an opportunity to harm the lives of others.

Redeemed Failures

Failure in the spiritual battle does not have to be the end. Scripture includes the accounts of several who experienced failure in a spiritual battle but went on to become victors. We will consider two notable examples.

Simon Peter was one of the disciples closest to Jesus. He was one of three invited to accompany Jesus when He went up on a mountain to pray. There Peter witnessed Jesus transfigured and conversing with Moses and Elijah, and there he heard the Father identify Jesus as His Son (Lk 9:28-35). Later he was again one of three invited to keep watch in Gethsemane with Jesus when He prayed (Mt 26:36-46). Yet in the heat of the spiritual battle after Jesus was arrested, Peter repeatedly denied knowing Him. This was a crushing failure for Peter, one that he had not thought possible (Mk 14:66-72).

Peter's failure was not permanent. After His resurrection Jesus gave Peter a repeated opportunity to reaffirm the relationship and his love for the Lord. Jesus responded by calling Peter afresh to ministry (Jn 21:15-17). Peter, who had failed in the battle, later became a victor. The same Peter who had denied knowing Jesus would proclaim that same Jesus in the power of the Spirit and see crowds of people turn to Christ. Peter's restoration seems to be focused on one question that goes to the heart of a relationship with Christ: "Do you love Me?"

A second example of one who was a victor after experiencing failure is John Mark, also called Mark. He had accompanied Paul and Barnabas on their first missionary journey. They left Antioch and headed to the island of Cypress, where Mark had opportunity to witness spiritual battles (Acts 13:4-13). After traveling through the island, they sailed north to the mainland where Mark left them to return home. Mark's departure became the focus of a serious disagreement between Paul and Barnabas over whether they should take him on a second journey (Acts 15:36-40). Paul was adamantly opposed to taking Mark. But years later, Paul requested Mark's presence and assistance (2 Tim 4:11). Interestingly Peter, who himself had failed, was instrumental in Mark's restoration. Though there was no blood relationship, Peter refers to Mark as "my son" (1 Pet 5:13). Peter, who had experienced God's grace in restoration, apparently helped Mark discover that same grace.

The Cloud of Witnesses

The writer of Hebrews includes a long list of God's people who remained faithful (Heb 11). Some are discussed in detail; others are mentioned only briefly. Their specific activities are varied, and they span a range of many centuries. What they had in common is acting in faith.

This is a long and impressive list, but it is not complete. There is not enough time, the writer said, to tell all that could be told (Heb 11:32).

We can easily point to moments of crisis in the lives of those mentioned in this chapter at which they had to decide whether to remain faithful. Often at such moments remaining faithful seems to be the more difficult choice; sometimes it seems much more difficult. But it is precisely at those challenging times when the battle seems most dangerous that we, like them, need to choose to remain faithful. Why should Noah keep building an ark? Why should Abraham and Sarah keep waiting for a son? Why should Gideon go into battle immensely outnumbered? Why should we keep battling the enemy when we are weary of the battle? Those who choose to remain faithful consider it worth it, and they discover that the God who is trustworthy when all is well is just as trustworthy in the heat of the battle.

The writer of Hebrews reminds us to be encouraged by this cloud of witnesses (Heb 12:1-3). We are called to let go of sin, to run the race before us with endurance, and to fix our eyes on Jesus. When we choose sin we give in to the enemy; we need to reject it and turn to the Lord. The Christian life is not a short sprint; it is a long-distance marathon that calls for endurance. That endurance becomes easier when we keep Jesus in view. He helps us remain faithful. He is the One who has brought us into a relationship with Himself, a relationship He values highly; He is the ultimate Victor. "Think of him," we are told, "so that you may not grow weary in your souls and give up" (Heb 12:3).

QUESTION 11

Who did Paul say had suffered shipwreck in regard to the faith? *(Select all that apply.)*

A. Alexander

B. Mark

C. Hymenaeus

D. Simon Peter

QUESTION 12

Why did Demas leave Paul?

A. He feared spiritual battles.

B. He loved the present age.

C. He went home to Jerusalem.

D. The Ephesian church needed him.

QUESTION 13

Who was instrumental in Mark's restoration?

A. Silas

B. Timothy

C. Peter

D. Demas

E. Alexander

QUESTION 14

Review the people who are listed as examples of faith in Hebrews 11. Choose at least three of them as personal models of faithfulness. Open your Life Notebook and explain for each one you choose how that person is an example for you.

QUESTION 15

Which of the following should we do since we are surrounded by a cloud of witnesses? *(Select all that apply.)*

A. Rid ourselves of sin

B. Carry the things that weigh us down

C. Run the race before us with endurance

D. Keep our eyes fixed on Jesus

E. Think about our failures

Topic 4: Promises to the Conqueror

In the spiritual battle finishing well is important. We saw in the last topic the importance of remaining faithful. God has promised to reward those who finish well; in Revelation He calls them "conquerors." In Revelation 21 the Lord told about the new heaven and the new earth (Rev 21:1). In this new creation, God Himself will live with humanity (Rev 21:3). After a brief but wonderful description of life in His presence, He said, "The one who conquers will inherit these things, and I will be his God and he will be my son" (Rev 21:7). God makes faithfulness in the spiritual battle worth it. His intention for us is that we enjoy an intimate relationship with Him. When we are victors in the spiritual battle, we can enjoy that relationship that He intends.

The nature of the battle is not the same in every time and place, but we still need to be victors. Read "The Victors of Revelation" and notice the encouragements given to those who conquer.

The Victors of Revelation

When John wrote the book of Revelation, his intended primary audience was embattled Christians who were trying to live out their faith in an often difficult and hostile world. The book is not only a revelation of how the future will unfold; it is a revelation of Christ Himself. The second and third chapters of the book consist of a series of short messages addressed to seven different churches in Asia Minor. While these churches faced different circumstances and challenges, they had the same Lord who offered commendation and correction—where appropriate—along with the encouragement to become victors in the specific battles they faced.

Their battles were not unique. While we may live in a different time and different place, we too can benefit from the encouragement that they received as we seek to be victors in the spiritual battles we face. The Lord of the church expected them to be victors. Each church's message includes a brief word of encouragement "to the one who conquers." As you consider these seven messages, it is likely that you will be able to identify with the circumstances of one or more of these churches. You too can find encouragement in the Lord's words to those who conquered in these churches.

Ephesus

Revelation 2:1-7

The Ephesian Christians lived in a city that was not only commercially important but was also a religious center with its temple to Artemis. Living as a Christian in that environment would have been challenging. Yet the believers had managed to maintain their commitment to truth. In the shadow of the temple of Artemis one might expect that their battle would have focused on drifting from the truth of the gospel. But instead, their arena of spiritual conflict focused on the fact that they had left their first love. A loveless relationship will soon wither, and it seemed that the enemy was winning in Ephesus. The Lord told them that their very existence as a church was in danger if they did not repent.

For the victors, those who conquer, there is a promise that echoes Eden. They are invited to eat of the tree of life in the paradise of God. This word of encouragement embodies both the gift of eternal life and the joy of God's presence. While the imagery seems to suggest eternity, both eternal life and enjoying God's presence are available to believers now through Christ's completed work on the cross. Victors, instead of leaving their first love, can enjoy a relationship with the Lord now and for all eternity.

Smyrna

Revelation 2:8-11

The Christians in Smyrna were the targets of persecution. This was a suffering church, and they were being told to expect more suffering. Smyrna is one of two churches for which there was no word of correction. Perhaps suffering had already purged the church of sinful practices. They were encouraged to remain faithful, even to the point of martyrdom. The church today is not beyond needing to hear that encouragement; Christians in many places still suffer persecution and even death for their faith. It is a sobering realization that one could be martyred and still be a victor. The word to victors in such circumstances is the important reminder that they will in no way be harmed by the second death. The second death is eternal separation from God that will be faced by unbelievers (Rev 20:14-15). These believers discover that God can be trusted even in death. For Christians, not even martyrdom can separate us from God!

Pergamum

Revelation 2:12-17

Pergamum was the capital of the Roman province of Asia. It had become a center for emperor worship as well as a host for assorted pagan religions. Christ's message to this church recognized that they lived in a place where Satan ruled. Spiritual syncretism seems to be the battle arena for these Christians. Some have tried to mix into their lives false teachings that included the acceptance of practices such as sexual immorality. Those who conquer in this spiritual battle will receive hidden manna and a white stone; written on the stone is a new name known only to the one who receives it. Victors can expect spiritual nourishment that the world will not understand. In this culture a person's name represented that person's character; those who conquer have been given a new nature that they can recognize. The white stone may have represented acquittal in a criminal trial. The Lord reminded those who conquer in this spiritual battle that they are justified, transformed, and nourished, and Christ Himself is the source of those blessings.

Thyatira

Revelation 2:18-28

A key factor in the spiritual battle in Thyatira was an influential woman who apparently claimed to be a believer but led Christians astray into sinful behavior. Much as in Pergamum, sinful behavior was accepted as normal. However, the evil influence in Thyatira may have been coming from within the church community. Some of the Christians were faithful while others were falling victim to the battle. The ongoing nature of the battle is emphasized when the promise is made to the one who not only conquers but who also "continues in my deeds until the end" (Rev 2:26). These victors will rule (or "shepherd") the nations with Christ, who gives them both that authority and "the morning star" (Rev 2:28). This is a term that Jesus used later to describe Himself (Rev 22:16). Once again, those who conquer are promised Christ Himself.

Sardis

Revelation 3:1-6

Sometimes a particular local church is described as "dead." Such a description usually means that they do not give evidence of vitality. There may be a lack of enthusiasm among the congregation and little ministry taking place. Such a description is often inaccurate. But when Sardis is described as "dead," the description is coming from the One who is the Head of the church, Jesus Christ. In this case the church appeared to others to be alive, while in reality it was characterized by people who were withdrawing from the spiritual battle. "Wake up," they are told, "and strengthen what remains that was about to die" (Rev 3:2). Their deeds were incomplete; they had stopped too soon.

Only a few in Sardis remained faithful. They will walk with Christ dressed in white. Those who heed the call, who wake up and become victors, will be like them. They will be cleansed, justified, and secure in Christ. This is a powerful promise. Though many at Sardis had given up on the battle, the Lord of the church had not given up on them.

Philadelphia

Revelation 3:7-13

The Christians at Philadelphia had remained faithful in the face of opposition and had carried out effective ministry with the little strength they had (Rev 3:8). Like Smyrna, Philadelphia receives no word of correction or rebuke. The message to the church at Philadelphia, which immediately follows the message to Sardis that had given up, is an encouragement to remain faithful. Sometimes we see the spiritual battle as the ultimate in testing, and we can become weary warriors. This church, however, was told that if they endured steadfastly, they would be kept from the hour of testing that the whole earth will experience. They were better off staying engaged in the battle. Those who conquer will be made pillars in the temple of God; they will be where God dwells. On them will be written new names—of God, of the New Jerusalem, and of Christ. This is a powerful image of an enduring relationship.

Laodicea

Revelation 3:14-22

Laodicea was an important commercial center and a relatively affluent city. But in the midst of that affluence—or perhaps because of it—the church had sunk into spiritual poverty. Its main characteristic seems to have been indifference. Content in their materialism, they had become blind to their own spiritual condition. No word of commendation was given to this church, only a call to repentance was included (Rev 3:19). They have drifted from an intimate relationship with Christ to the point that He pictured Himself standing at their door knocking, ready to come in and share a meal, if invited (Rev 3:20). The condition of this church seems even more serious than the "dead" church in Sardis.

But even in the midst of indifference, in a church described as neither hot nor cold, it is possible to become a victor. There is in Christ's message to this church the clear hope that among the hopelessly lukewarm, there will be those who hear Him knocking and respond. And those who become victors will sit with Christ on His throne. Yet again, and even to those who have been trapped in their own bondage to materialism, those who conquer enjoy the presence of Christ.

Summary

In each one of these seven very different churches, the spiritual battle is evident. In each of the seven, those who conquer are rewarded; and always at the heart of the reward is Christ Himself. The battles we face are like theirs. Our need to remain faithful is no less than theirs. And the focus of our reward when we are victors is the same as theirs: enjoying an unfettered and eternal relationship with Jesus Christ.

QUESTION 16

Which of the churches in Revelation 2–3 did not receive a word of correction? *(Select all that apply.)*

A. Ephesus

B. Smyrna

C. Thyatira

D. Sardis

E. Philadelphia

QUESTION 17

Match the church with what was promised to those in that church who conquer.

Church	*What Was Promised*
Ephesus	Made a pillar in temple of God
Smyrna	In no way harmed by the second death
Pergamum	Dressed in white clothing; never erased from book of life
Thyatira	Hidden manna and a white stone with a new name
Sardis	Permission to sit with Christ on His throne
Philadelphia	Authority over the nations; the morning star
Laodicea	Eat from the tree of life

QUESTION 18

The common theme in what is promised to those who conquer in the churches of Revelation 2–3 is Christ Himself. *True or False?*

The churches in Revelation 2–3 each faced a different set of circumstances. The spiritual battles they experienced differed from one another. Review these two chapters, and then answer the following question.

QUESTION 19

Open your Life Notebook and identify which church (or churches) in Revelation 2–3 most closely resembles your current circumstances. How does the message to this church (or churches) encourage you?

Topic 5: Ordinary Victors

Christians should take the matter of spiritual battles seriously. It's part of what is involved in being a Christian. But we may wonder whether it really matters, because it's not as though the future of Christianity is at stake. However, believers would do well to remember that what is at stake in our spiritual battles is the condition of our relationship with Christ. And that's worth fighting for.

The last topic showed us the variety of battles faced by the churches of Asia Minor in Revelation. Not every Christian will conquer in all the ways described in Revelation 2–3. Not everyone will be in a position to make some of the great sacrifices the heroes of the faith in Hebrews 11 did. Not everyone is called to forfeit his life as Stephen did after a fiery, Holy Spirit-inspired indictment of Israel's leaders for crucifying their Christ (Acts 7). Not everyone will be a Peter who reportedly died as a martyr hanging upside down on a cross, refusing the "honor" of dying upright as Jesus did (Jn 21:18-23). But all of us will face spiritual battles no matter how ordinary our lives may seem. And all of us have the opportunity to be victors in those battles.

If the circumstances of a Christian's life are as dramatic as those of Peter or Paul, it would be normal to expect spiritual battles. Those of us whose lives seem more ordinary (at least to ourselves) might be tempted to think that spiritual battles are for other people. But we are not exempt from the battles, and our victories are no less significant because our lives seem more ordinary.

The heart of the Christian life is a relationship with Jesus. No matter the circumstances of our lives we are still called to remain faithful in that relationship. It is possible that the shape of our faithfulness may seem insignificant to us; nevertheless, faithfulness is our calling, and we must strive to be faithful. Scripture provides plenty of examples of believers who have done just that.

Read "Ordinary Victors" before answering the questions below.

Ordinary Victors

The heroes of the faith are easy to remember; they are great men called to great tasks. Abraham, Moses, and David helped form the nation Israel while Peter and Paul helped shape the identity of the early church. But what about some of the more obscure people whose appearance in Scripture almost seems to be an afterthought? What was the impact of these ordinary believers, and could their faithfulness really make a difference?

While some Christians may be among the material, social, or political elite, and others are in places of obvious influence, most believers are ordinary people. That reality is not an accident. Paul spoke to the ordinariness of the Corinthian Christians in his first letter to them (1 Cor 1:26-31). When God works through ordinary people who have been called into a relationship with Christ, it is easier to see that God is the One who is at work. The Bible includes many people who did not have a dramatic role in the front lines of the spiritual battle, but whose faithfulness in the battle still made a difference. We will consider a few examples.

Mary, Joanna, Susanna

Most Christians are aware of Jesus' twelve disciples and are especially familiar with those who were prominent, such as Peter and John. Luke tells us about a less recognized group of women who accompanied Jesus and the Twelve, who by their faithfulness carried out an important role. As far as we know, they did not preach, heal, or cast out demons, though they had been on the receiving end of that ministry. They played a supportive role that enabled Jesus and the disciples to devote time to ministry. Out of their own resources they provided for the physical needs of Jesus and His followers.

There is always a cost involved in following Jesus, and it would have been no different for these women. Some of them were unlikely followers of Jesus. Mary Magdalene had been freed from multiple demons. Joanna's husband was the household manager for Herod Antipas, who ruled Galilee. Susanna and others joined them, determined to do what they could. They made a choice, and their participation made a difference.

Joseph of Arimathea

Joseph of Arimathea had been a follower of Jesus, though most who knew him would not have known that (Jn 19:38). He had kept it secret, fearing the reaction of the Jewish authorities. He was a member of the Sanhedrin, and his allegiance to Jesus would not have endeared him to others who were opposed to Jesus (Lk 23:50-52). Joseph requested the crucified body of Jesus from Pilate, and, along with Nicodemus, he prepared the body for burial in an unused garden tomb.

Politically this was not a good time for Joseph to reveal his secret allegiance to Jesus. Those opposed to Him had seemingly won, and Jesus was dead. For Joseph to have remained quiet would have been far easier. Instead, he and Nicodemus, took a stand. Whatever was involved in Joseph's quiet spiritual battle, he became a victor.

Ananias and Barnabas

Most Christians recognize the significance of Paul. Fewer are aware of two other believers who played key roles in Paul's life. After Paul's miraculous encounter with the Lord on the road to Damascus, he was led blind into Damascus, not knowing what would happen next (Acts 9:1-9). Ananias was a believer in Damascus who was to become Paul's first Christian contact (Acts 9:10-22). Given the task of going to Paul (called Saul at that time), Ananias at first objected; after all, Saul had devoted himself to persecuting Christians. In this spiritual battle fear played a role, but Ananias became a victor and obeyed God's call. As a result, Paul's sight was restored, and he was introduced to the community of believers at Damascus who helped him escape when the Jews plotted to kill him (Acts 9:23-25).

When Saul returned to Jerusalem, he was not well received by the Christians there. They were every bit as suspicious as Ananias had been. But Barnabas interceded on behalf of this new believer, introducing him to the disciples there and telling them of the change God had accomplished in his life (Acts 9:26-27). Though Ananias and Barnabas do not receive credit for Paul's ministry and writings, both of them played a key role in his life because they were faithful to the Lord.

Though the spiritual battles of ordinary people may seem less dramatic or significant than those of the heroes of the faith, the nature of the battle and the value of the victory are no less significant. The arena for spiritual battles is most often the mind; that is true for all Christians (2 Cor 11:3). Believers in this fallen world are surrounded by ungodly value systems that can seem attractive. When their thinking is shaped by ungodly values, it leads to ungodly choices and spiritual defeats. When Paul wrote to the ordinary Christians in Corinth who had their share of spiritual failures, he reminded them that their battle was not physical but spiritual, and he encouraged them to "take every thought captive to make it obey Christ" (2 Cor 10:3-5). Bringing every thought into captivity to Christ helps ordinary Christians become victors.

The pages of Scripture are punctuated with ordinary people who decided to be faithful and whose decisions often made an extraordinary difference. At Bethany, when a woman in an act of extravagant worship broke her jar of fragrant oil and anointed Jesus, most who witnessed it criticized her. Jesus, however, praised her and said that she did what she could (Mk 14:3-9). Her act not only ministered to Jesus but also became an encouragement to believers through the ages; wherever the gospel is proclaimed, what she did for her Savior will be told. Doing what we can is always a good choice for ordinary believers who are willing to be faithful in the battle. We know that God does not forget the faithful actions or lives of His children and these will be rewarded.

QUESTION 20

How many women accompanied Jesus and the disciples and provided for them?

A. 1

B. 2

C. 3

D. More than 3

QUESTION 21

Match the persons below with their descriptions.

Person	*Description*
Joanna	Formerly secret disciple who claimed the body of Jesus
Joseph of Arimathea	Introduced Paul to Christians in Jerusalem
Ananias	Provided for Jesus and the disciples
Barnabas	Paul's initial Christian contact in Damascus

QUESTION 22

There are many other believers in Scripture who may have been ordinary or obscure but who chose to remain faithful. Choose at least one of these people. Open your Life Notebook and describe the results of their faithfulness.

Topic 6: Conclusion

A person becomes a Christian by trusting Jesus Christ as his Savior. The same faith that is active at the beginning of a relationship with Christ remains an integral ingredient as that relationship is lived out day-by-day. In the midst of the battle we may find ourselves wrongly thinking that Christ is somehow less than He is, that we are irredeemable, or that our relationship with Christ is of little consequence. That is when we must choose to believe what is true.

The goal of the enemy in the battles we face in the Christian life is to hinder our relationship with Christ and try to separate us from Him. In Romans 8:31-39 Paul listed several things that will not be able to separate us from the love of Christ. He declared that "in all these things we have complete victory through Him who loved us!" (Rom 8:37). Paul expressed his strong conviction that *nothing* could separate him from the love of God in Christ Jesus.

Though we are engaged in a spiritual battle, we too can experience complete victory through Christ. Our relationship with Him is the focal point of the spiritual battle and it is also the key to our victory.

QUESTION 23

Spend some time reading and meditating on Romans 8:31-39. Of the items listed that might try to separate us from the love of Christ, which seem to be currently the most threatening to you? Pray about these items. Then open your Life Notebook and reflect on your conversation with the Lord.

Lesson 12 Self Check: The Christian Life

QUESTION 1

Spiritual warfare is a battle over truth. *True or False?*

QUESTION 2

What is the single offensive weapon in the Christian's armor that can neutralize the effectiveness of the enemy?

A. Faith

B. Gospel of peace

C. Salvation

D. Word of God

QUESTION 3

What is the role of prayer in the Christian's spiritual battles?

A. It is essential.

B. It should be avoided to protect privacy.

C. It is irrelevant; prayer will not make any difference.

D. It is optional; we can pray if we want to.

QUESTION 4

Prayer, authority, and truth were all used by Jesus in facing spiritual battles. *True or False?*

QUESTION 5

Who did Paul say was shipwrecked in regard to the faith?

A. Mark

B. Hymenaeus and Alexander

C. Ananias and Barnabas

D. Himself

QUESTION 6

Which of the following is NOT something we should do because we are surrounded by the cloud of witnesses?

A. Run the race before us with endurance

B. Fix our eyes on Jesus

C. Think about our failures in the battle

D. Rid ourselves of sin

QUESTION 7

Mark and Simon Peter are examples of people who failed in a significant spiritual battle and later experienced victory. *True or False?*

QUESTION 8

Which of the following embattled churches of Revelation did NOT receive a specific word of correction from the Lord?

A. Ephesus
B. Smyrna
C. Pergamum
D. Thyatira

QUESTION 9

The theme of the letters to the churches in Revelation 2-3 is that the heart of the reward is Christ Himself. *True or False?*

QUESTION 10

Who was Paul's initial Christian contact at Damascus?

A. Joseph of Arimathea
B. Barnabas
C. Peter
D. Ananias

Unit 4 Exam: The Christian Life

QUESTION 1

When in the Bible did Satan tempt the Son of God?

A. Before the creation of the world
B. When Satan first rebelled against God
C. During Jesus' life on earth
D. After Jesus was resurrected and ascended to the Father

QUESTION 2

According to the vision in Revelation 12, who flees into the wilderness to escape Satan's persecution?

A. The church
B. People without the sign of the beast
C. Israel during the tribulation
D. Israel during Jesus' ministry on earth

QUESTION 3

Why were the believers in the book of Hebrews tempted to shrink away from Christ?

A. They were ashamed of Jesus and His words.
B. They were not living by faith.
C. They were in danger of returning to the world.
D. They were threatened by the Jewish council (the Sanhedrin).

QUESTION 4

According to the explanation of the word Smyrna, when would believers be a pleasing fragrance for Christ?

A. While under distress
B. When they successfully endured until the end
C. When reading God's Word daily
D. When doing things in love

QUESTION 5

According to 2 Timothy 4:10 the "colaborer" with Paul who deserted him because "he loved this present age" was __________.

A. Apollos
B. Demas
C. Epaphrus
D. Mark

QUESTION 6

When did Jesus weep?

A. When empathizing with His friends' grief
B. When He was exhausted
C. When His mother was insulted as a fornicator
D. When suffering hunger and thirst

QUESTION 7

How did Paul describe the Christian's suffering when he talked about an eternal perspective in 2 Corinthians 4:16-18?

A. Momentary and light
B. Painful and purifying
C. Unnecessary and avoidable
D. Deep and lasting

QUESTION 8

Maintaining an attitude of gratitude helps prepare a person to endure suffering. *True or False?*

QUESTION 9

When God spoke to Job, He explained the reason for Job's suffering. *True or False?*

QUESTION 10

All of creation is groaning and suffering because of man's sin. *True or False?*

QUESTION 11

What did Jesus pray for His disciples in John 17:14-16?

A. That they would be kept safe in the world
B. That they would be taken out of the world
C. That they would be loved by the world
D. That they would belong in the world

QUESTION 12

How should Christians think of themselves in relationship to their old sin nature?

A. They should consider themselves sin's ruler.
B. They should consider themselves sin's servant.
C. They should consider themselves dead to sin.
D. Since they are redeemed, they don't need to be concerned with the sin nature.

QUESTION 13

When we give in to temptation, we are giving in to a dead, disarmed, or defeated foe. *True or False?*

QUESTION 14

In Paul's struggle with the flesh, he found it easy to conquer the will to sin. *True or False?*

QUESTION 15

What does Peter say our response should be to Satan, whom he describes as a roaring lion?

A. Flee him
B. Feed him
C. Ignore him
D. Resist him

QUESTION 16

Satan is limited in what he can do. *True or False?*

QUESTION 17

Which of the following is NOT true according to 1 Corinthians 10:13?

A. God is faithful.
B. God will limit our trials.
C. Sometimes we encounter temptations that are unique to us.
D. God provides a way through our trial without sinning.

QUESTION 18

What did Jesus tell the disciples to do while He was praying in the Garden of Gethsemane?

A. Sleep because they were tired.
B. Pray that they not fall into temptation.
C. Eat since they were hungry.
D. Leave to avoid those who were coming to arrest Jesus.

QUESTION 19

A Christian equipped with the armor of God should be praying for other people. *True or False?*

QUESTION 20

How did Jesus respond to each of Satan's temptations?

A. With fear
B. In silence
C. By quoting Scripture
D. By ignoring Satan

QUESTION 21

Jesus' spiritual battle was limited to three temptations from Satan. *True or False?*

QUESTION 22

Who was instrumental in helping to restore Mark?

A. Demas
B. Peter
C. Alexander
D. Timothy

QUESTION 23

Which of the churches in Revelation 2–3 received no commendation from the Lord?

A. Ephesus

B. Philadelphia

C. Sardis

D. Laodicea

QUESTION 24

A common theme in what is promised to conquerors is Christ Himself. *True or False?*

QUESTION 25

What can separate us from the love of Christ?

A. Nothing in creation

B. Persecution

C. Danger

D. Death

Lesson 12 Answers to Questions

QUESTION 1: *Your answer*

QUESTION 2

B. Strength

C. The full armor of God

D. The need to stand

QUESTION 3: Stand

QUESTION 4

Reference	*Teaching*
Ephesians 6:14	The belt of truth and breastplate of righteousness
Ephesians 6:15	Feet prepared with the good news of peace
Ephesians 6:16	The shield of faith
Ephesians 6:17	The helmet of salvation and the Word of God
Ephesians 6:18	Praying in the Spirit for all the saints

QUESTION 5: *Your answer*

QUESTION 6

A. Their actions

B. Their values

C. Their ability to succeed in spiritual battles

QUESTION 7

Scripture	*Encouragement*
1 Peter 2:21	Christ also suffered for you, leaving an example for you to follow in His steps
1 Corinthians 11:1	Be imitators of me just as I also am of Christ.
Ephesians 5:1-2	Live in love just as Christ also loved us.
Colossians 2:6-7	Continue to live your lives in Him rooted and built up in Him.

QUESTION 8: False

QUESTION 9

A. Prayer

C. Memorized Scripture

D. Authority

E. Truth

QUESTION 10: *Your answer*

QUESTION 11

A. Alexander

C. Hymenaeus

QUESTION 12

B. He loved the present age.

QUESTION 13

C. C. Peter [Interestingly, Peter, who himself had failed, was instrumental in Mark's restoration. Though there was no blood relationship, Peter refers to Mark as "my son" (1 Pet 5:13).]

QUESTION 14: *Your answer*

QUESTION 15

C. Run the race before us with endurance

D. Keep our eyes fixed on Jesus

QUESTION 16

B. Smyrna

E. Philadelphia

QUESTION 17

Church	*What Was Promised*
Ephesus	Eat from the tree of life
Smyrna	In no way harmed by the second death
Pergamum	Hidden manna and a white stone with a new name
Thyatira	Authority over the nations; the morning star
Sardis	Dressed in white clothing; never erased from book of life
Philadelphia	Made a pillar in temple of God
Laodicea	Permission to sit with Christ on His throne

QUESTION 18: True

QUESTION 19: *Your answer*

QUESTION 20

D. More than 3

QUESTION 21

Person	*Description*
Joanna	Provided for Jesus and the disciples
Joseph of Arimathea	Formerly secret disciple who claimed the body of Jesus
Ananias	Paul's initial Christian contact in Damascus
Barnabas	Introduced Paul to Christians in Jerusalem

QUESTION 22: *Your answer*

QUESTION 23: *Your answer*

Lesson 12 Self Check Answers

QUESTION 1: True

QUESTION 2

D. Word of God

QUESTION 3

A. It is essential.

QUESTION 4: True

QUESTION 5

B. Hymenaeus and Alexander

QUESTION 6

C. Think about our failures in the battle

QUESTION 7: True

QUESTION 8

B. Smyrna

QUESTION 9: True

QUESTION 10

D. Ananias

Unit 4 Exam Answers

QUESTION 1

C. During Jesus' life on earth

QUESTION 2

C. Israel during the tribulation

QUESTION 3

B. They were not living by faith.

QUESTION 4

A. While under distress

QUESTION 5

B. Demas

QUESTION 6

A. When empathizing with His friends' grief

QUESTION 7

A. Momentary and light

QUESTION 8: True

QUESTION 9: False

QUESTION 10: True

QUESTION 11

A. That they would be kept safe in the world

QUESTION 12

C. They should consider themselves dead to sin.

QUESTION 13: True

QUESTION 14: False

QUESTION 15

D. Resist him

QUESTION 16: True

QUESTION 17

C. Sometimes we encounter temptations that are unique to us.

QUESTION 18

B. Pray that they not fall into temptation.

QUESTION 19: True

QUESTION 20

C. By quoting Scripture

QUESTION 21: False

QUESTION 22

B. Peter

QUESTION 23

D. Laodicea

QUESTION 24: True

QUESTION 25

A. Nothing in creation

Made in the USA
Middletown, DE
17 July 2022